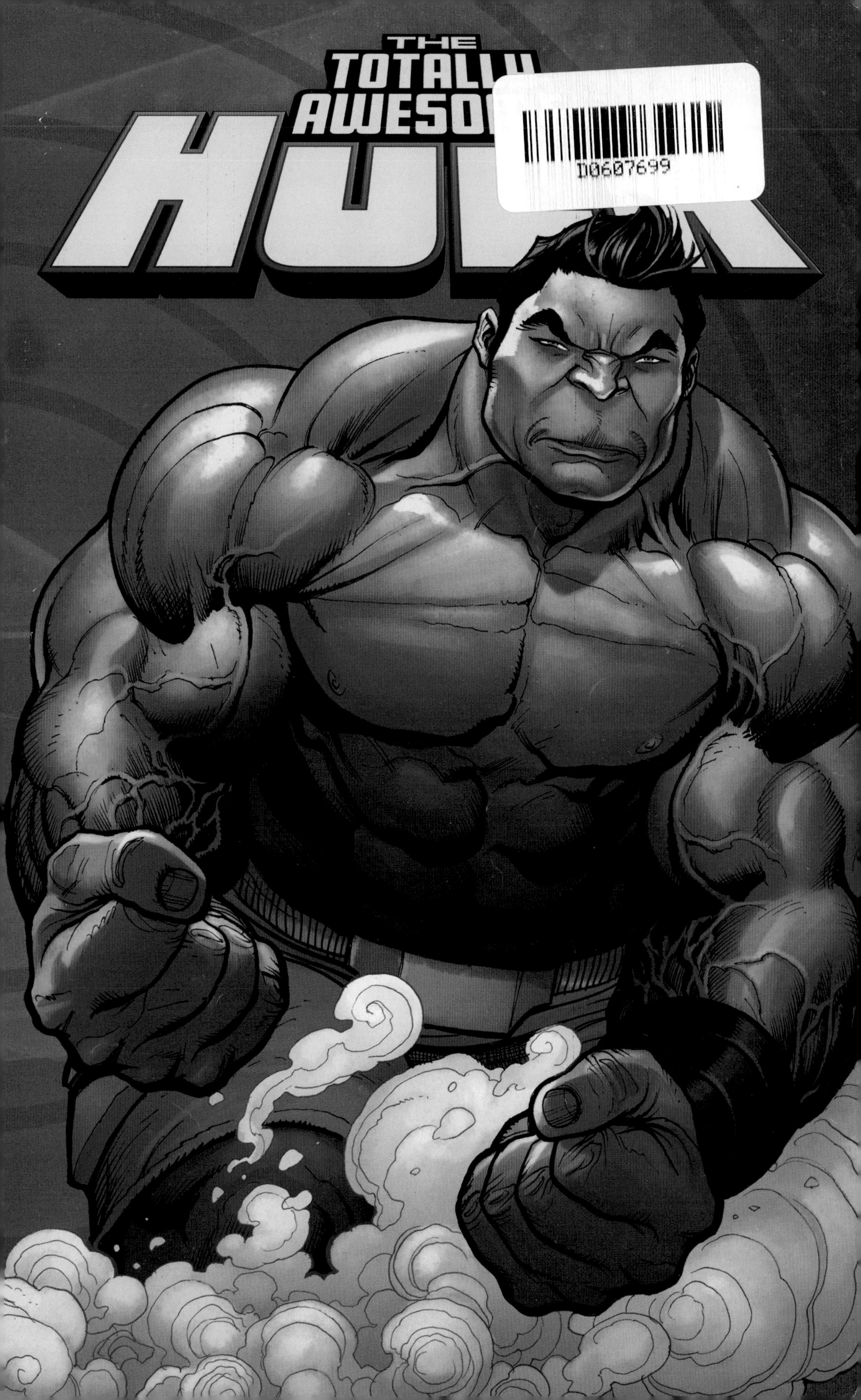
THE
TOTALL
AWESO
HU

AWESOME HULK

GREG PAK
WRITER

FRANK CHO (#1-4) & **MIKE CHOI** (#5-6)
ARTISTS

SONIA OBACK (#1-4),
FRANK MARTIN (#5) &
ANDREW CROSSLEY (#6)
COLOR ARTISTS

**FRANK CHO &
DAVID CURIEL** (#1) AND
**FRANK CHO &
SONIA OBACK** (#2-6)
COVER ART

VC's CORY PETIT
LETTERER

CHRIS ROBINSON
ASSISTANT EDITOR

DARREN SHAN
ASSOCIATE EDITOR

MARK PANICCIA
EDITOR

"PHOENIX BURNING"

GREG PAK
WRITER

TAKESHI MIYAZAWA
ARTIST

RACHELLE ROSENBERG
COLOR ARTIST

VC's TRAVIS LANHAM
LETTERER

LEONARD KIRK & TAMRA BONVILLAIN
COVER ART

CHRIS ROBINSON
ASSISTANT EDITOR

DARREN SHAN
ASSOCIATE EDITOR

HULK CREATED BY **STAN LEE** & **JACK KIRBY**

HI! I'M MADDY CHO, SISTER OF SUPER-GENIUS
TEENAGER **AMADEUS CHO**. WELL, *THIS* ISN'T
ME...I'M ACTUALLY...NEVER MIND, YOU'LL SEE.
ANYWAY, AMADEUS ALWAYS BELIEVED
THE HULK WAS THE WORLD'S GREATEST HERO,
NOT ITS MOST TERRIFYING MONSTER. NOW IT'S
UP TO AMADEUS TO PROVE IT AS...

THE TOTALLY AWESOME HULK

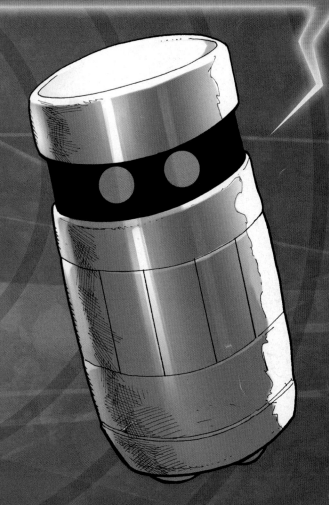

COLLECTION EDITOR **JENNIFER GRÜNWALD**
ASSOCIATE EDITOR **SARAH BRUNSTAD**
ASSOCIATE MANAGING EDITOR **ALEX STARBUCK**
EDITOR, SPECIAL PROJECTS **MARK D. BEAZLEY**

VP, PRODUCTION & SPECIAL PROJECTS **JEFF YOUNGQUIST**
SVP PRINT, SALES & MARKETING **DAVID GABRIEL**
BOOK DESIGNER **ADAM DEL RE**

EDITOR IN CHIEF **AXEL ALONSO**
CHIEF CREATIVE OFFICER **JOE QUESADA**
PUBLISHER **DAN BUCKLEY**
EXECUTIVE PRODUCER **ALAN FINE**

THE TOTALLY AWESOME HULK VOL. 1: CHO TIME. Contains material originally published in magazine form as THE TOTALLY AWESOME HULK #1-6 and PLANET HULK #1. First printing 2016. ISBN# 978-0-7851-9609-9. Published by MARVEL WORLDWIDE, INC., a subsidiary of MARVEL ENTERTAINMENT, LLC. OFFICE OF PUBLICATION: 135 West 50th Street, New York, NY 10020. Copyright © 2016 MARVEL. No similarity between any of the names, characters, persons, and/or institutions in this magazine with those of any living or dead person or institution is intended, and any such similarity which may exist is purely coincidental. **Printed in the U.S.A.** ALAN FINE, President, Marvel Entertainment; DAN BUCKLEY, President, TV, Publishing & Brand Management; JOE QUESADA, Chief Creative Officer; TOM BREVOORT, SVP of Publishing; DAVID BOGART, SVP of Business Affairs & Operations, Publishing & Partnership; C.B. CEBULSKI, VP of Brand Management & Development, Asia; DAVID GABRIEL, SVP of Sales & Marketing, Publishing; JEFF YOUNGQUIST, VP of Production & Special Projects; DAN CARR, Executive Director of Publishing Technology; ALEX MORALES, Director of Publishing Operations; SUSAN CRESPI, Production Manager; STAN LEE, Chairman Emeritus. For information regarding advertising in Marvel Comics or on Marvel.com, please contact Vit DeBellis, Integrated Sales Manager, at vdebellis@marvel.com. For Marvel subscription inquiries, please call 888-511-5480. **Manufactured between 5/20/2016 and 6/27/2016 by R.R. DONNELLEY, INC., SALEM, VA, USA.**

10 9 8 7 6 5 4 3 2 1

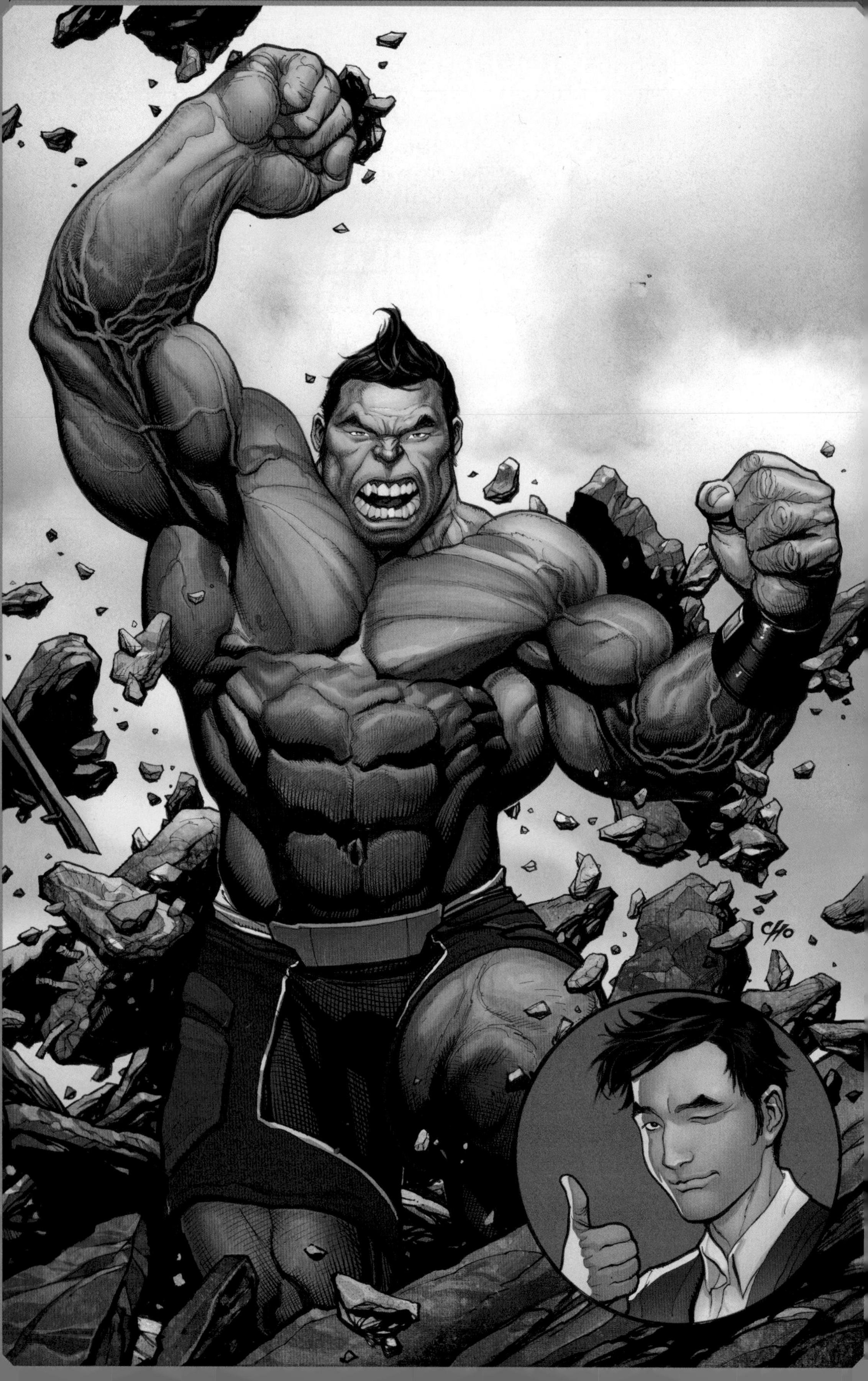
CHO

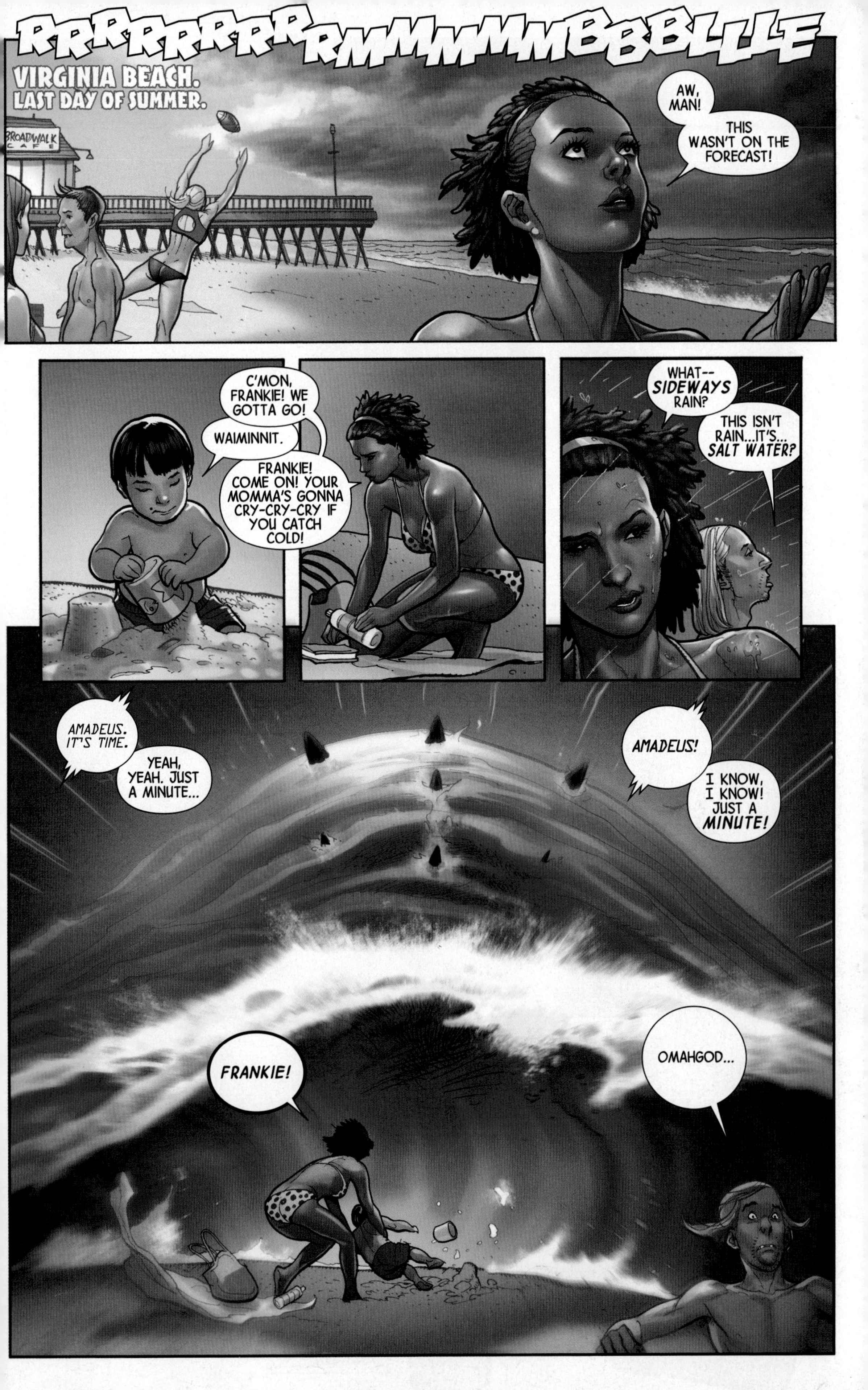
RRRRRRRRRMMMMMMMBBBLLLE
VIRGINIA BEACH.
LAST DAY OF SUMMER.
BROADWALK CAFE
AW, MAN!
THIS WASN'T ON THE FORECAST!
C'MON, FRANKIE! WE GOTTA GO!
WAIMINNIT.
FRANKIE! COME ON! YOUR MOMMA'S GONNA CRY-CRY-CRY IF YOU CATCH COLD!
WHAT-- SIDEWAYS RAIN?
THIS ISN'T RAIN...IT'S... SALT WATER?
AMADEUS. IT'S TIME.
YEAH, YEAH. JUST A MINUTE...
AMADEUS!
I KNOW, I KNOW! JUST A MINUTE!
FRANKIE!
OMAHGOD...

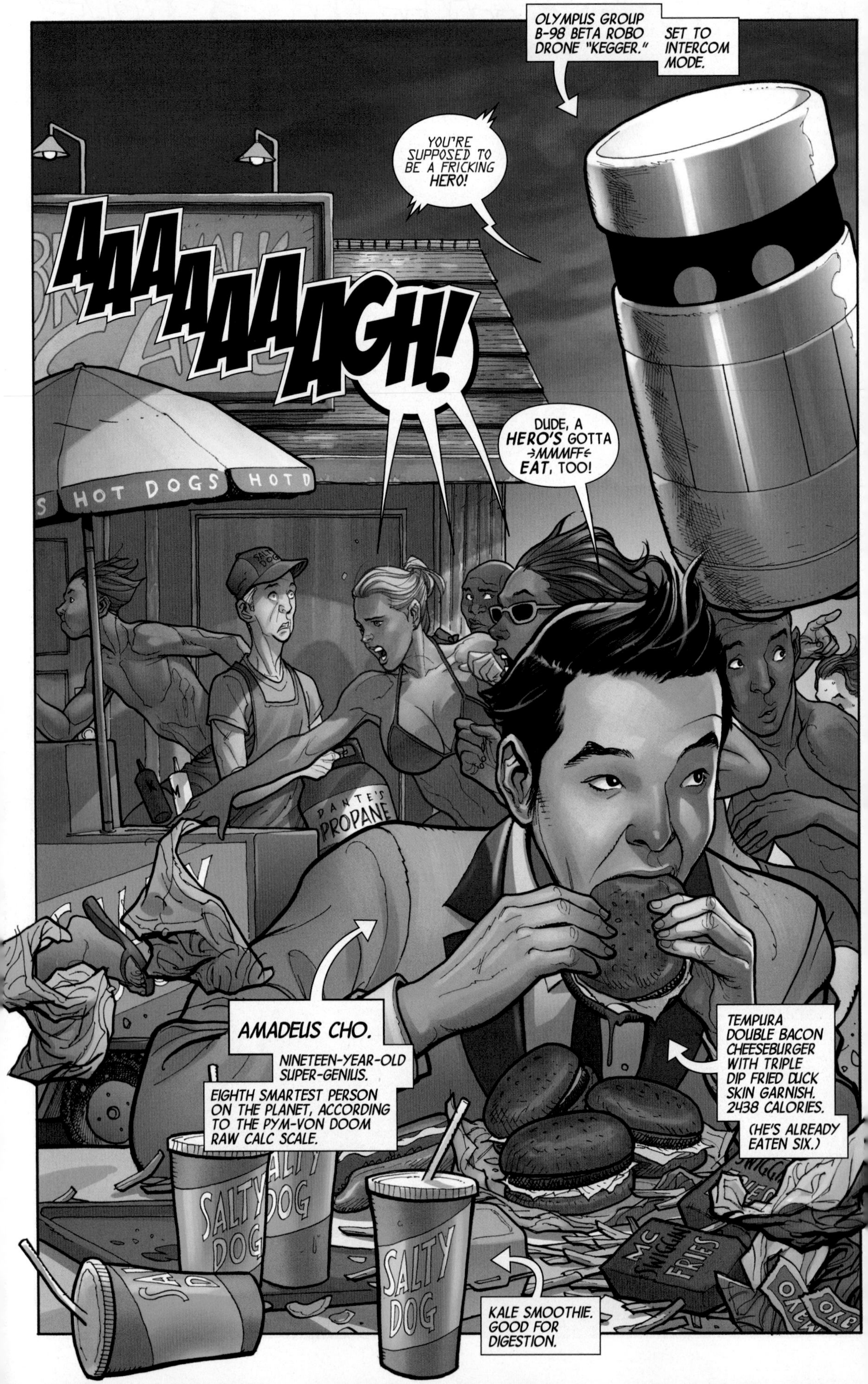
OLYMPUS GROUP B-98 BETA ROBO DRONE "KEGGER."
SET TO INTERCOM MODE.
YOU'RE SUPPOSED TO BE A FRICKING HERO!
AAAAAAAAGH!
DUDE, A HERO'S GOTTA →MMMFF← EAT, TOO!
HOT DOGS HOT D
DANTE'S PROPANE
AMADEUS CHO.
NINETEEN-YEAR-OLD SUPER-GENIUS.
EIGHTH SMARTEST PERSON ON THE PLANET, ACCORDING TO THE PYM-VON DOOM RAW CALC SCALE.
TEMPURA DOUBLE BACON CHEESEBURGER WITH TRIPLE DIP FRIED DUCK SKIN GARNISH. 2438 CALORIES.
(HE'S ALREADY EATEN SIX.)
SALTY DOG
MC SWIGGIN FRIES
KALE SMOOTHIE. GOOD FOR DIGESTION.

FTOOOM

GRRRRAAAAAAAAAAAAAA!

FRANKIE!

TURTLE!

AMADEUS! THAT KID--

CHILL.

I'VE FED MY MONSTER...

CLIK

...AND THE MONSTER'S READY.

AND NO LITTLE KID'S GETTING HURT ON MY WATCH...

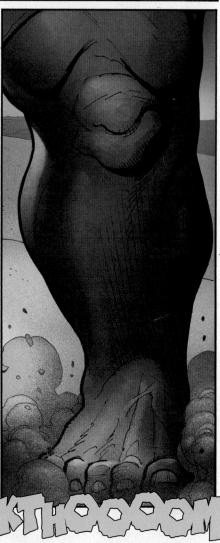

KTHOOOOM

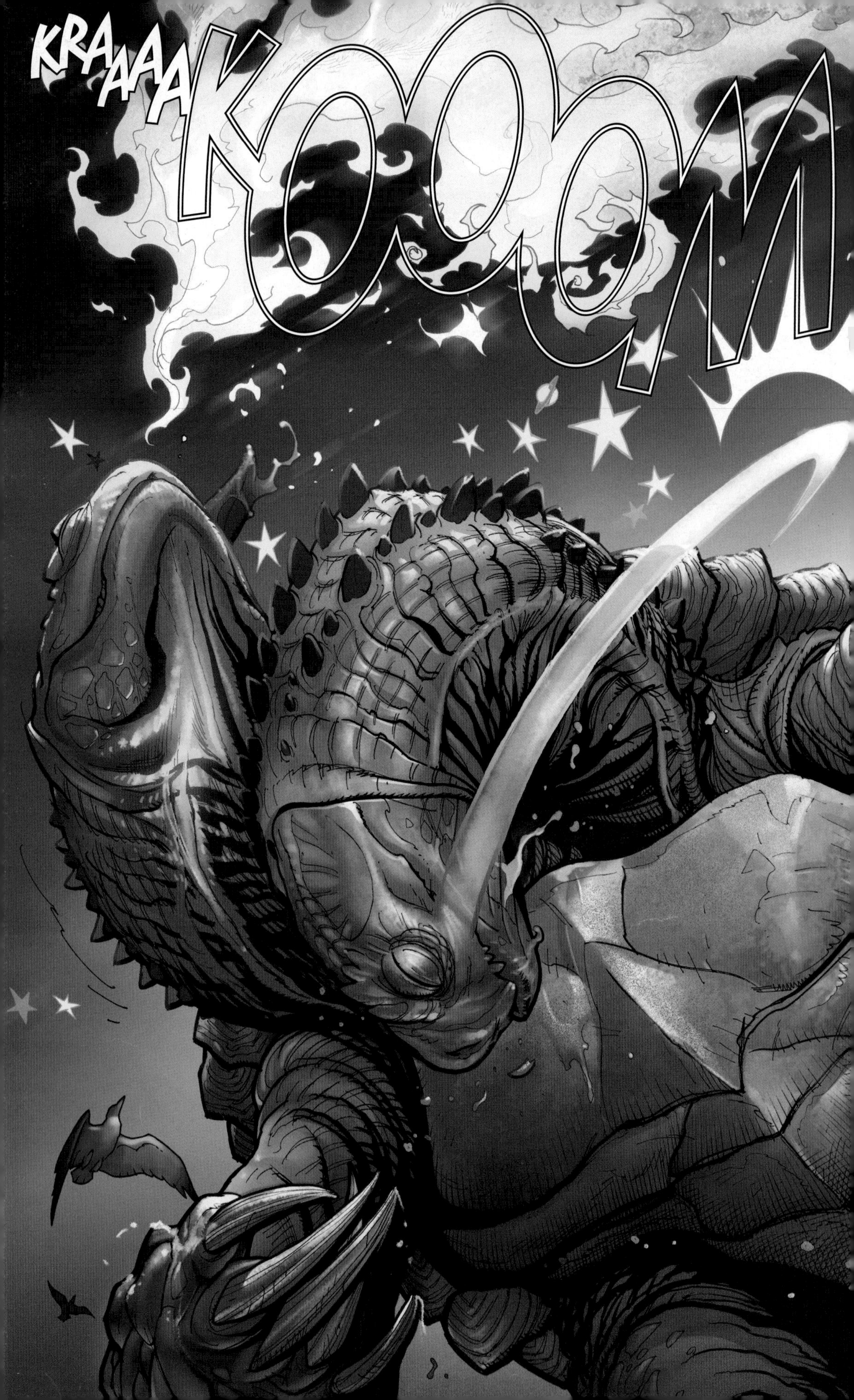
KRAAAAKOOOOM

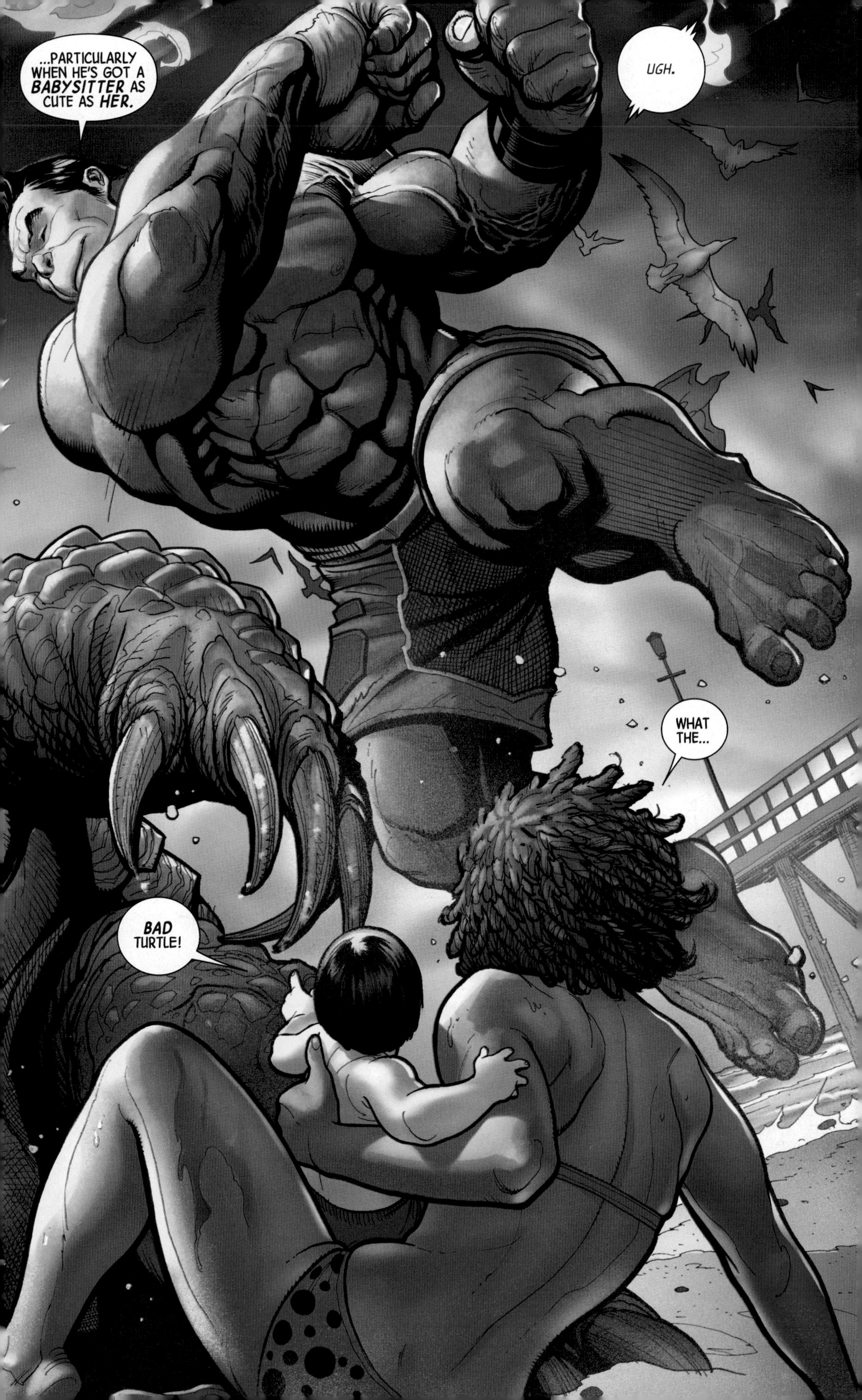

...PARTICULARLY WHEN HE'S GOT A *BABYSITTER* AS CUTE AS *HER.*
UGH.
WHAT THE...
BAD TURTLE!

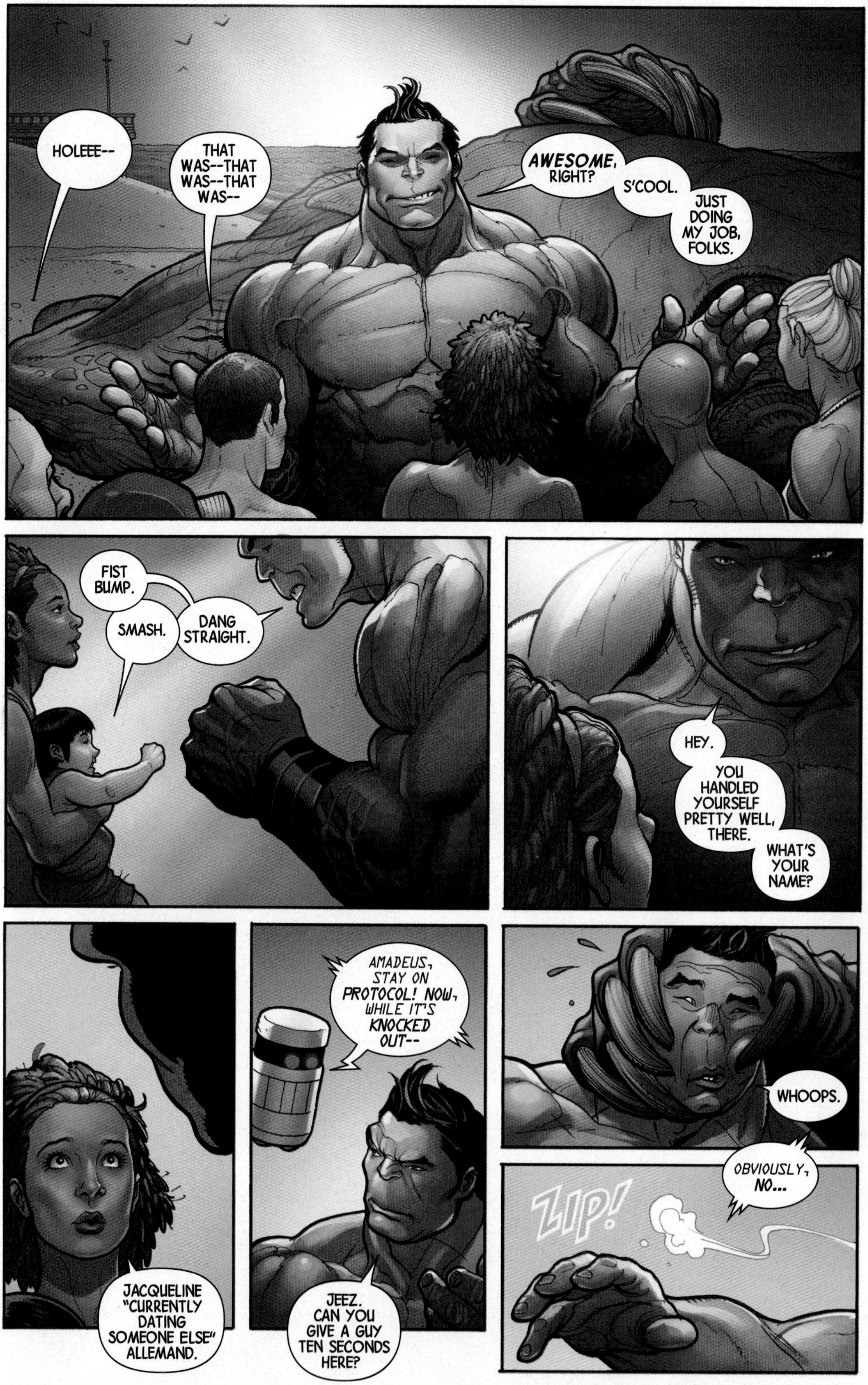
HOLEEE--
THAT WAS--THAT WAS--THAT WAS--
AWESOME, RIGHT?
S'COOL.
JUST DOING MY JOB, FOLKS.
FIST BUMP.
SMASH.
DANG STRAIGHT.
HEY.
YOU HANDLED YOURSELF PRETTY WELL, THERE.
WHAT'S YOUR NAME?
JACQUELINE "CURRENTLY DATING SOMEONE ELSE" ALLEMAND.
AMADEUS, STAY ON PROTOCOL! NOW, WHILE IT'S KNOCKED OUT--
JEEZ. CAN YOU GIVE A GUY TEN SECONDS HERE?
WHOOPS.
OBVIOUSLY, NO...
ZIP!

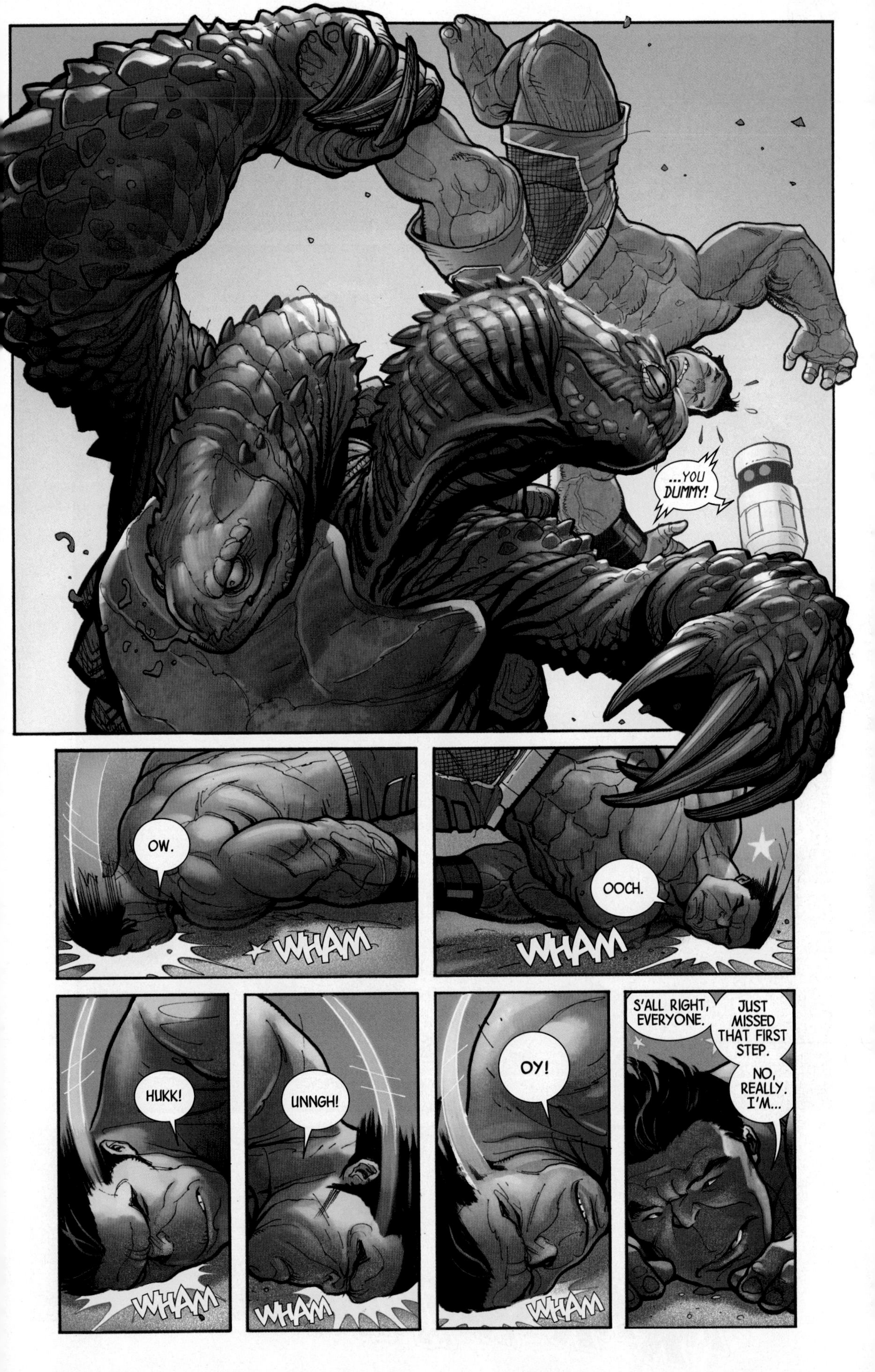
...YOU DUMMY!
OW.
WHAM
OOCH.
WHAM
HUKK!
WHAM
UNNGH!
WHAM
OY!
WHAM
S'ALL RIGHT, EVERYONE.
JUST MISSED THAT FIRST STEP.
NO, REALLY. I'M...

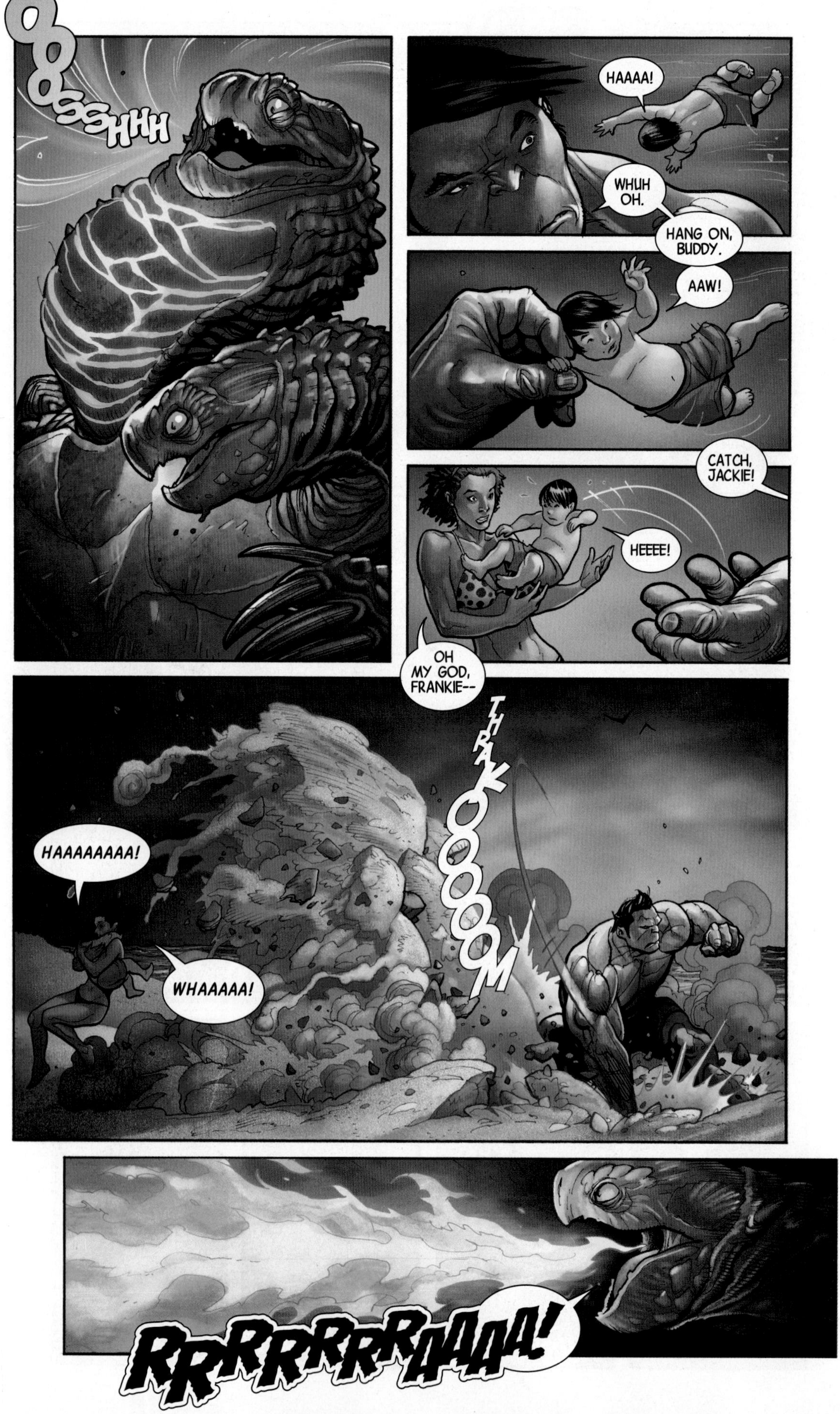

FSSSHHH
HAAAA!
WHUH OH.
HANG ON, BUDDY.
AAW!
CATCH, JACKIE!
HEEEE!
OH MY GOD, FRANKIE--
THRAKOOOOOM
HAAAAAAAA!
WHAAAAA!
RRRRRRRRAAAA!

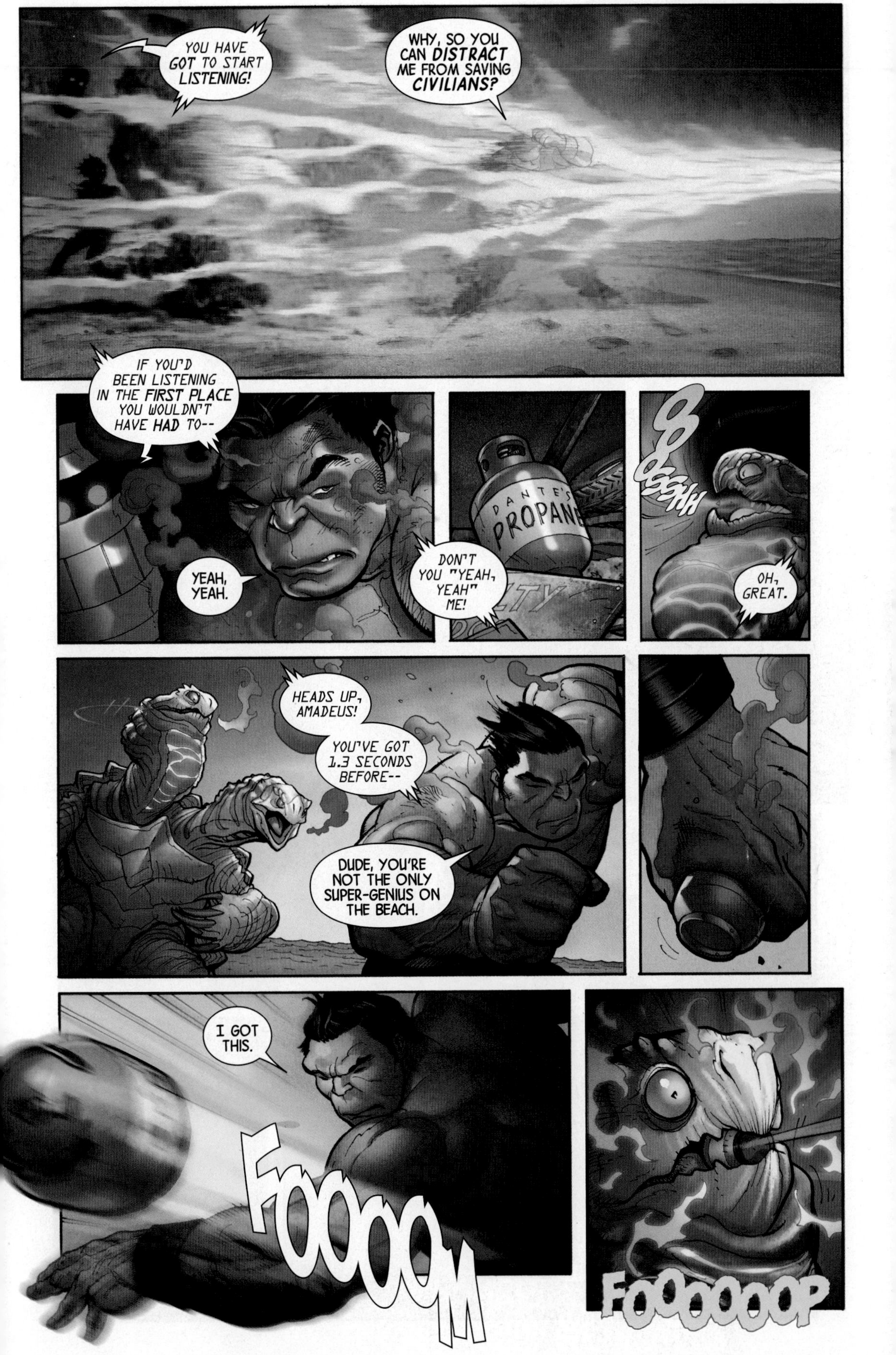

YOU HAVE GOT TO START LISTENING!
WHY, SO YOU CAN DISTRACT ME FROM SAVING CIVILIANS?
IF YOU'D BEEN LISTENING IN THE FIRST PLACE YOU WOULDN'T HAVE HAD TO--
YEAH, YEAH.
DANTE'S PROPANE
DON'T YOU "YEAH, YEAH" ME!
OOOHH
OH, GREAT.
HEADS UP, AMADEUS!
YOU'VE GOT 1.3 SECONDS BEFORE--
DUDE, YOU'RE NOT THE ONLY SUPER-GENIUS ON THE BEACH.
I GOT THIS.
FOOOOM
FOOOOOOP

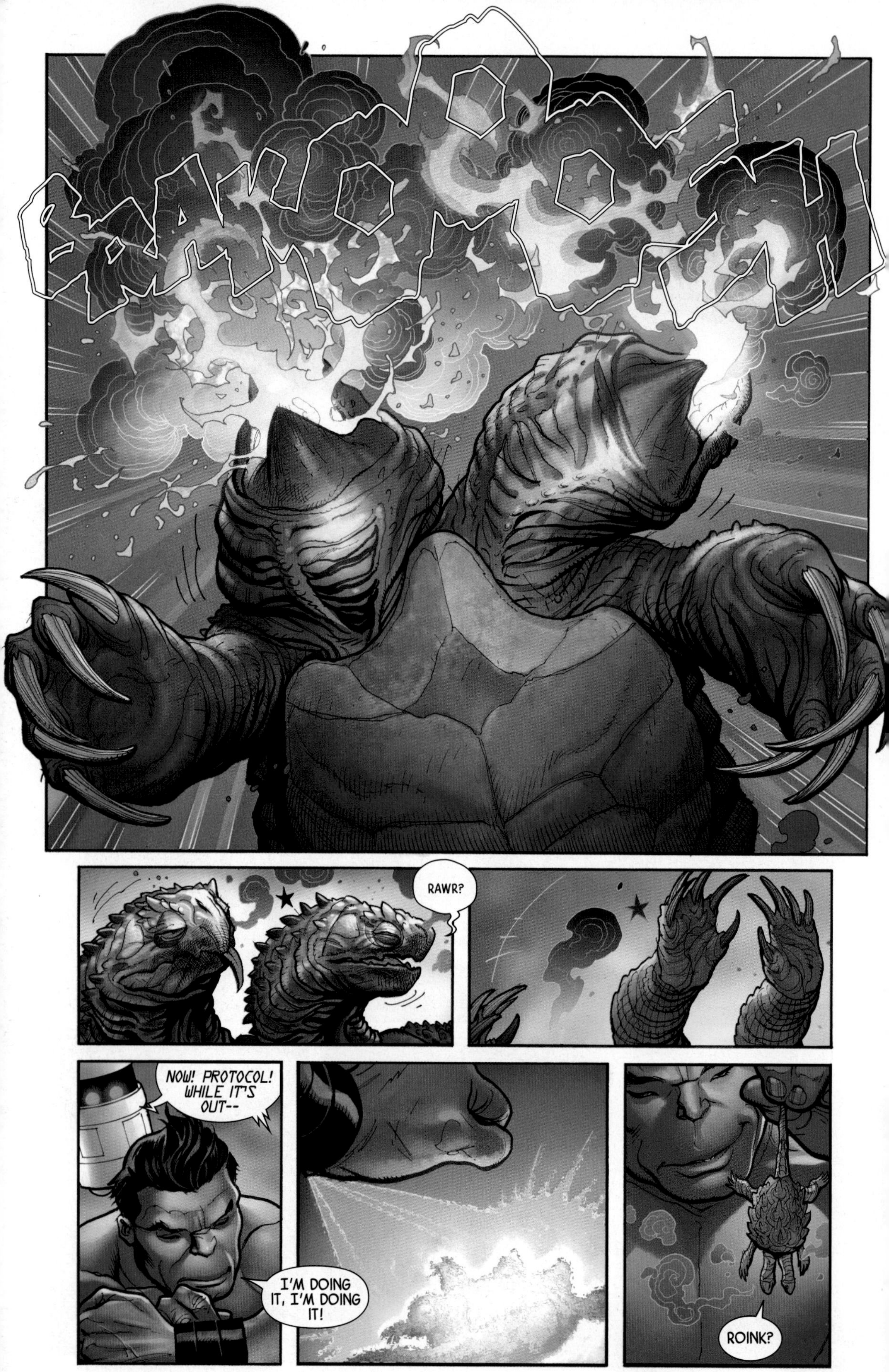
RAWR?
NOW! PROTOCOL! WHILE IT'S OUT--
I'M DOING IT, I'M DOING IT!
ROINK?

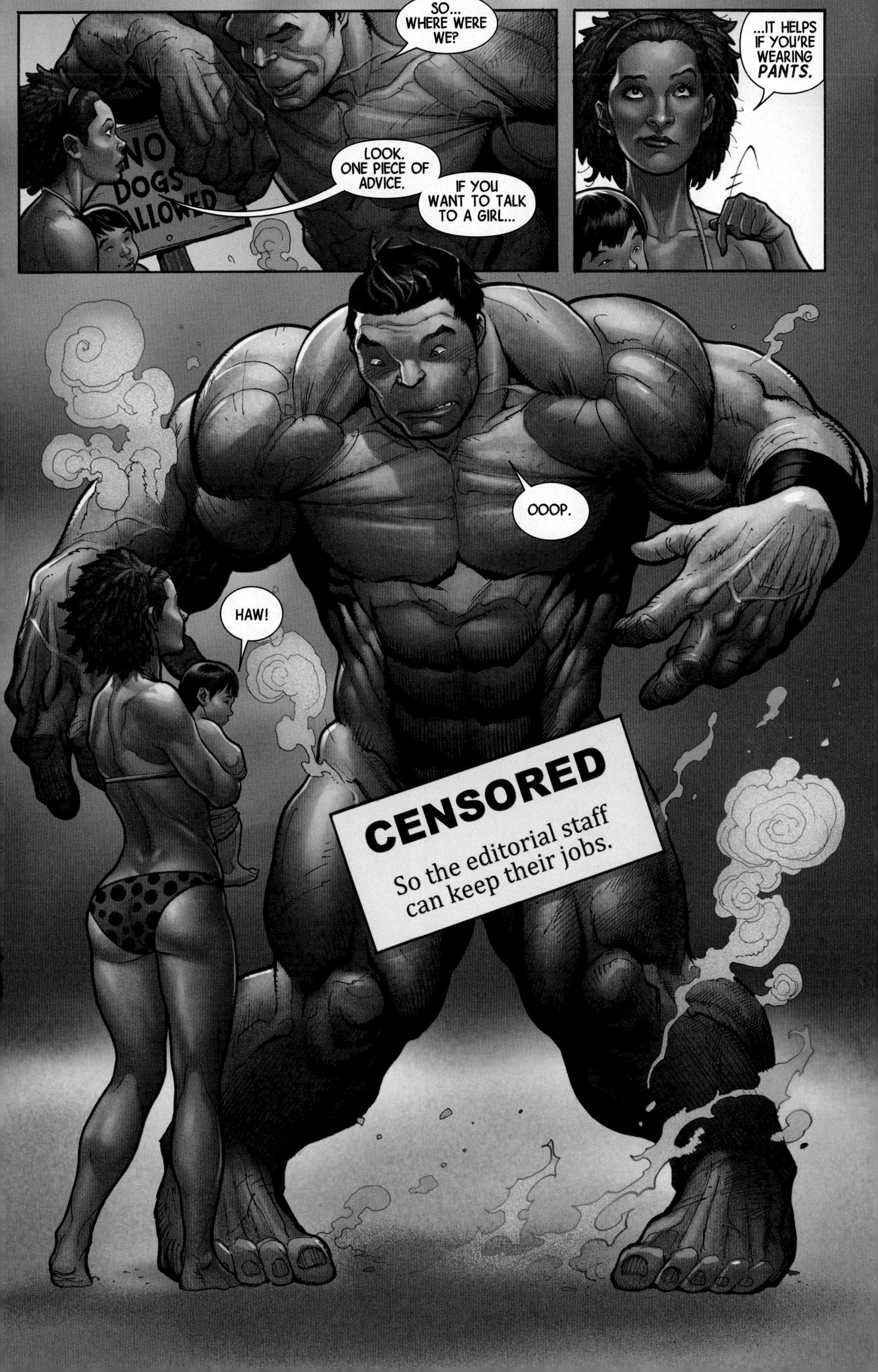

SO... WHERE WERE WE?
LOOK. ONE PIECE OF ADVICE.
IF YOU WANT TO TALK TO A GIRL...
...IT HELPS IF YOU'RE WEARING *PANTS.*
OOOP.
HAW!
CENSORED
So the editorial staff can keep their jobs.

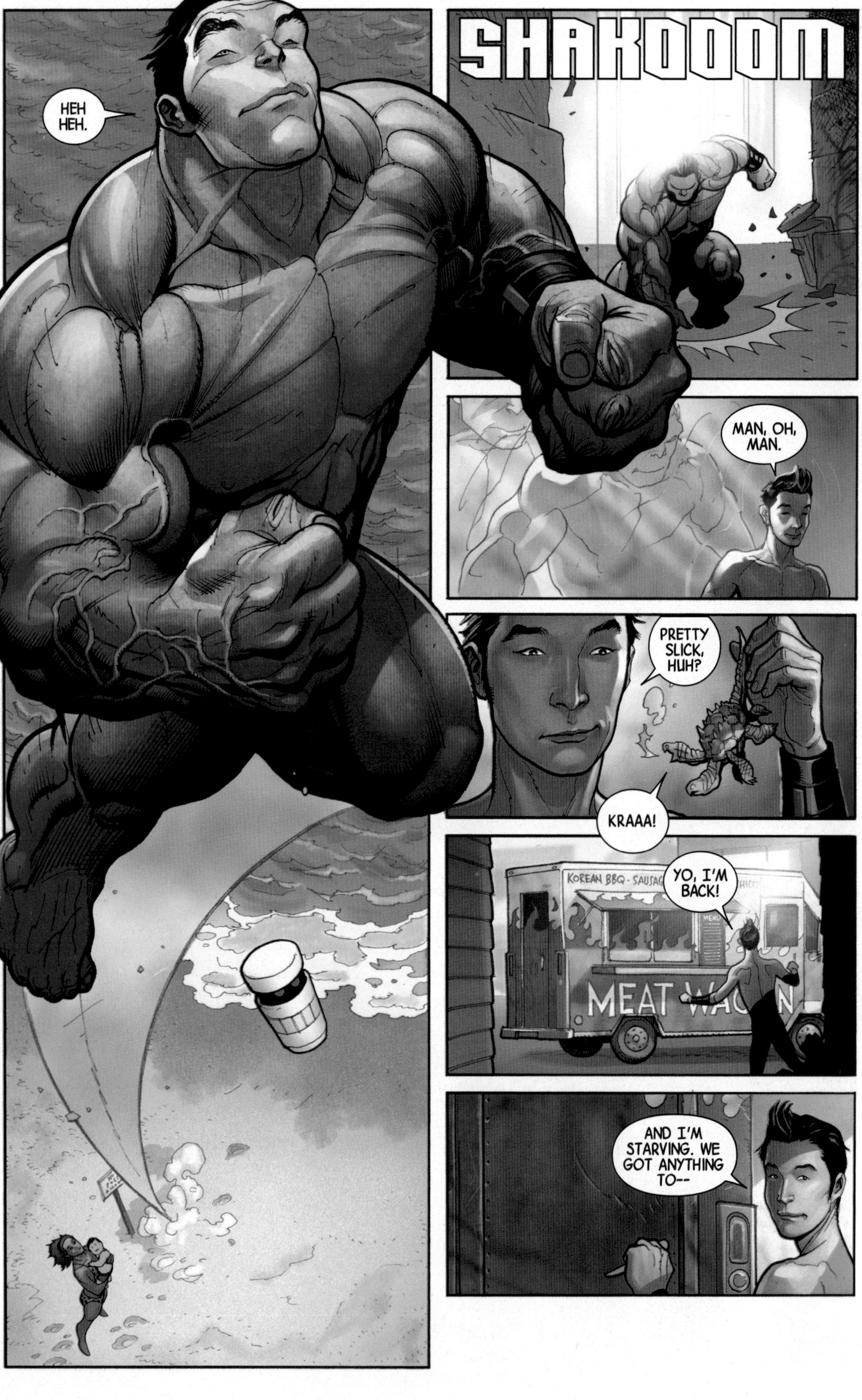
HEH HEH.
SHAKOOOM
MAN, OH, MAN.
PRETTY SLICK, HUH?
KRAAA!
KOREAN BBQ · SAUSAG
YO, I'M BACK!
MEAT WAGON
AND I'M STARVING. WE GOT ANYTHING TO--

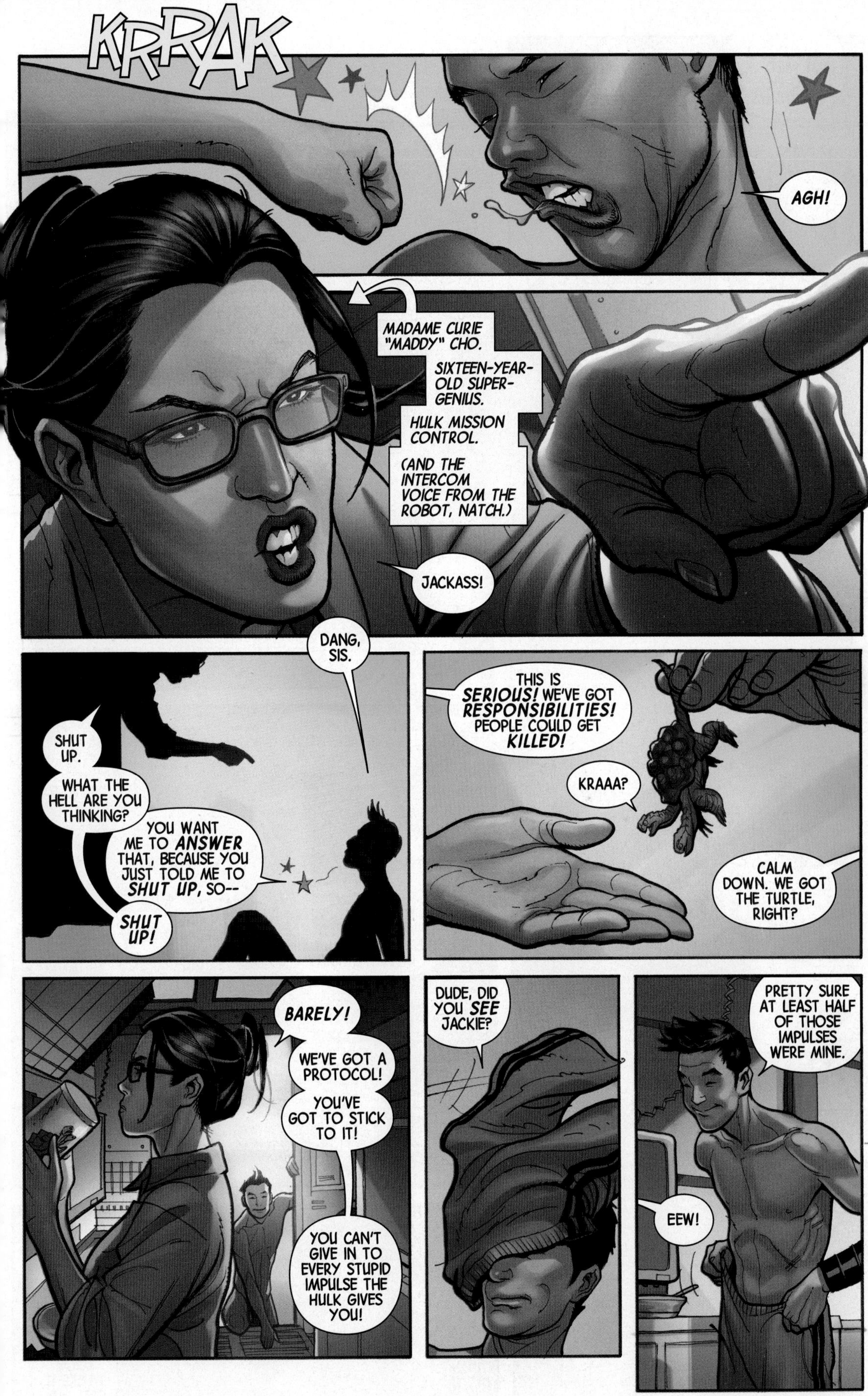
KRRAK
AGH!
MADAME CURIE "MADDY" CHO.
SIXTEEN-YEAR-OLD SUPER-GENIUS.
HULK MISSION CONTROL.
(AND THE INTERCOM VOICE FROM THE ROBOT, NATCH.)
JACKASS!
DANG, SIS.
SHUT UP.
WHAT THE HELL ARE YOU THINKING?
YOU WANT ME TO ANSWER THAT, BECAUSE YOU JUST TOLD ME TO SHUT UP, SO--
SHUT UP!
THIS IS SERIOUS! WE'VE GOT RESPONSIBILITIES! PEOPLE COULD GET KILLED!
KRAAA?
CALM DOWN. WE GOT THE TURTLE, RIGHT?
BARELY!
WE'VE GOT A PROTOCOL!
YOU'VE GOT TO STICK TO IT!
YOU CAN'T GIVE IN TO EVERY STUPID IMPULSE THE HULK GIVES YOU!
DUDE, DID YOU SEE JACKIE?
PRETTY SURE AT LEAST HALF OF THOSE IMPULSES WERE MINE.
EEW!

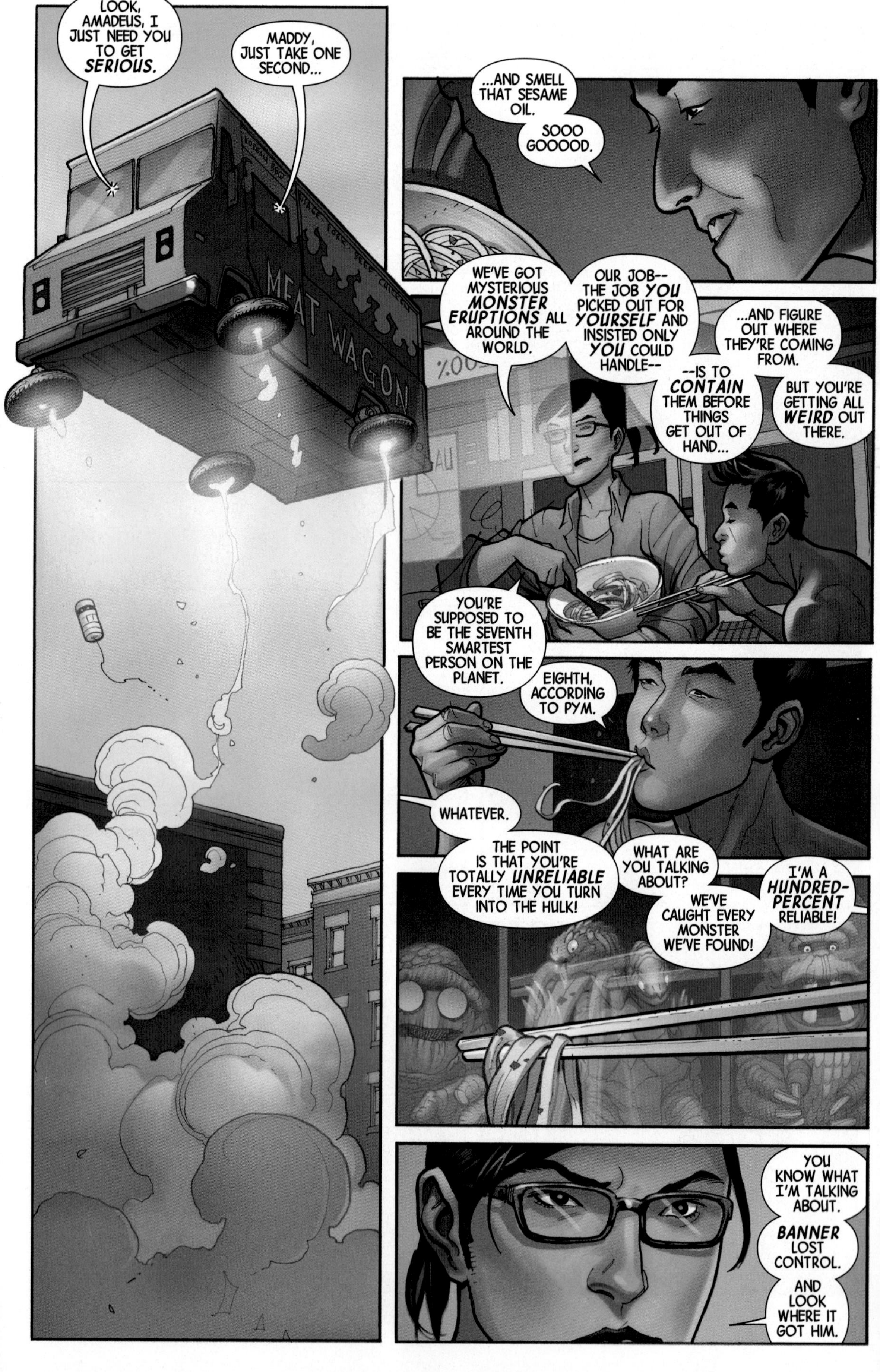
LOOK, AMADEUS, I JUST NEED YOU TO GET SERIOUS.
MADDY, JUST TAKE ONE SECOND...
MEAT WAGON
...AND SMELL THAT SESAME OIL.
SOOO GOOOOD.
WE'VE GOT MYSTERIOUS MONSTER ERUPTIONS ALL AROUND THE WORLD.
OUR JOB-- THE JOB YOU PICKED OUT FOR YOURSELF AND INSISTED ONLY YOU COULD HANDLE--
--IS TO CONTAIN THEM BEFORE THINGS GET OUT OF HAND...
...AND FIGURE OUT WHERE THEY'RE COMING FROM.
BUT YOU'RE GETTING ALL WEIRD OUT THERE.
YOU'RE SUPPOSED TO BE THE SEVENTH SMARTEST PERSON ON THE PLANET.
EIGHTH, ACCORDING TO PYM.
WHATEVER.
THE POINT IS THAT YOU'RE TOTALLY UNRELIABLE EVERY TIME YOU TURN INTO THE HULK!
WHAT ARE YOU TALKING ABOUT?
WE'VE CAUGHT EVERY MONSTER WE'VE FOUND!
I'M A HUNDRED-PERCENT RELIABLE!
YOU KNOW WHAT I'M TALKING ABOUT.
BANNER LOST CONTROL.
AND LOOK WHERE IT GOT HIM.

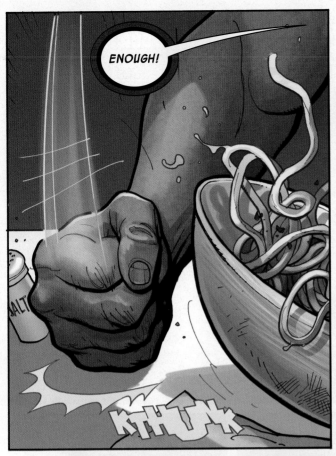

ENOUGH!

KTHUNK

HEY! YOU DON'T TALK TO ME LIKE THAT!

AND YOU'RE NOT FIGHTING *MONSTERS* RIGHT NOW, SO ENOUGH WITH THE *SMASHING*--

I'M NOT BANNER.

GAMMA ALERT! GAMMA ALERT!

AMADEUS! THIS IS WHAT I'M TALKING ABOUT!

GET AHOLD OF YOURSELF!

I SAID...

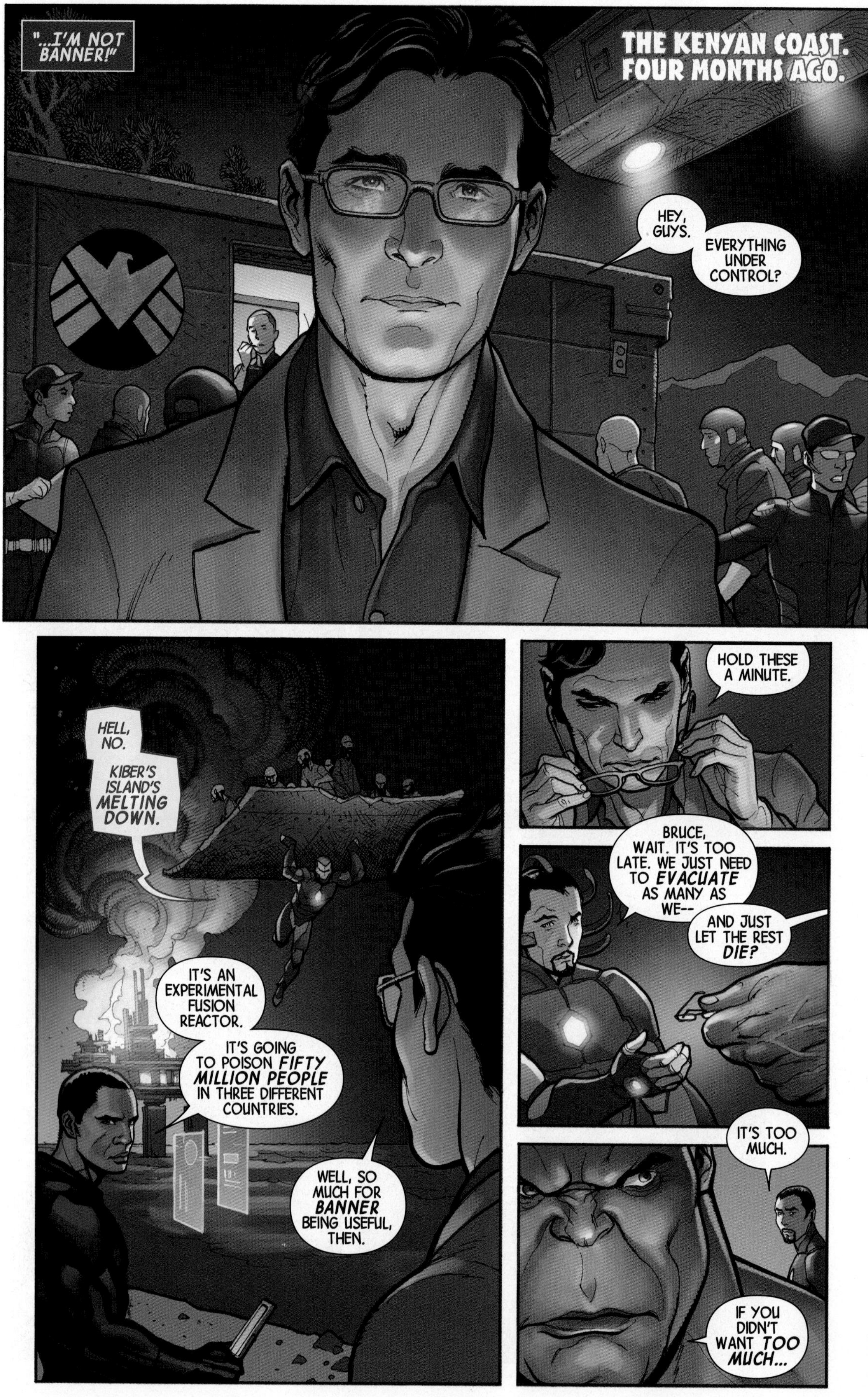
"...I'M NOT BANNER!"
THE KENYAN COAST. FOUR MONTHS AGO.
HEY, GUYS.
EVERYTHING UNDER CONTROL?
HELL, NO.
KIBER'S ISLAND'S MELTING DOWN.
IT'S AN EXPERIMENTAL FUSION REACTOR.
IT'S GOING TO POISON FIFTY MILLION PEOPLE IN THREE DIFFERENT COUNTRIES.
WELL, SO MUCH FOR BANNER BEING USEFUL, THEN.
HOLD THESE A MINUTE.
BRUCE, WAIT. IT'S TOO LATE. WE JUST NEED TO EVACUATE AS MANY AS WE--
AND JUST LET THE REST DIE?
IT'S TOO MUCH.
IF YOU DIDN'T WANT TOO MUCH...

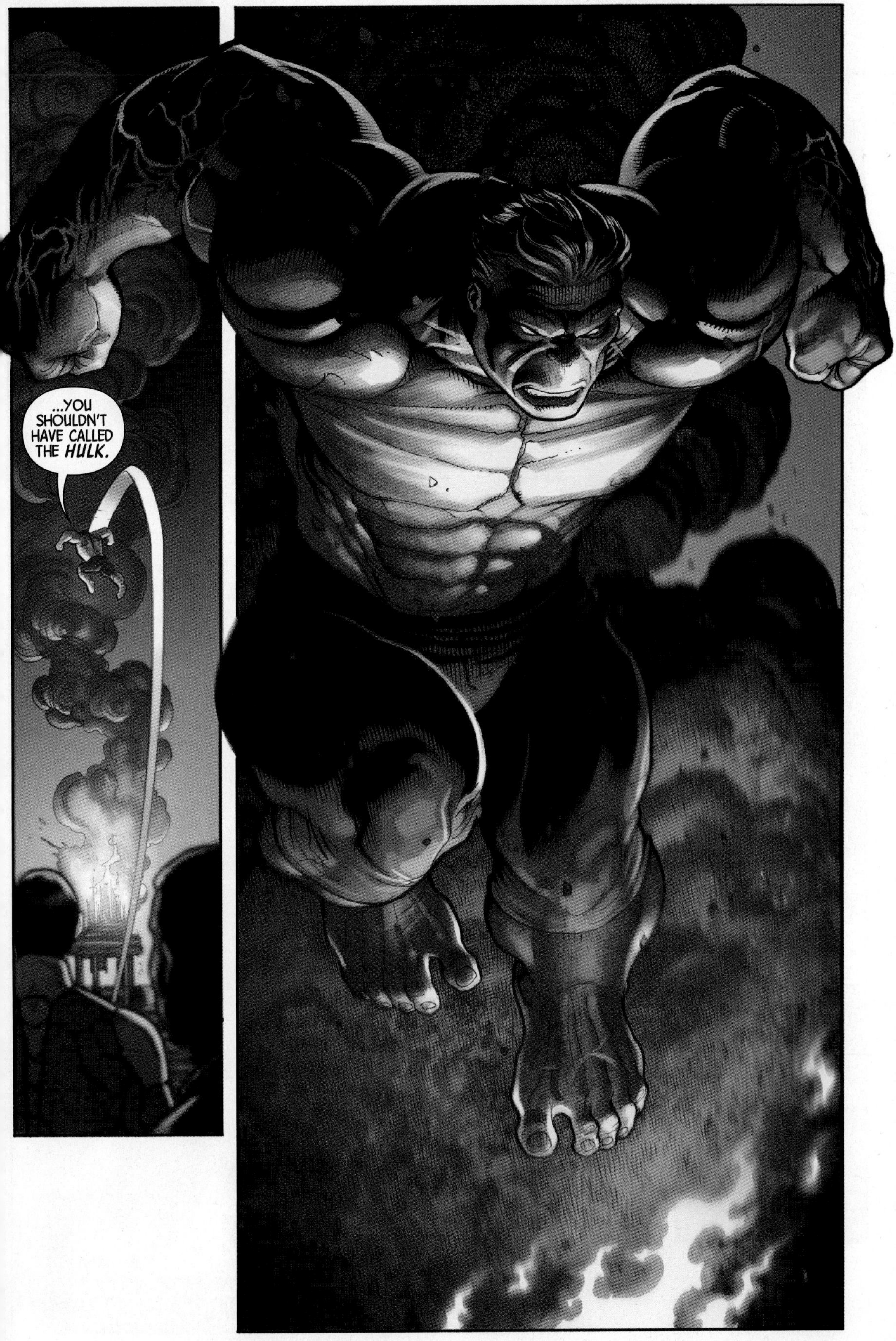
...YOU SHOULDN'T HAVE CALLED THE HULK.

DAMMIT.

COME ON, STARK! WE'VE GOT TO HELP WHOMEVER WE CAN--

WAIT, T'CHALLA...

HE'S *ABSORBING* THE *RADIATION.*

THIS...

144% RADIATION

...THIS IS VERY BAD.

102% RADI

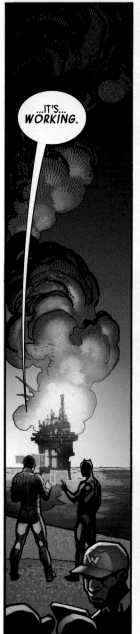

...IT'S... *WORKING.*

WHAT ARE YOU TALKING ABOUT? IT FITS THE THEORIES. WE JUST DIDN'T KNOW HE COULD ABSORB THIS *MUCH*--

NO.

LOOK.

"THIS IS A KIBER FUSION REACTOR...

"...WHICH GENERATES ENERGIES COMPLETELY *DIFFERENT* FROM THE *GAMMA* RADIATION THAT CREATED THE HULK."

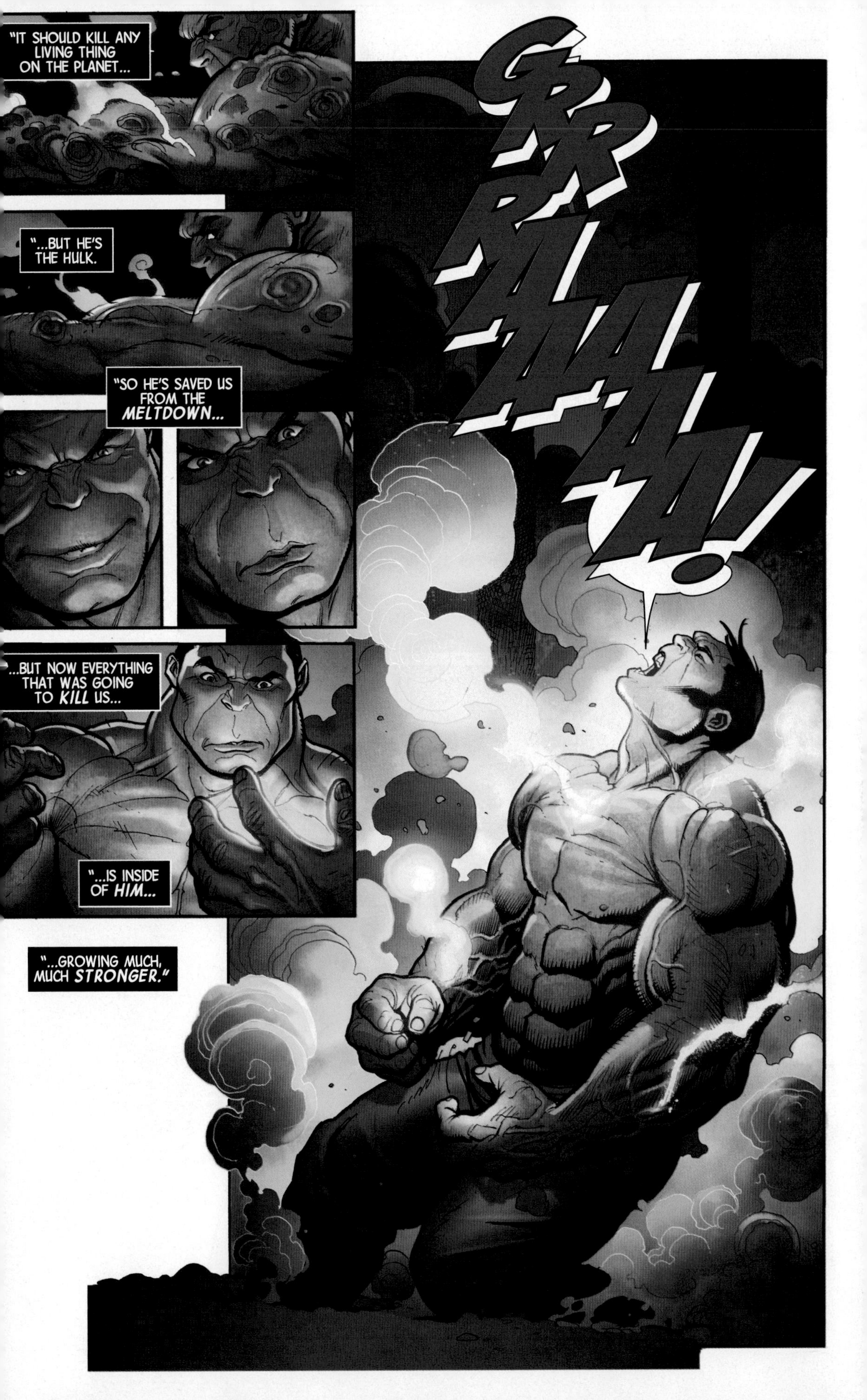
"IT SHOULD KILL ANY LIVING THING ON THE PLANET...
"...BUT HE'S THE HULK.
"SO HE'S SAVED US FROM THE MELTDOWN...
...BUT NOW EVERYTHING THAT WAS GOING TO KILL US...
"...IS INSIDE OF HIM...
"...GROWING MUCH, MUCH STRONGER."
GRRRAAAAAAAAAH!

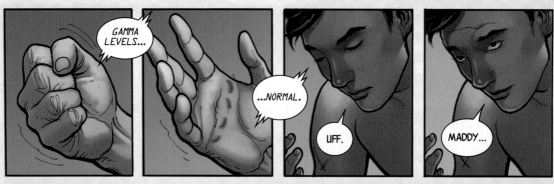

GAMMA LEVELS...

...NORMAL.

UFF.

MADDY...

...SORRY ABOUT THAT.

AMMY.

DON'T CALL ME AMMY.

AMMY...

...YOU'VE ALWAYS BEEN A GOOF. I'M YOUR SISTER. I KNOW THAT.

BUT YOU'RE NOT NORMALLY THIS RIDICULOUS.

I BELIEVE IN YOU. I WOULDN'T BE HERE IF I DIDN'T.

BUT WITH THE POWER YOU CAN DRAW ON...

...YOU... YOU JUST HAVE TO BE CAREFUL.

OKAY.

OKAY?

OKAY.

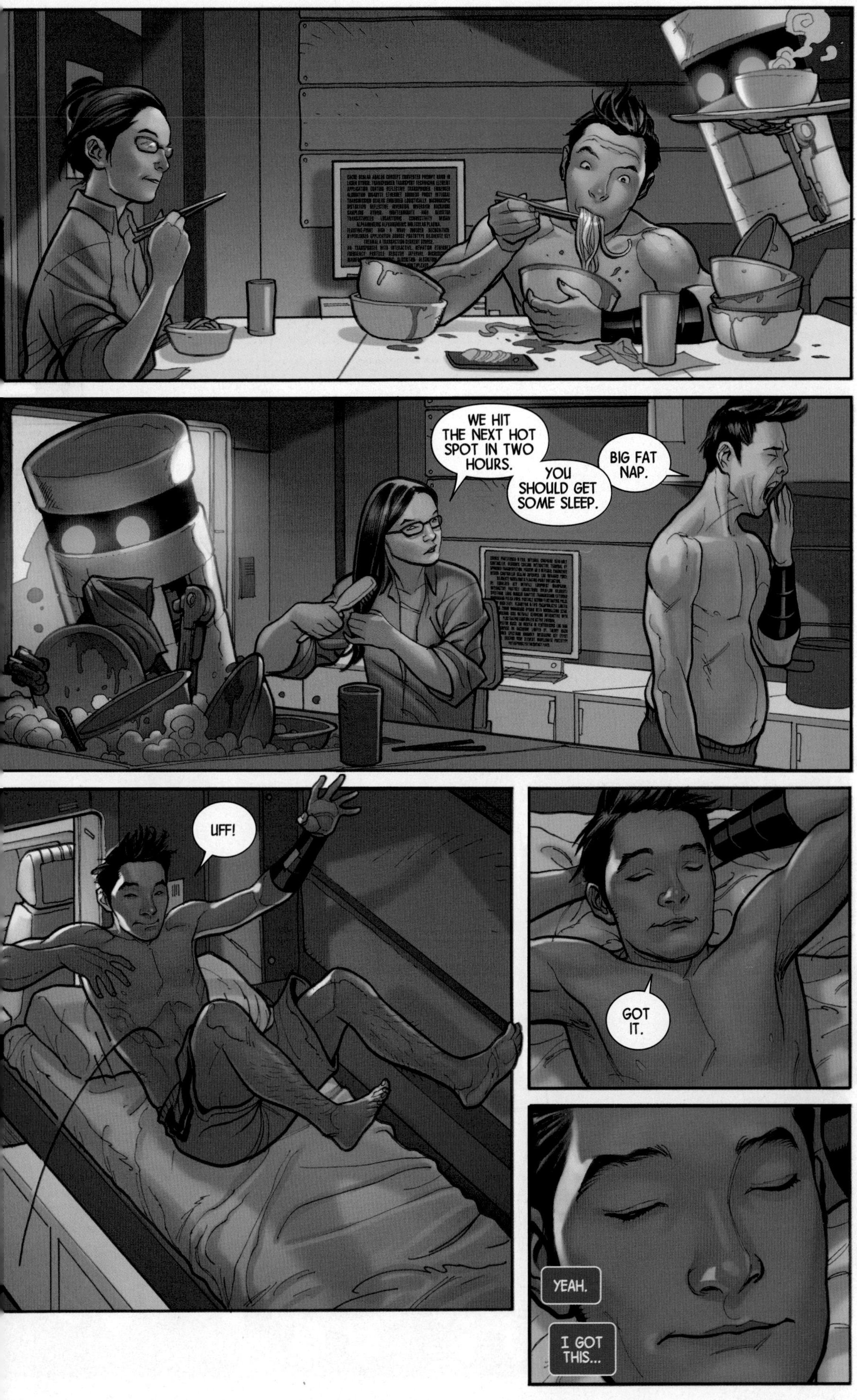

WE HIT THE NEXT HOT SPOT IN TWO HOURS.
YOU SHOULD GET SOME SLEEP.
BIG FAT NAP.
UFF!
GOT IT.
YEAH.
I GOT THIS...

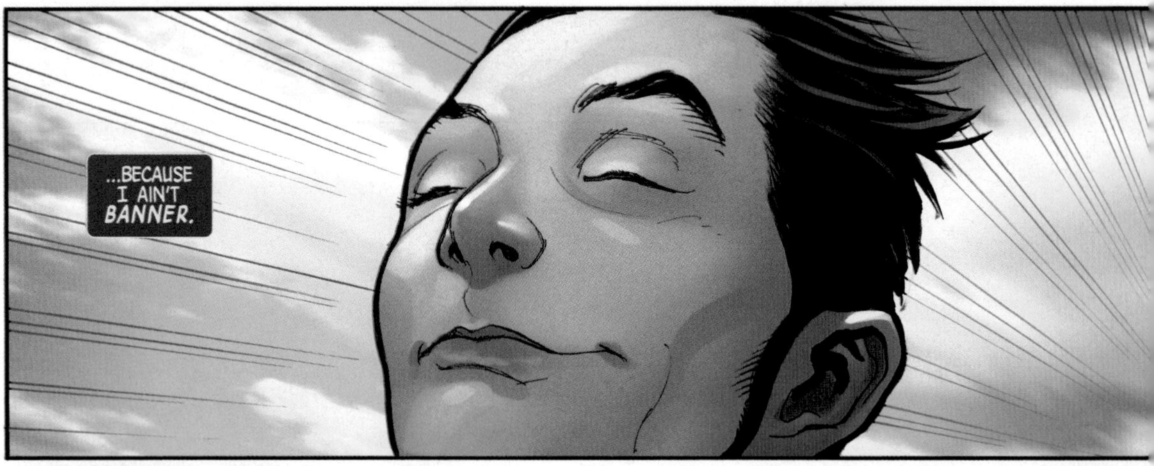
...BECAUSE I AIN'T BANNER.

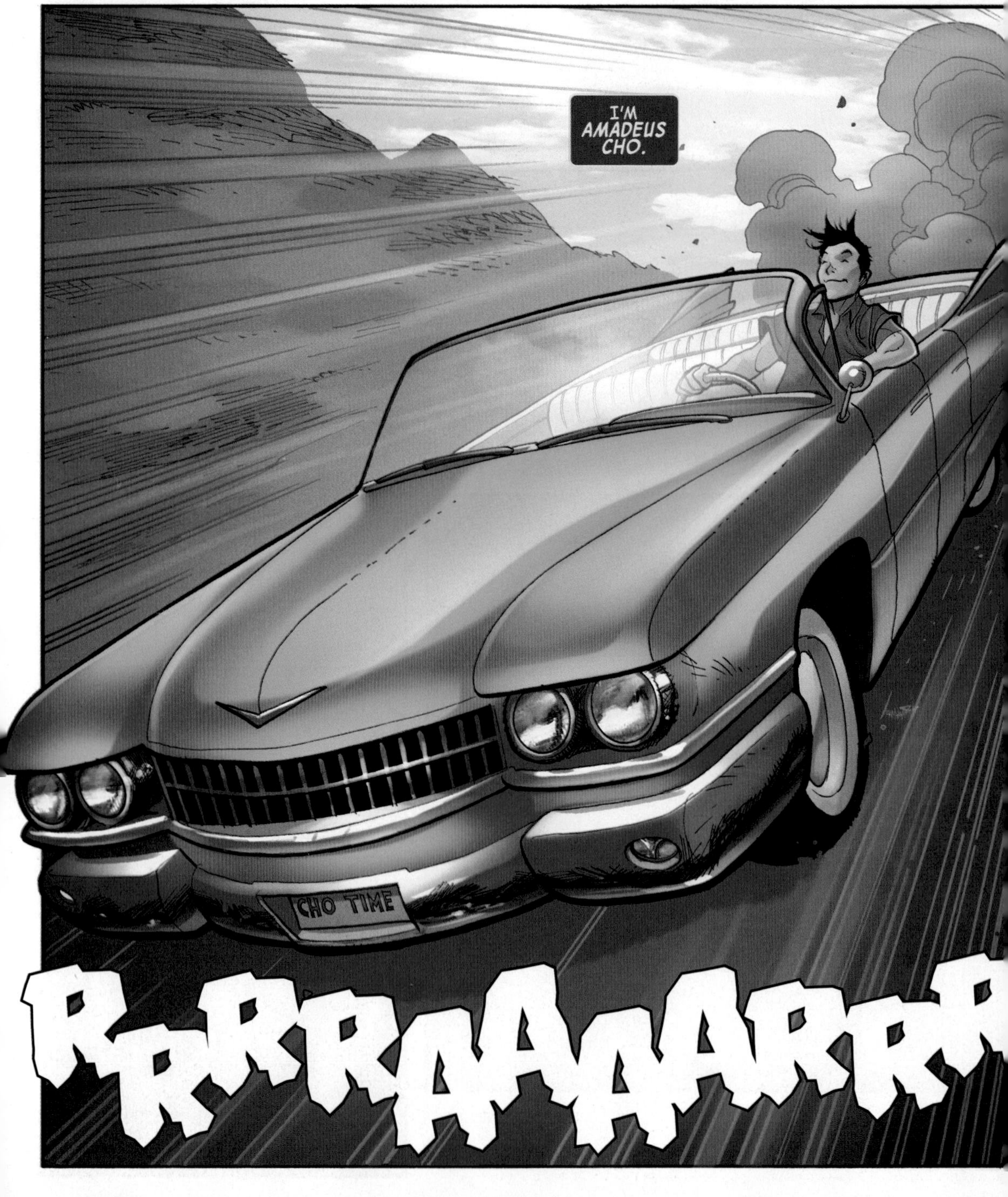
I'M AMADEUS CHO.
CHO TIME
RRRRAAAAARRR

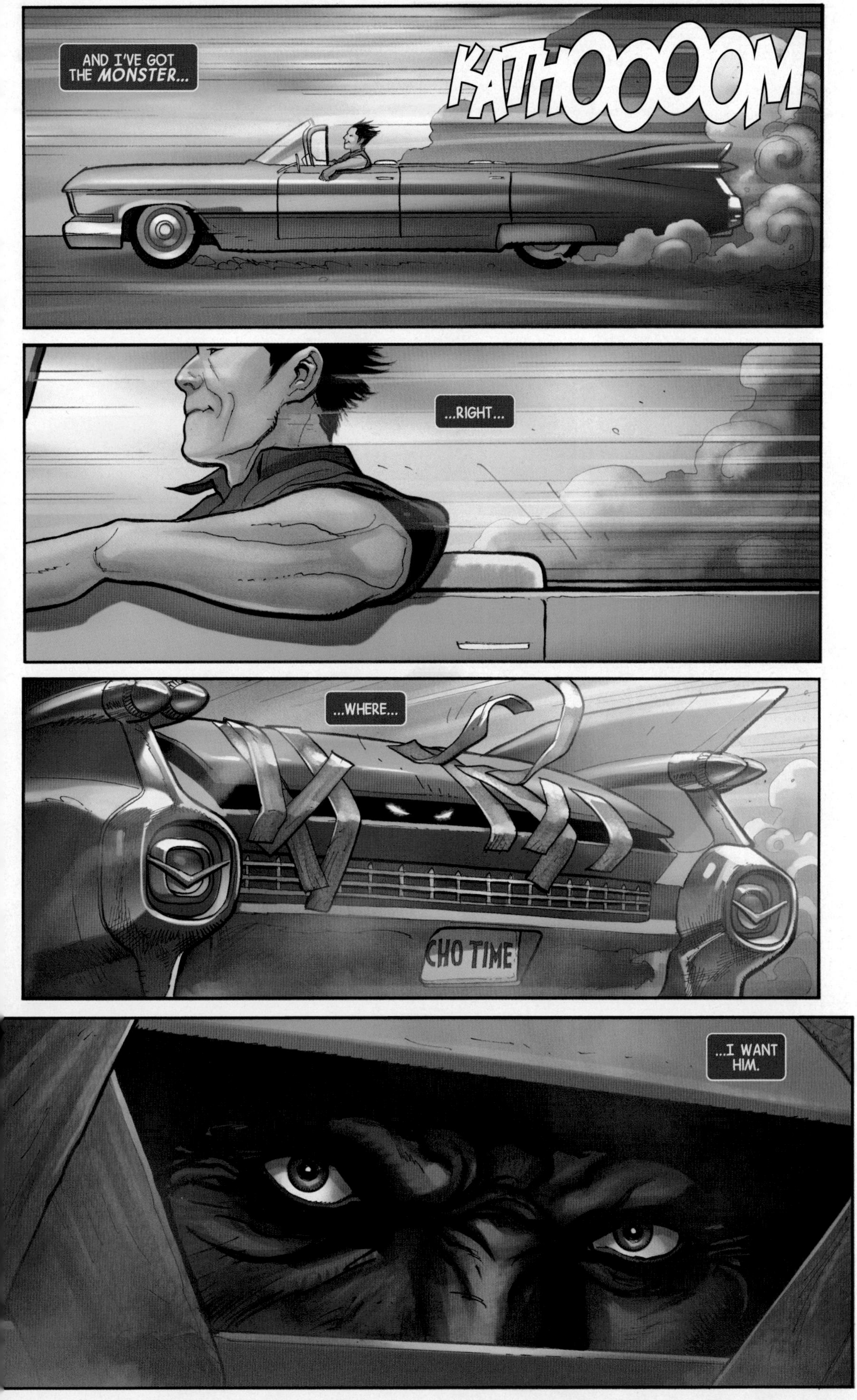
AND I'VE GOT THE MONSTER...
KATHOOOOOM
...RIGHT...
...WHERE...
CHO TIME
...I WANT HIM.

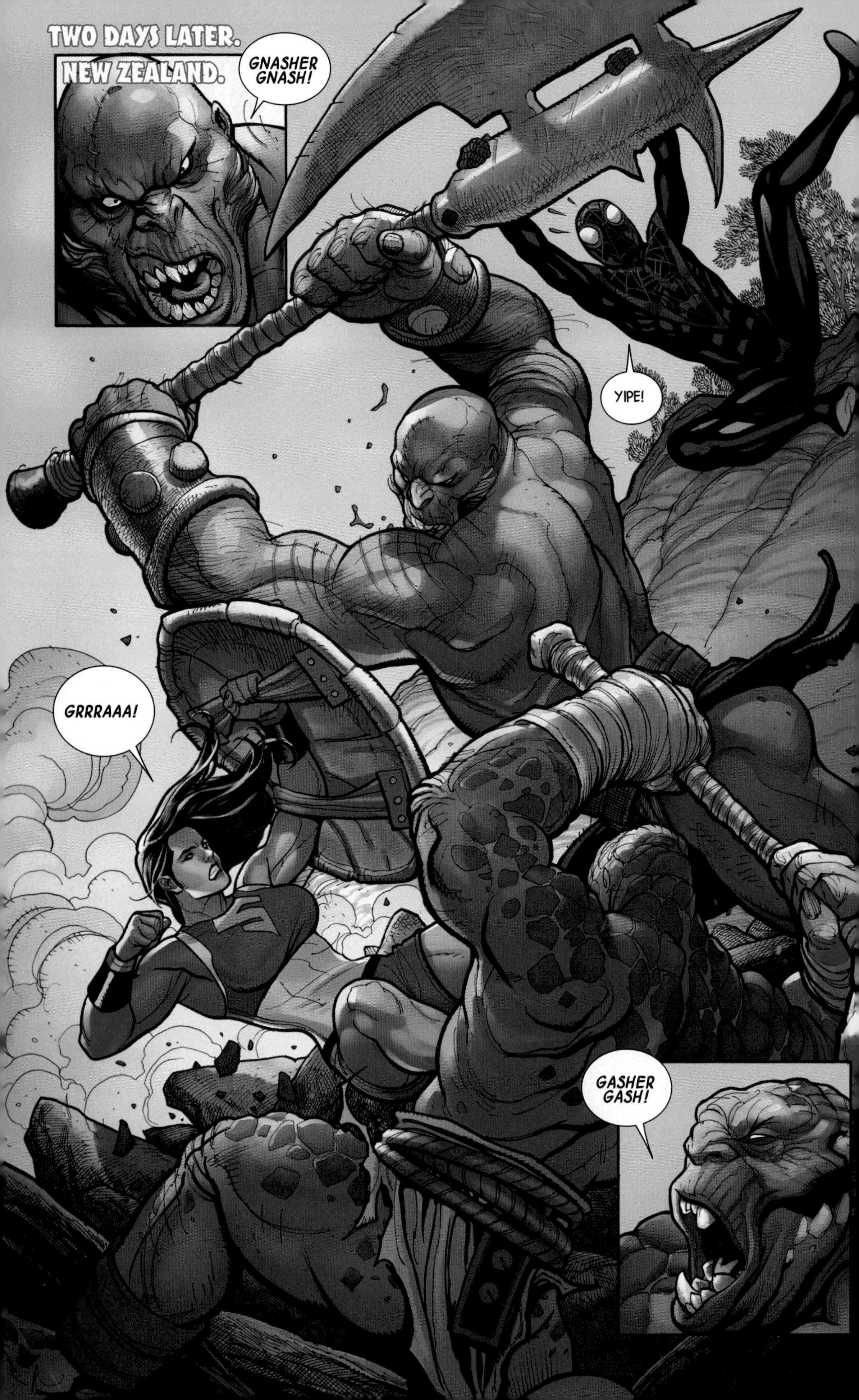
TWO DAYS LATER.
NEW ZEALAND.
GNASHER GNASH!
YIPE!
GRRRAAA!
GASHER GASH!

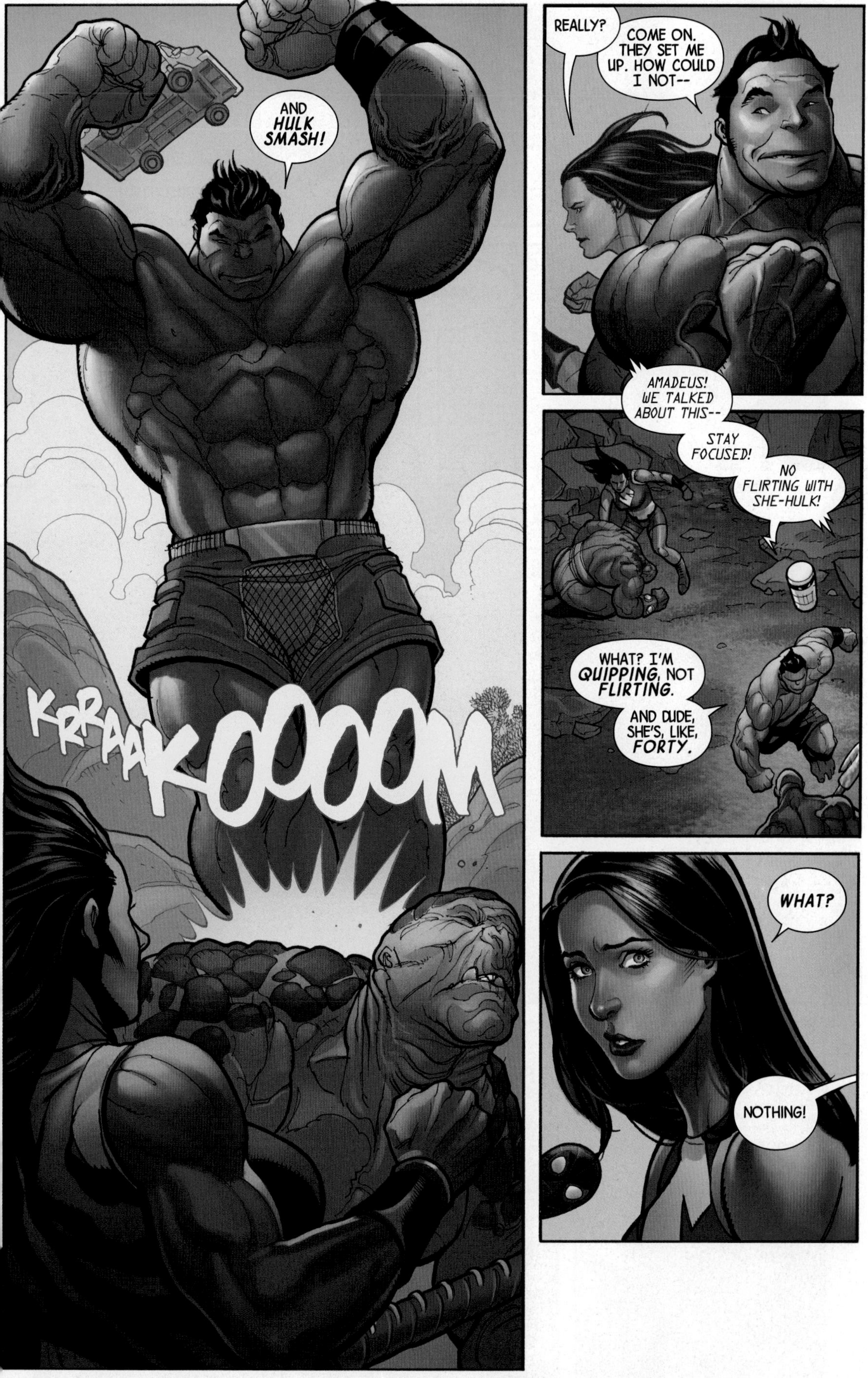
AND HULK SMASH!
KRRAAKOOOOM
REALLY?
COME ON. THEY SET ME UP. HOW COULD I NOT--
AMADEUS! WE TALKED ABOUT THIS--
STAY FOCUSED!
NO FLIRTING WITH SHE-HULK!
WHAT? I'M QUIPPING, NOT FLIRTING.
AND DUDE, SHE'S, LIKE, FORTY.
WHAT?
NOTHING!

FINE.

KKRRRAAKK

BRRAAAK

SERIOUSLY!

GRRAAAAAAAAA!

SKKKRRRAAAKK

POW

AND *STAY* DOWN!

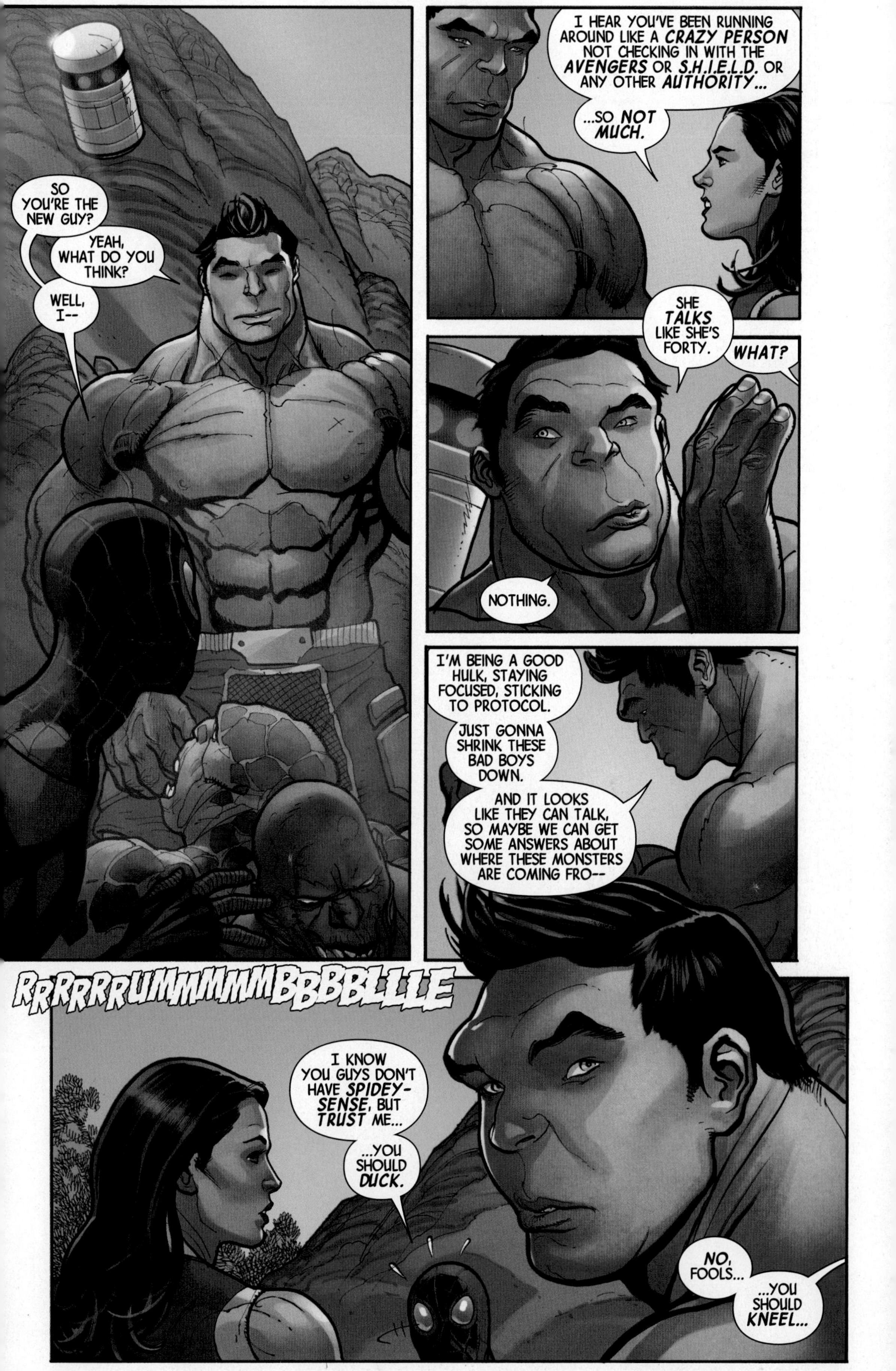
SO YOU'RE THE NEW GUY?
YEAH, WHAT DO YOU THINK?
WELL, I--
I HEAR YOU'VE BEEN RUNNING AROUND LIKE A CRAZY PERSON NOT CHECKING IN WITH THE AVENGERS OR S.H.I.E.L.D. OR ANY OTHER AUTHORITY...
...SO NOT MUCH.
SHE TALKS LIKE SHE'S FORTY.
WHAT?
NOTHING.
I'M BEING A GOOD HULK, STAYING FOCUSED, STICKING TO PROTOCOL.
JUST GONNA SHRINK THESE BAD BOYS DOWN.
AND IT LOOKS LIKE THEY CAN TALK, SO MAYBE WE CAN GET SOME ANSWERS ABOUT WHERE THESE MONSTERS ARE COMING FRO--
RRRRRRUMMMMMMBBBBLLLE
I KNOW YOU GUYS DON'T HAVE SPIDEY-SENSE, BUT TRUST ME...
...YOU SHOULD DUCK.
NO, FOOLS...
...YOU SHOULD KNEEL...

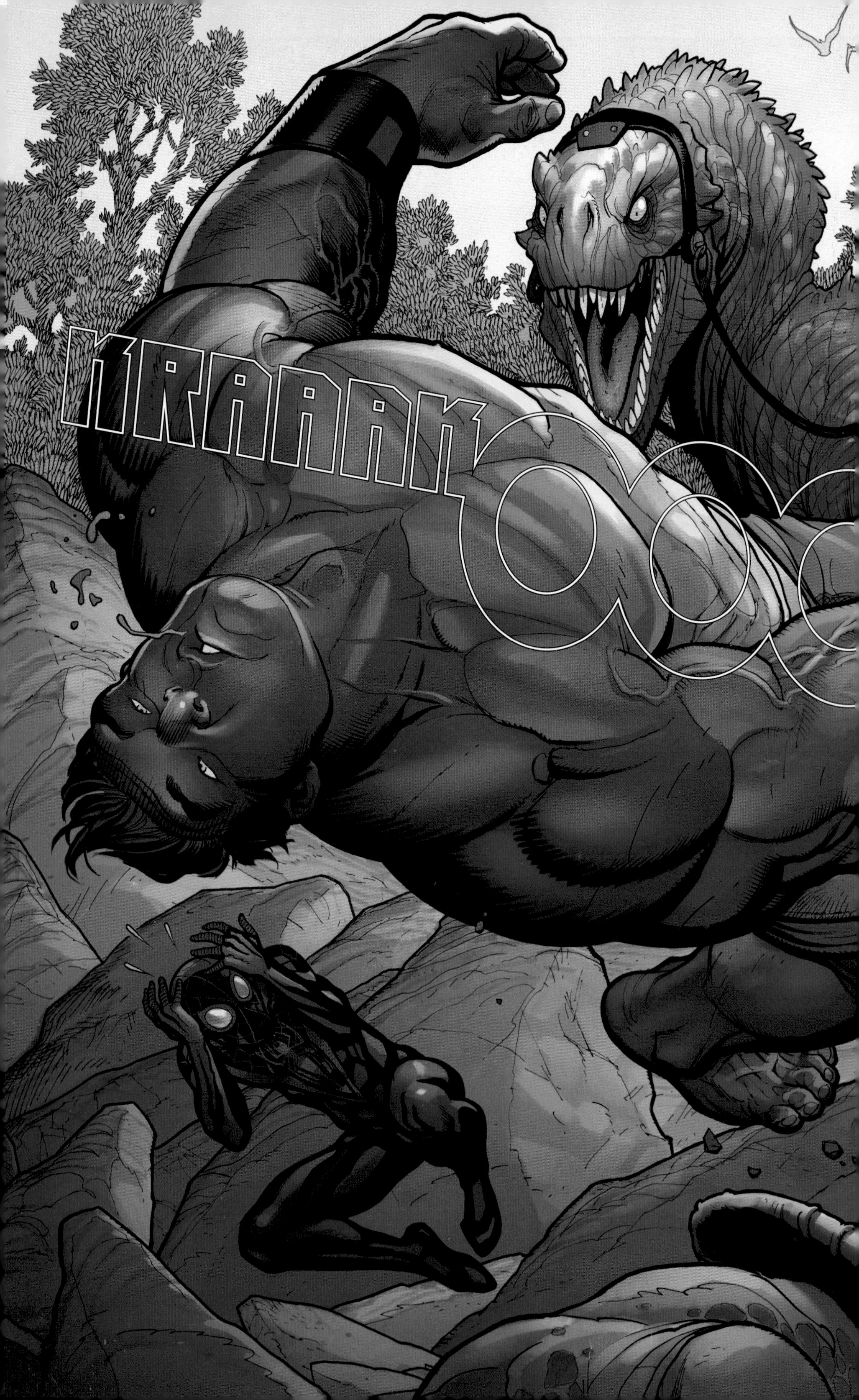
KRAAAKOOO

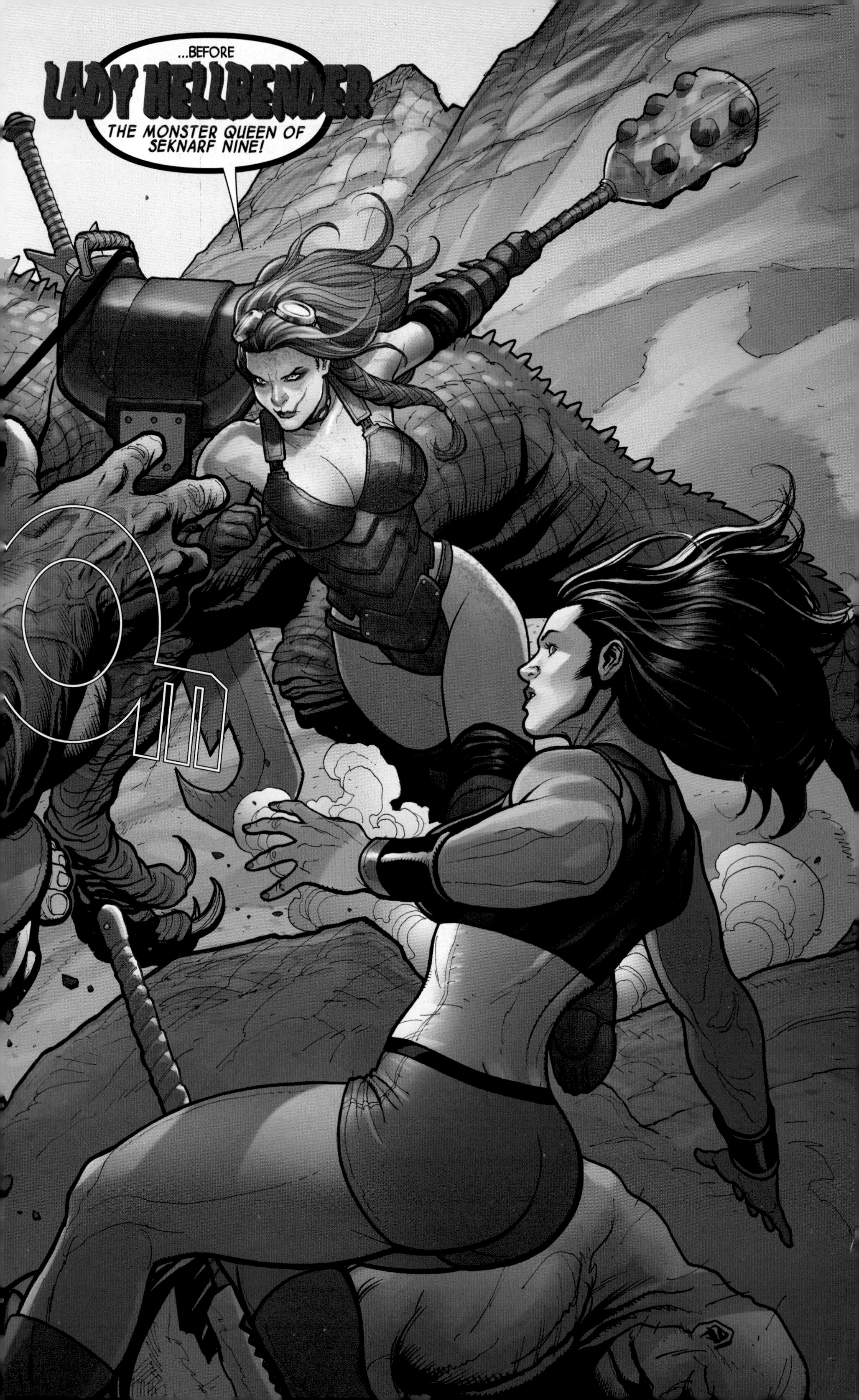
...BEFORE
LADY HELLBENDER
THE MONSTER QUEEN OF SEKNARF NINE!

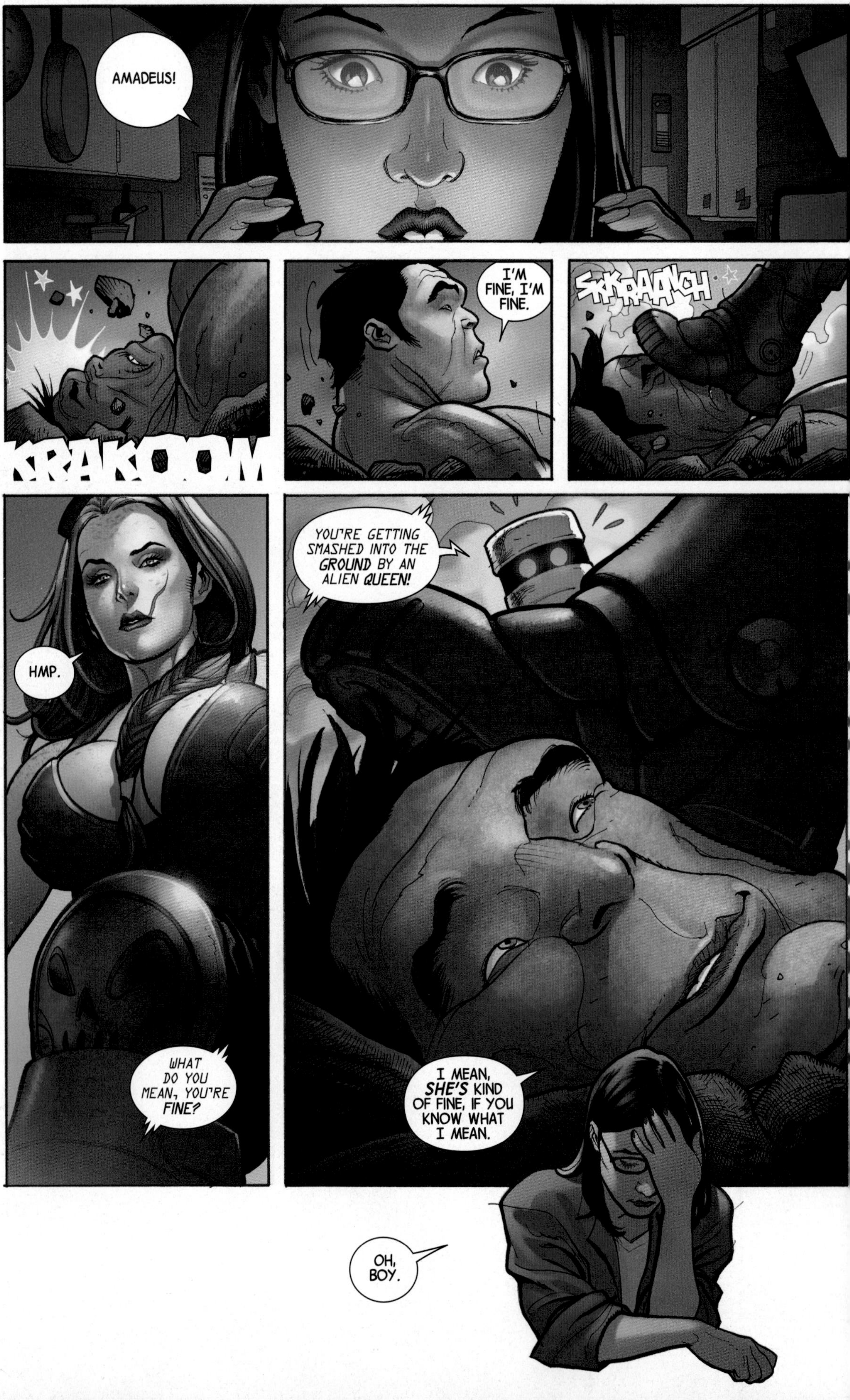
AMADEUS!
KRAKOOM
I'M FINE, I'M FINE.
SKKRAAANCH
YOU'RE GETTING SMASHED INTO THE GROUND BY AN ALIEN QUEEN!
HMP.
WHAT DO YOU MEAN, YOU'RE FINE?
I MEAN, SHE'S KIND OF FINE, IF YOU KNOW WHAT I MEAN.
OH, BOY.

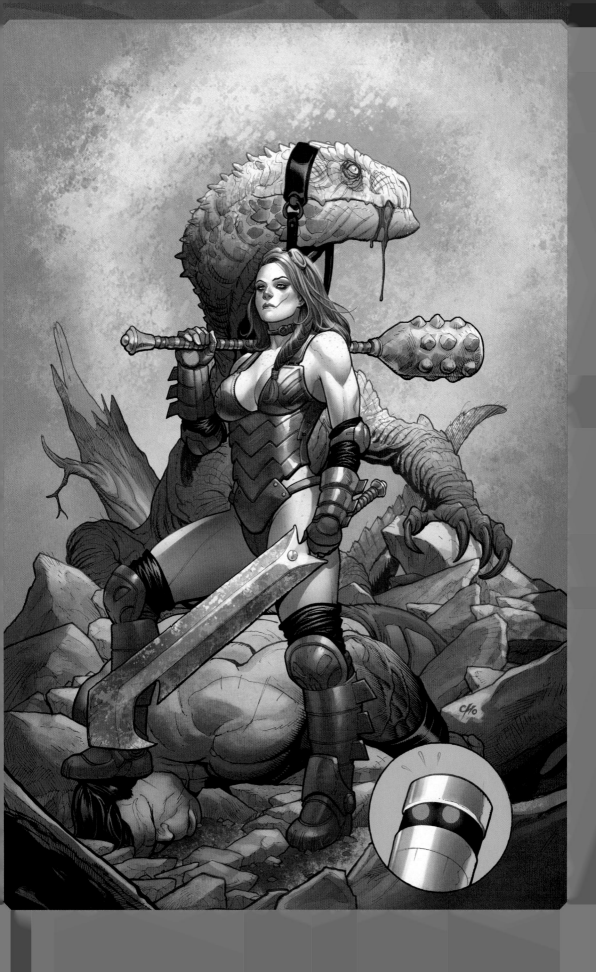

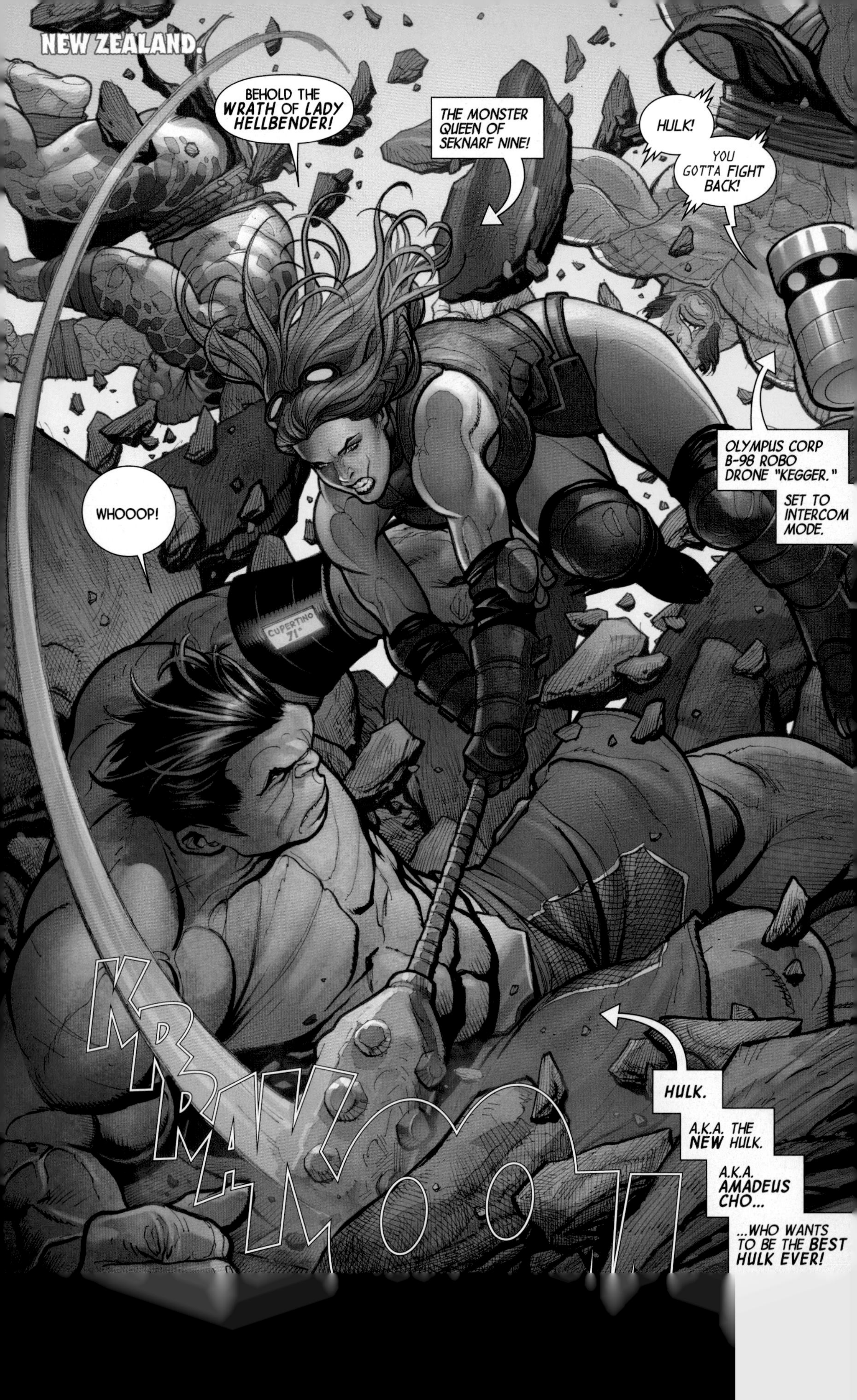
NEW ZEALAND.
BEHOLD THE WRATH OF LADY HELLBENDER!
THE MONSTER QUEEN OF SEKNARF NINE!
HULK!
YOU GOTTA FIGHT BACK!
OLYMPUS CORP B-98 ROBO DRONE "KEGGER."
SET TO INTERCOM MODE.
WHOOOP!
CUPERTINO 71°
KRBAMMOOM
HULK.
A.K.A. THE NEW HULK.
A.K.A. AMADEUS CHO...
...WHO WANTS TO BE THE BEST HULK EVER!

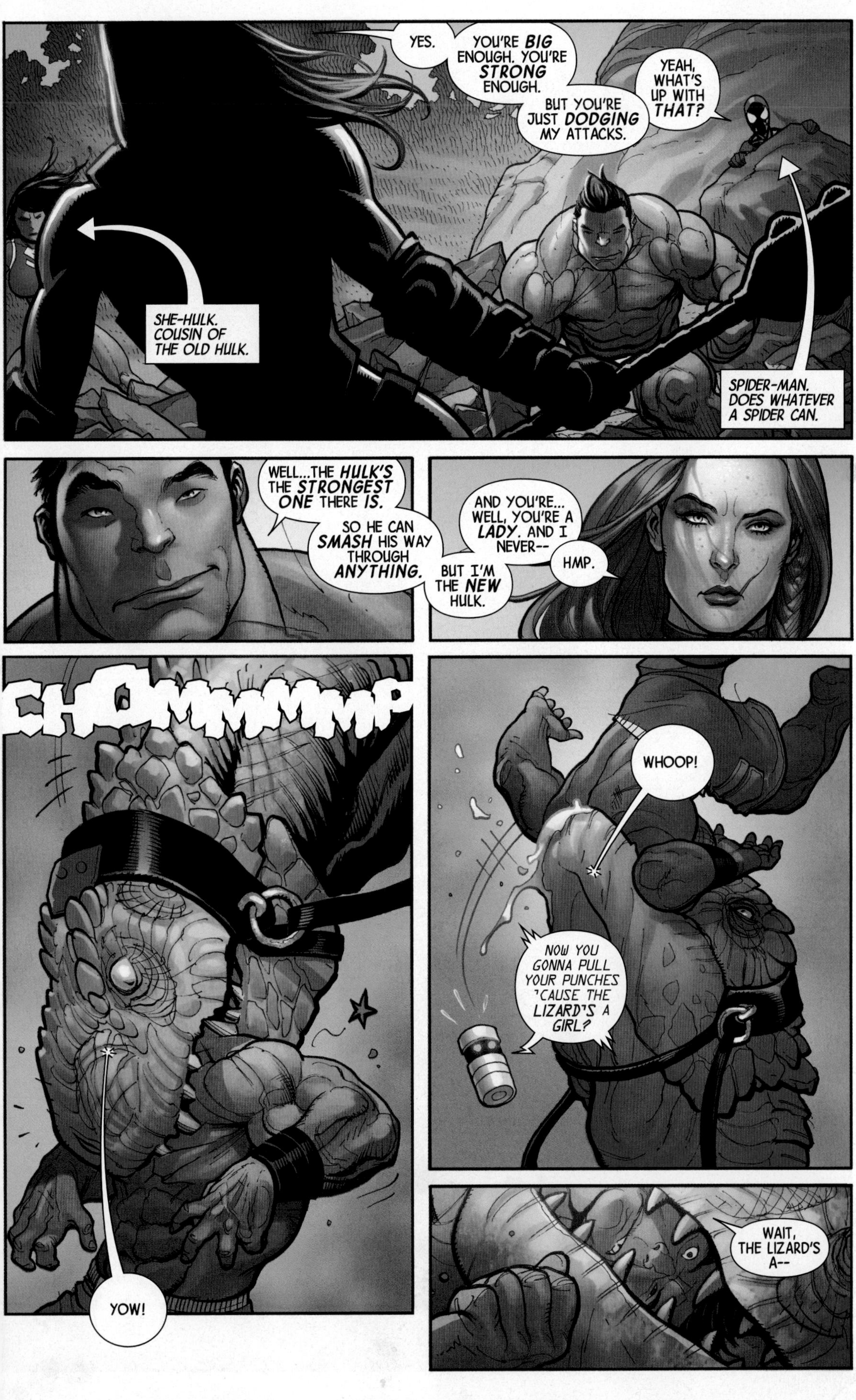
YES.
YOU'RE BIG ENOUGH. YOU'RE STRONG ENOUGH.
BUT YOU'RE JUST DODGING MY ATTACKS.
YEAH, WHAT'S UP WITH THAT?
SHE-HULK. COUSIN OF THE OLD HULK.
SPIDER-MAN. DOES WHATEVER A SPIDER CAN.
WELL...THE HULK'S THE STRONGEST ONE THERE IS.
SO HE CAN SMASH HIS WAY THROUGH ANYTHING.
BUT I'M THE NEW HULK.
AND YOU'RE... WELL, YOU'RE A LADY. AND I NEVER--
HMP.
CHOMMMMMP
YOW!
WHOOP!
NOW YOU GONNA PULL YOUR PUNCHES 'CAUSE THE LIZARD'S A GIRL?
WAIT, THE LIZARD'S A--

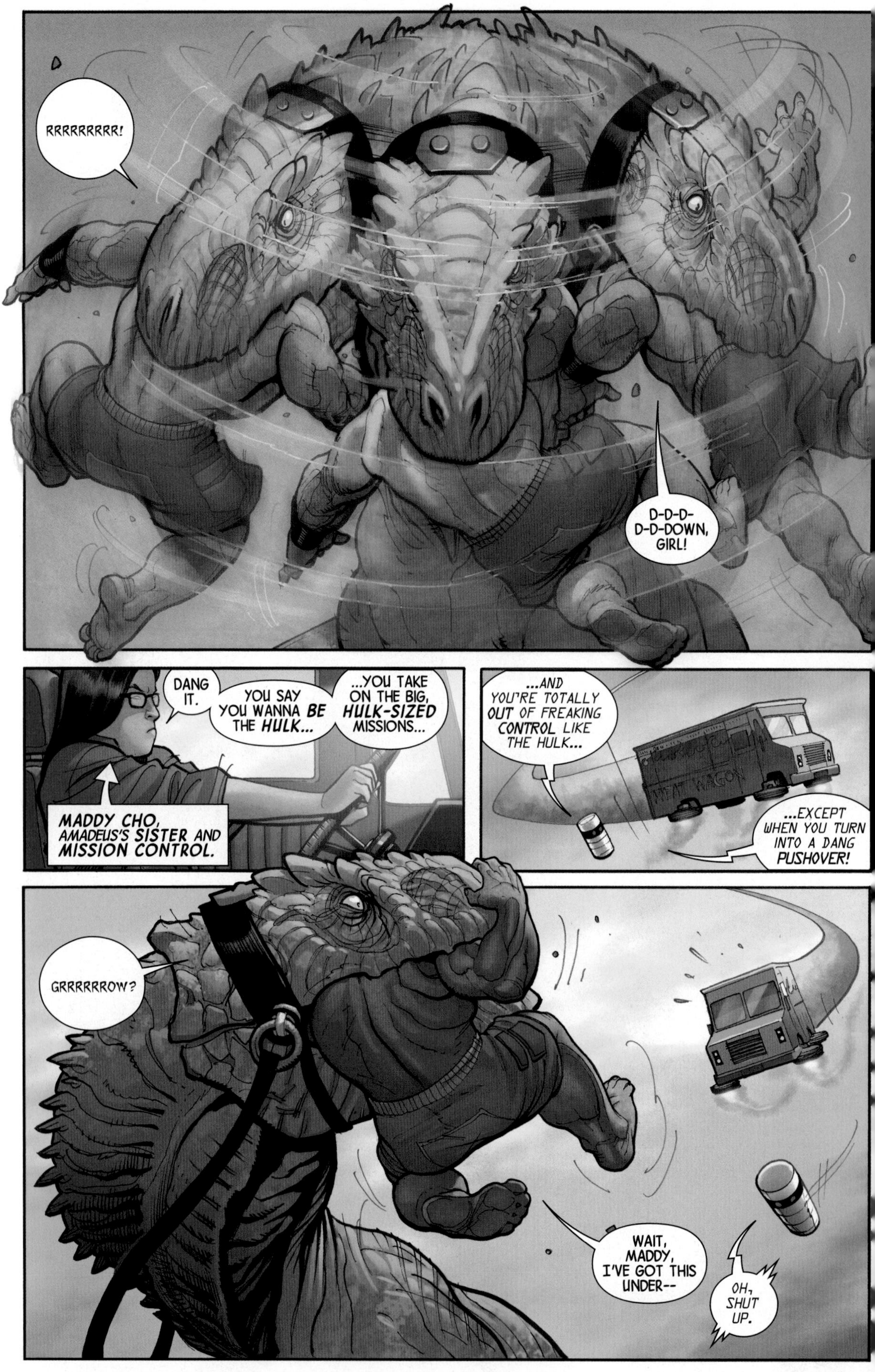
RRRRRRRRR!
D-D-D-D-D-DOWN, GIRL!
DANG IT.
YOU SAY YOU WANNA BE THE HULK...
...YOU TAKE ON THE BIG, HULK-SIZED MISSIONS...
MADDY CHO, AMADEUS'S SISTER AND MISSION CONTROL.
...AND YOU'RE TOTALLY OUT OF FREAKING CONTROL LIKE THE HULK...
MEAT WAGON
...EXCEPT WHEN YOU TURN INTO A DANG PUSHOVER!
GRRRRRROW?
WAIT, MADDY, I'VE GOT THIS UNDER--
OH, SHUT UP.

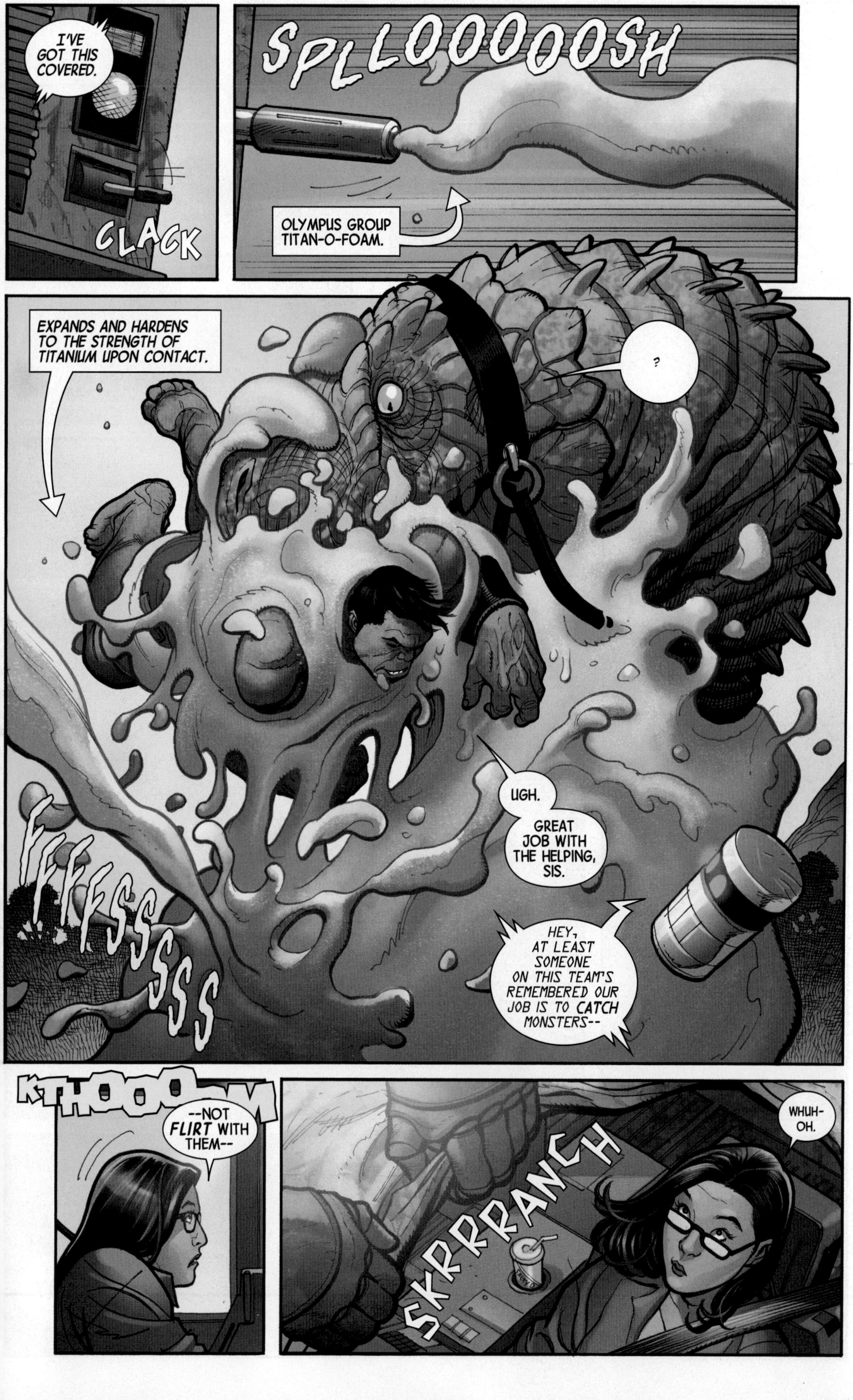

I'VE GOT THIS COVERED.
CLACK
SPLLOOOOOOSH
OLYMPUS GROUP TITAN-O-FOAM.
EXPANDS AND HARDENS TO THE STRENGTH OF TITANIUM UPON CONTACT.
?
UGH.
GREAT JOB WITH THE HELPING, SIS.
FFFFSSSSSSS
HEY, AT LEAST SOMEONE ON THIS TEAM'S REMEMBERED OUR JOB IS TO CATCH MONSTERS--
KTHOOOOM
--NOT FLIRT WITH THEM--
WHUH-OH.
SKRRRANCH

HA HAAAAA!

GAH!

KOREAN BBQ · HAMBURGER · PORK · BEEF · CHICKEN

MEAT WAGON

MADDY!

I'LL GET HER!

THWAP

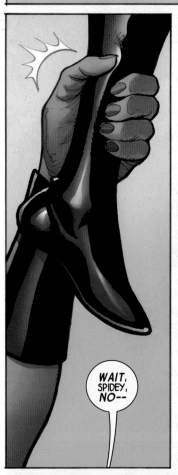

WAIT, SPIDEY, NO--

WHAT THE HECK?!

LOOK AT THE HULK!

TRUST ME, I KNOW THAT LOOK, AND--

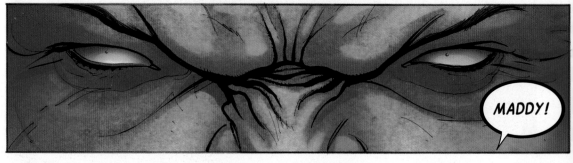

MADDY!

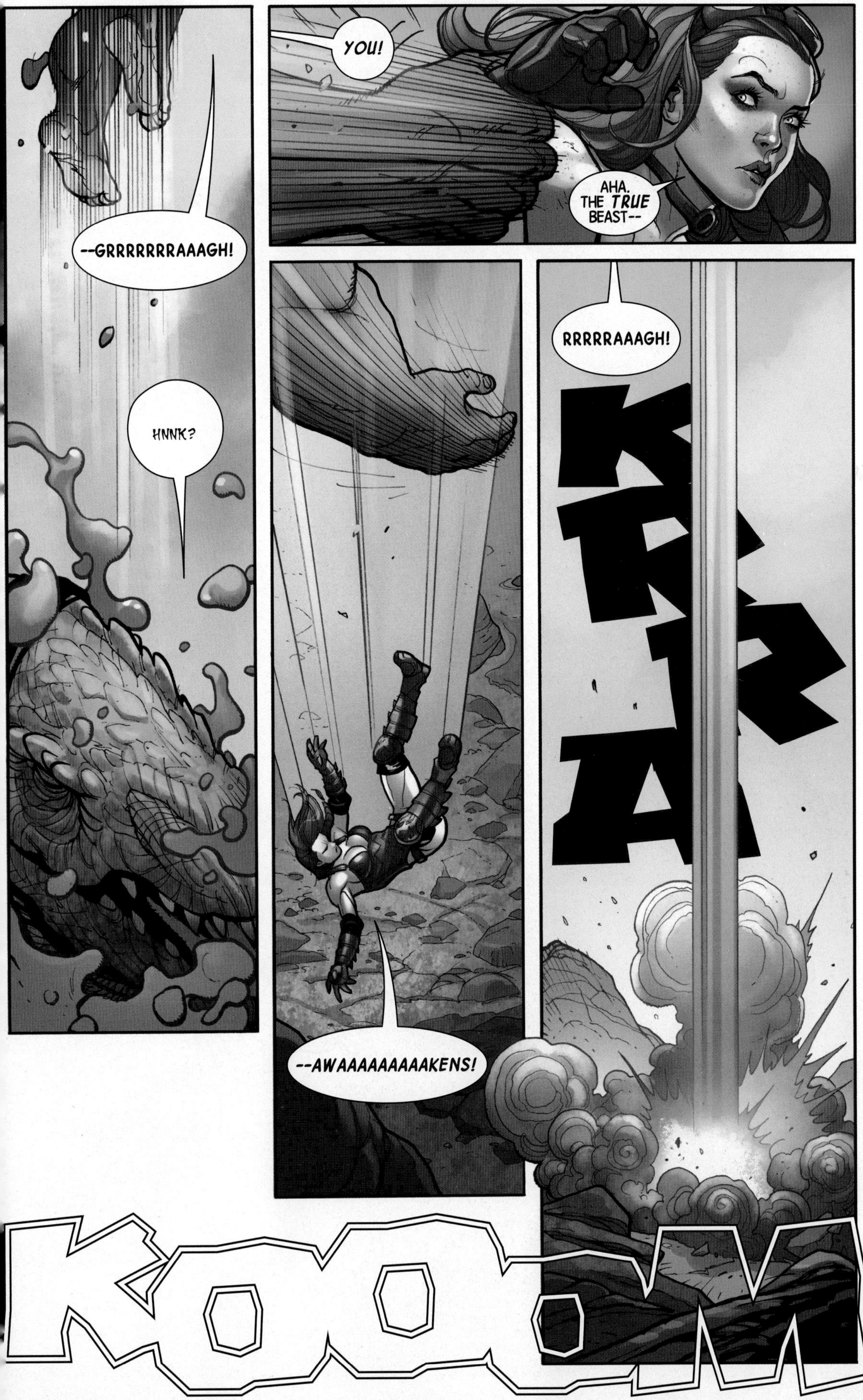
YOU!
AHA. THE *TRUE* BEAST--
--GRRRRRRRAAAGH!
HNNK?
--AWAAAAAAAAAKENS!
RRRRRAAAGH!
KRRA
KOOOM

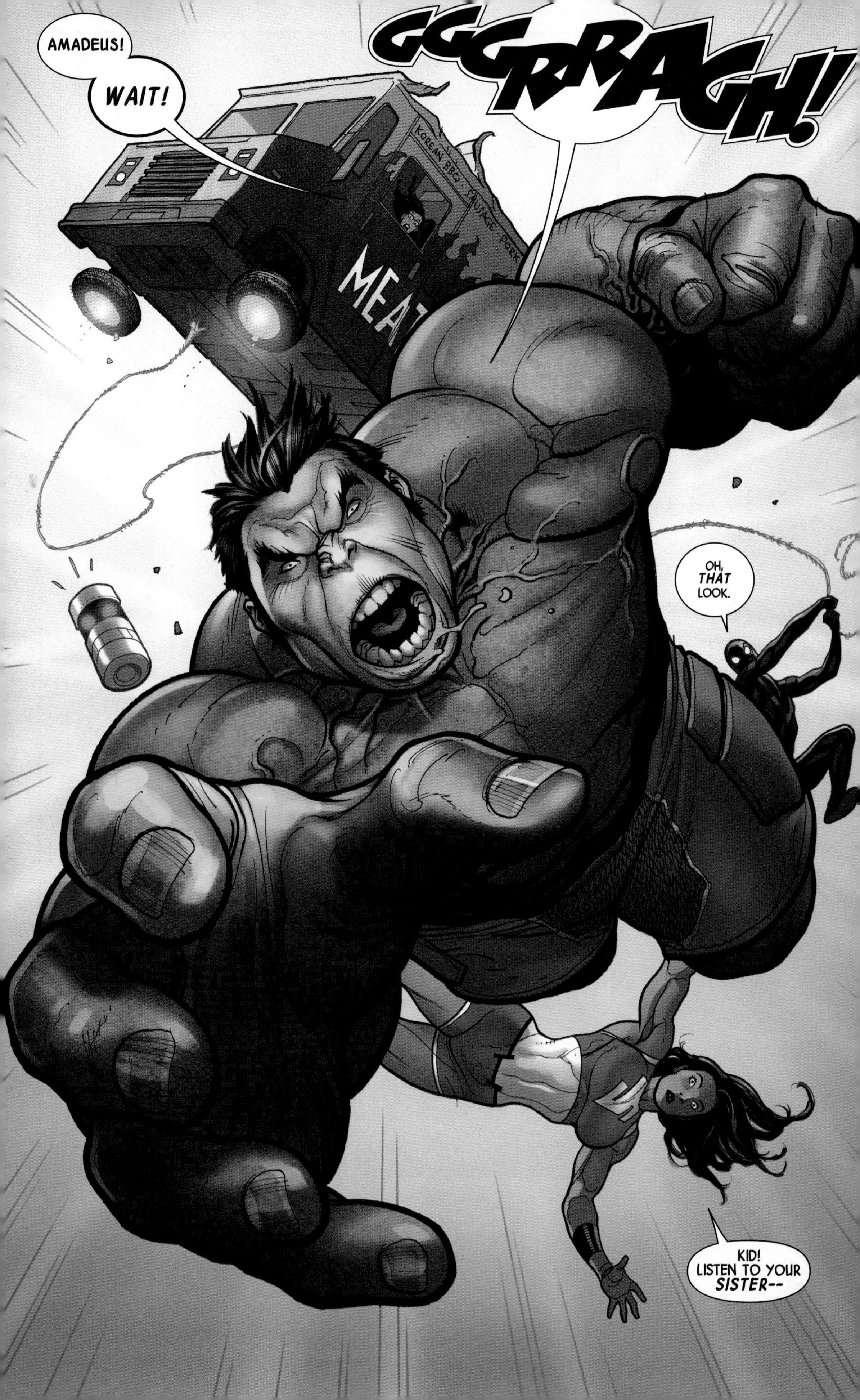
AMADEUS!
WAIT!
GGGRRAGH!
KOREAN BBQ · SAUSAGE · PORK
MEAT
OH, THAT LOOK.
KID! LISTEN TO YOUR SISTER--

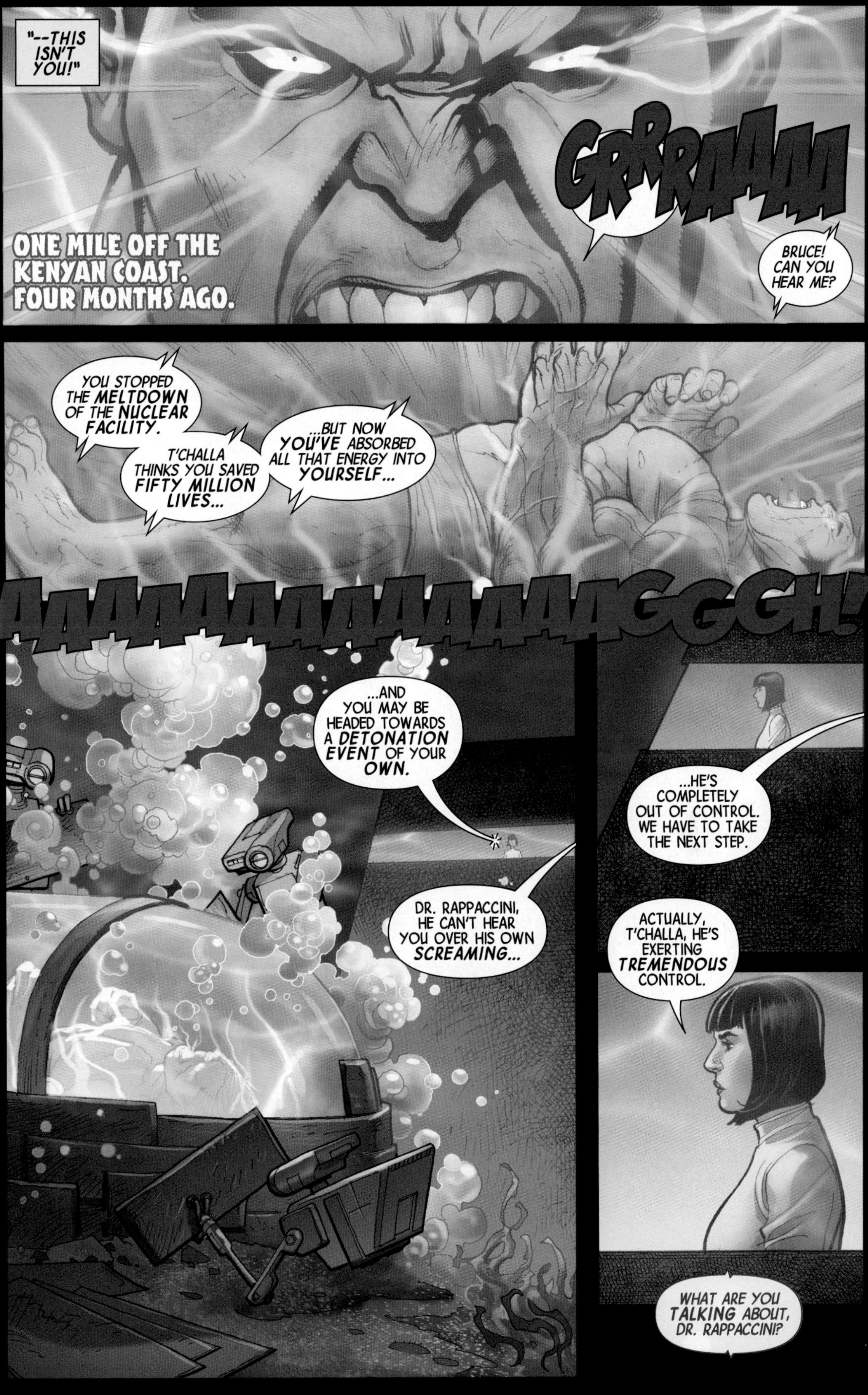
"--THIS ISN'T YOU!"
GRRRAAAAA
ONE MILE OFF THE KENYAN COAST. FOUR MONTHS AGO.
BRUCE! CAN YOU HEAR ME?
YOU STOPPED THE MELTDOWN OF THE NUCLEAR FACILITY.
T'CHALLA THINKS YOU SAVED FIFTY MILLION LIVES...
...BUT NOW YOU'VE ABSORBED ALL THAT ENERGY INTO YOURSELF...
AAAAAAAAAAAAAAAGGGH!
...AND YOU MAY BE HEADED TOWARDS A DETONATION EVENT OF YOUR OWN.
DR. RAPPACCINI, HE CAN'T HEAR YOU OVER HIS OWN SCREAMING...
...HE'S COMPLETELY OUT OF CONTROL. WE HAVE TO TAKE THE NEXT STEP.
ACTUALLY, T'CHALLA, HE'S EXERTING TREMENDOUS CONTROL.
WHAT ARE YOU TALKING ABOUT, DR. RAPPACCINI?

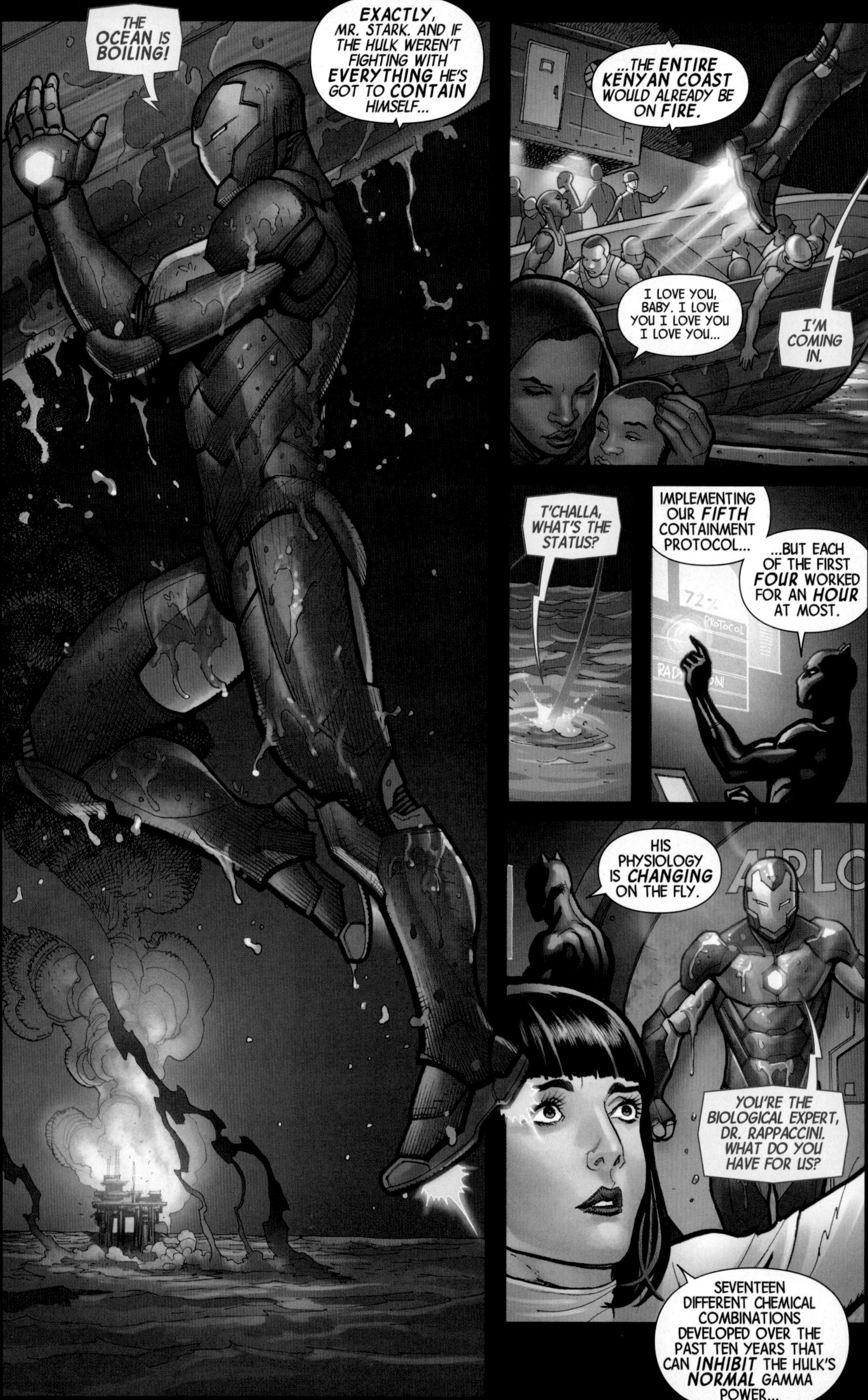

THE OCEAN IS BOILING!
EXACTLY, MR. STARK. AND IF THE HULK WEREN'T FIGHTING WITH EVERYTHING HE'S GOT TO CONTAIN HIMSELF...
...THE ENTIRE KENYAN COAST WOULD ALREADY BE ON FIRE.
I LOVE YOU, BABY. I LOVE YOU I LOVE YOU I LOVE YOU...
I'M COMING IN.
T'CHALLA, WHAT'S THE STATUS?
IMPLEMENTING OUR FIFTH CONTAINMENT PROTOCOL...
...BUT EACH OF THE FIRST FOUR WORKED FOR AN HOUR AT MOST.
72%
PROTOCOL
HIS PHYSIOLOGY IS CHANGING ON THE FLY.
AIRLO
YOU'RE THE BIOLOGICAL EXPERT, DR. RAPPACCINI. WHAT DO YOU HAVE FOR US?
SEVENTEEN DIFFERENT CHEMICAL COMBINATIONS DEVELOPED OVER THE PAST TEN YEARS THAT CAN INHIBIT THE HULK'S NORMAL GAMMA POWER...

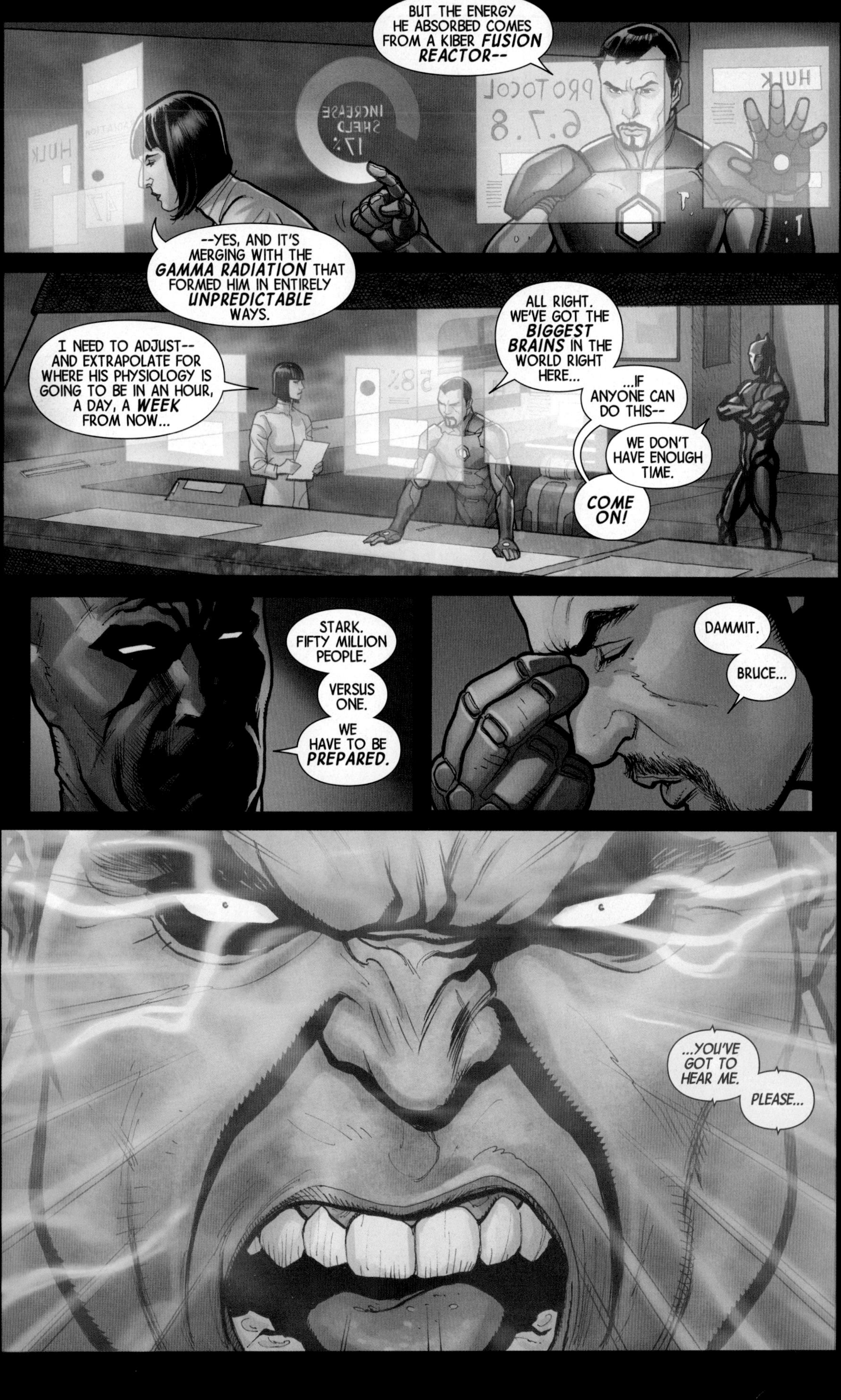
BUT THE ENERGY HE ABSORBED COMES FROM A KIBER FUSION REACTOR--
--YES, AND IT'S MERGING WITH THE GAMMA RADIATION THAT FORMED HIM IN ENTIRELY UNPREDICTABLE WAYS.
I NEED TO ADJUST-- AND EXTRAPOLATE FOR WHERE HIS PHYSIOLOGY IS GOING TO BE IN AN HOUR, A DAY, A WEEK FROM NOW...
ALL RIGHT. WE'VE GOT THE BIGGEST BRAINS IN THE WORLD RIGHT HERE...
...IF ANYONE CAN DO THIS--
WE DON'T HAVE ENOUGH TIME.
COME ON!
STARK. FIFTY MILLION PEOPLE.
VERSUS ONE.
WE HAVE TO BE PREPARED.
DAMMIT.
BRUCE...
...YOU'VE GOT TO HEAR ME.
PLEASE...

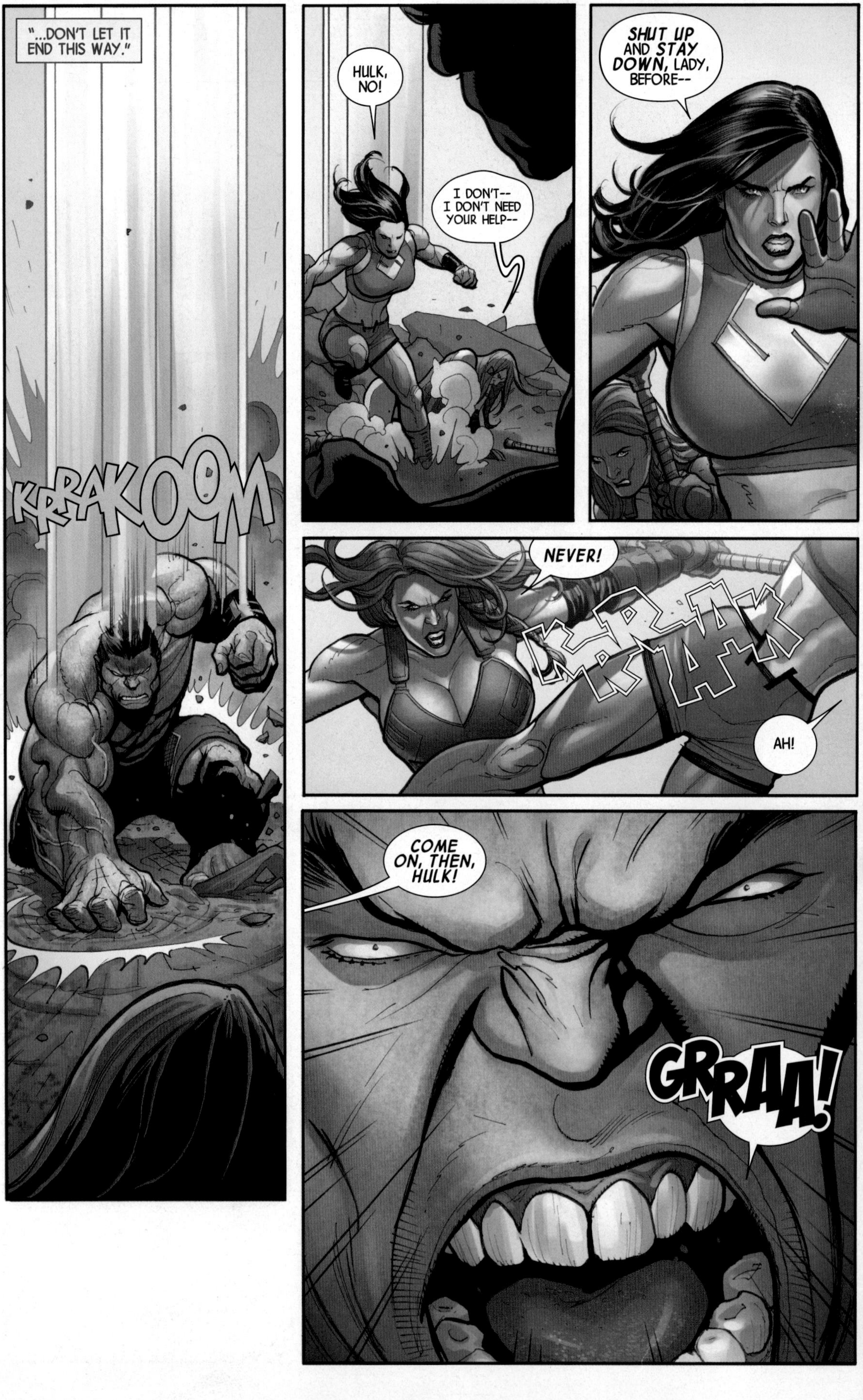
"...DON'T LET IT END THIS WAY."
KRRAKOOM
HULK, NO!
I DON'T-- I DON'T NEED YOUR HELP--
SHUT UP AND STAY DOWN, LADY, BEFORE--
NEVER!
KRAAK
AH!
COME ON, THEN, HULK!
GRRAA!

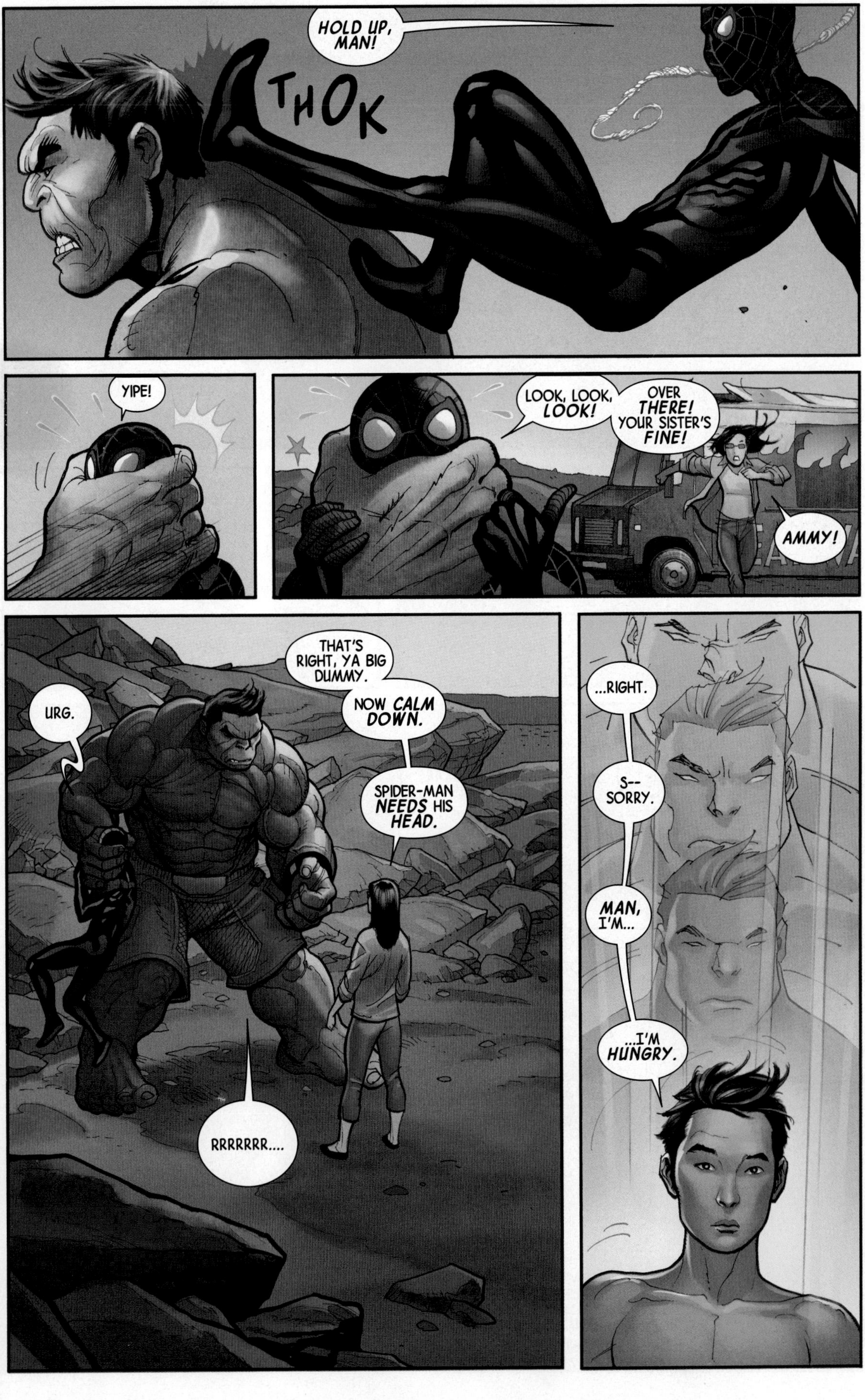
HOLD UP, MAN!
THOK
YIPE!
LOOK, LOOK, LOOK!
OVER THERE! YOUR SISTER'S FINE!
AMMY!
THAT'S RIGHT, YA BIG DUMMY.
NOW CALM DOWN.
SPIDER-MAN NEEDS HIS HEAD.
URG.
RRRRRRR....
...RIGHT.
S-- SORRY.
MAN, I'M...
...I'M HUNGRY.

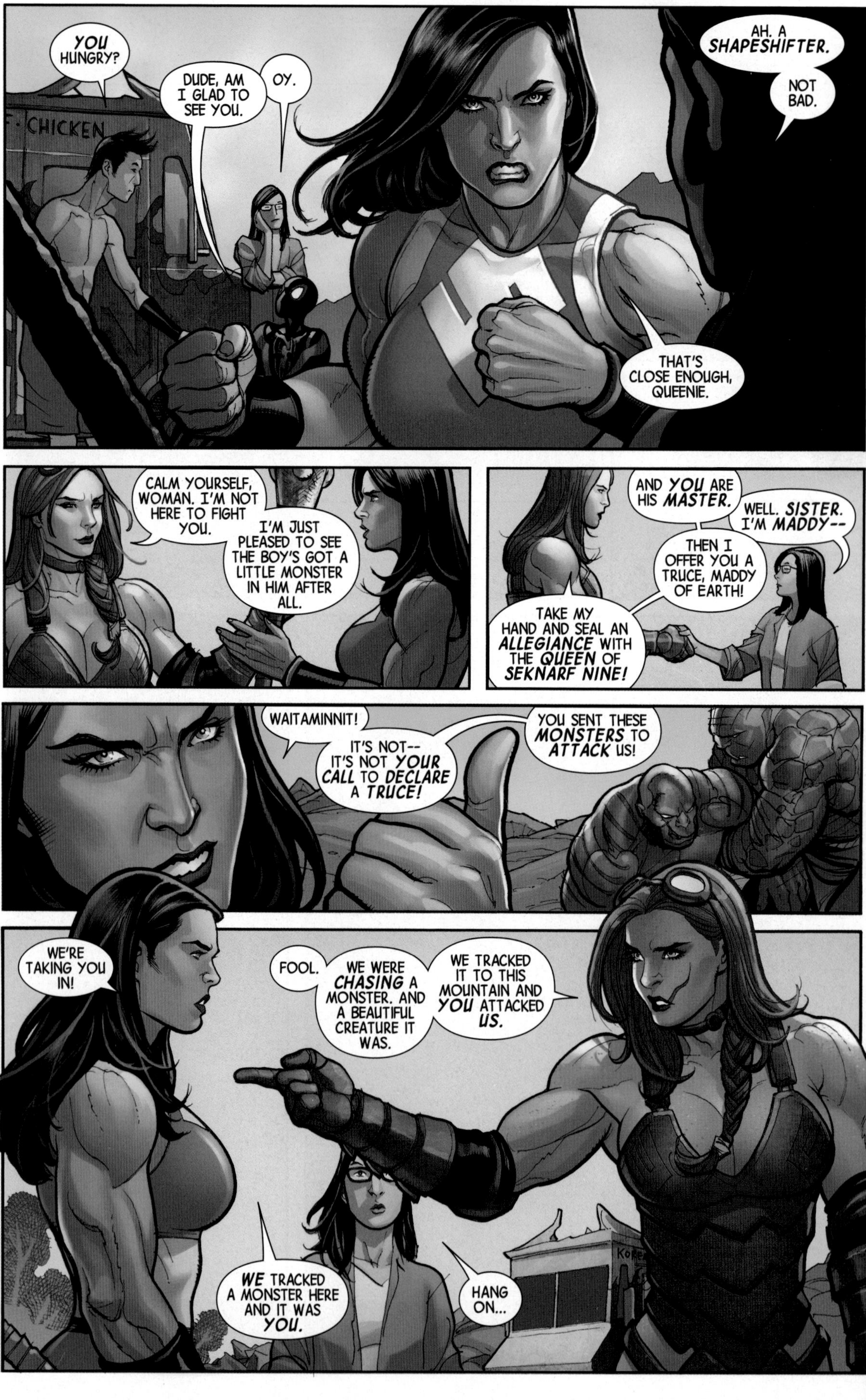
YOU HUNGRY?
DUDE, AM I GLAD TO SEE YOU.
OY.
F·CHICKEN
AH. A SHAPESHIFTER.
NOT BAD.
THAT'S CLOSE ENOUGH, QUEENIE.
CALM YOURSELF, WOMAN. I'M NOT HERE TO FIGHT YOU.
I'M JUST PLEASED TO SEE THE BOY'S GOT A LITTLE MONSTER IN HIM AFTER ALL.
AND YOU ARE HIS MASTER.
WELL. SISTER. I'M MADDY--
THEN I OFFER YOU A TRUCE, MADDY OF EARTH!
TAKE MY HAND AND SEAL AN ALLEGIANCE WITH THE QUEEN OF SEKNARF NINE!
WAITAMINNIT!
IT'S NOT-- IT'S NOT YOUR CALL TO DECLARE A TRUCE!
YOU SENT THESE MONSTERS TO ATTACK US!
WE'RE TAKING YOU IN!
FOOL.
WE WERE CHASING A MONSTER. AND A BEAUTIFUL CREATURE IT WAS.
WE TRACKED IT TO THIS MOUNTAIN AND YOU ATTACKED US.
WE TRACKED A MONSTER HERE AND IT WAS YOU.
HANG ON...

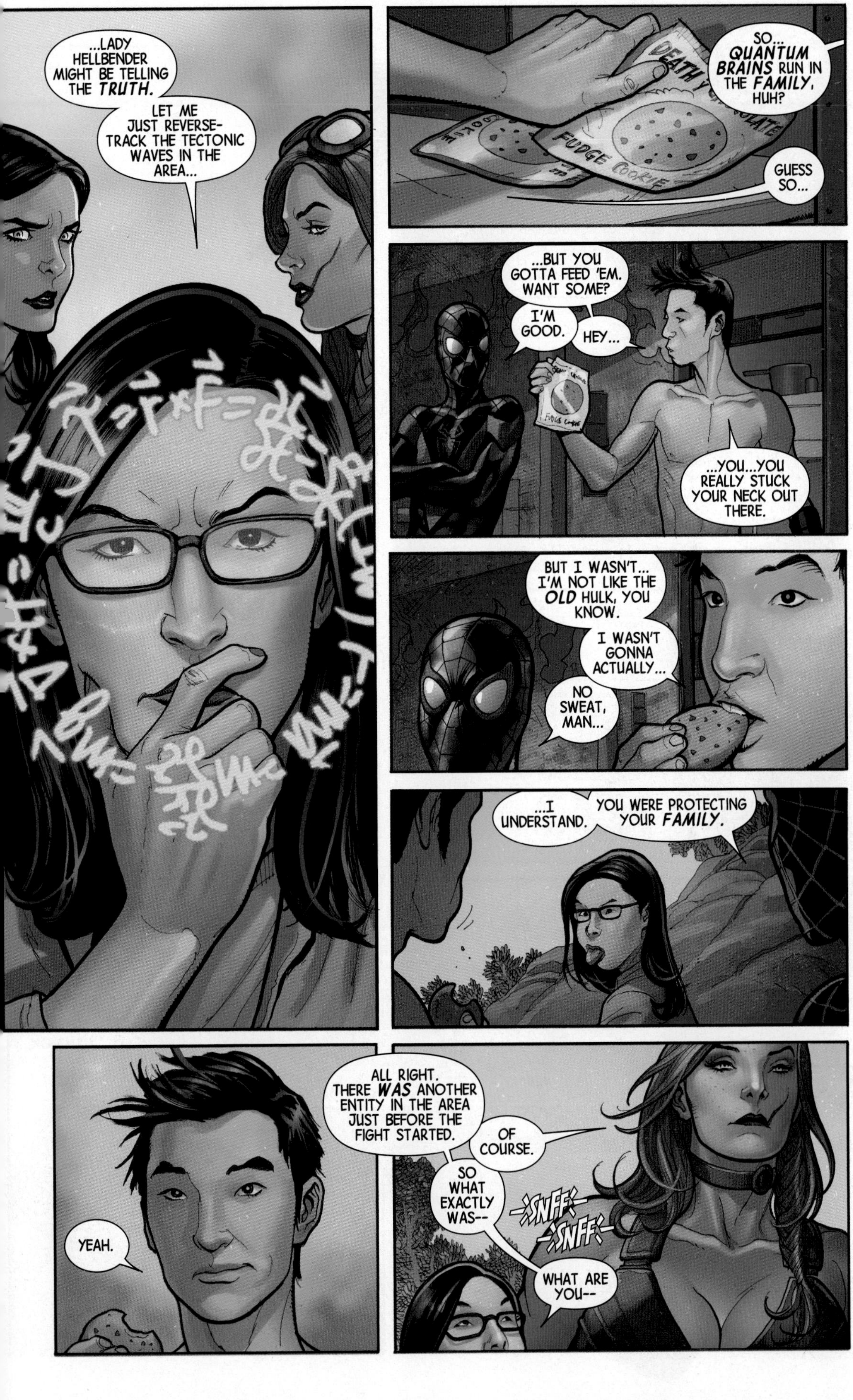
...LADY HELLBENDER MIGHT BE TELLING THE TRUTH.
LET ME JUST REVERSE-TRACK THE TECTONIC WAVES IN THE AREA...
SO... QUANTUM BRAINS RUN IN THE FAMILY, HUH?
FUDGE COOKIE
GUESS SO...
...BUT YOU GOTTA FEED 'EM. WANT SOME?
I'M GOOD.
HEY...
...YOU...YOU REALLY STUCK YOUR NECK OUT THERE.
BUT I WASN'T... I'M NOT LIKE THE OLD HULK, YOU KNOW.
I WASN'T GONNA ACTUALLY...
NO SWEAT, MAN...
...I UNDERSTAND.
YOU WERE PROTECTING YOUR FAMILY.
YEAH.
ALL RIGHT. THERE WAS ANOTHER ENTITY IN THE AREA JUST BEFORE THE FIGHT STARTED.
OF COURSE.
SO WHAT EXACTLY WAS--
SNFF
SNFF
WHAT ARE YOU--

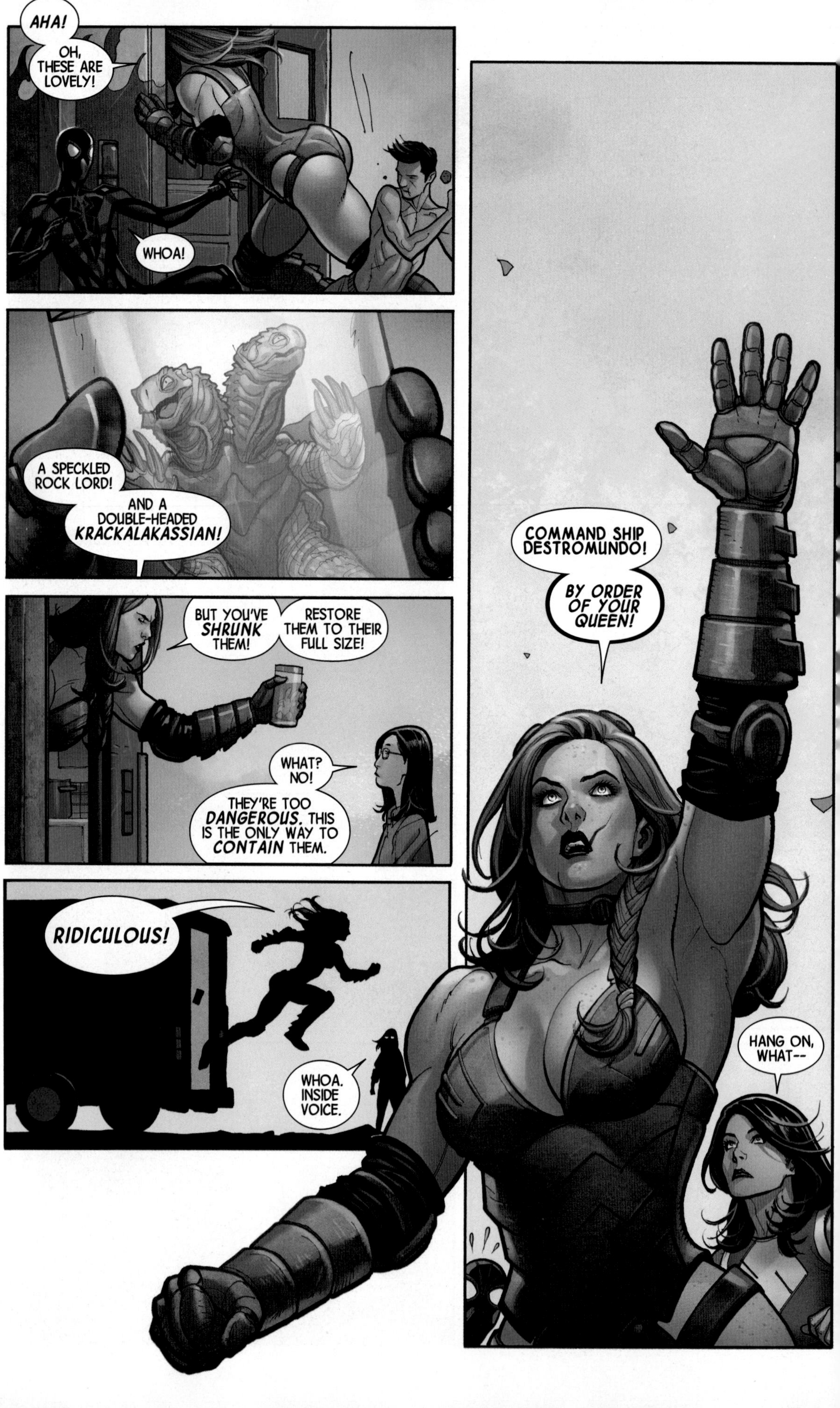
AHA!
OH, THESE ARE LOVELY!
WHOA!
A SPECKLED ROCK LORD!
AND A DOUBLE-HEADED KRACKALAKASSIAN!
BUT YOU'VE SHRUNK THEM!
RESTORE THEM TO THEIR FULL SIZE!
WHAT? NO!
THEY'RE TOO DANGEROUS. THIS IS THE ONLY WAY TO CONTAIN THEM.
RIDICULOUS!
WHOA. INSIDE VOICE.
COMMAND SHIP DESTROMUNDO!
BY ORDER OF YOUR QUEEN!
HANG ON, WHAT--

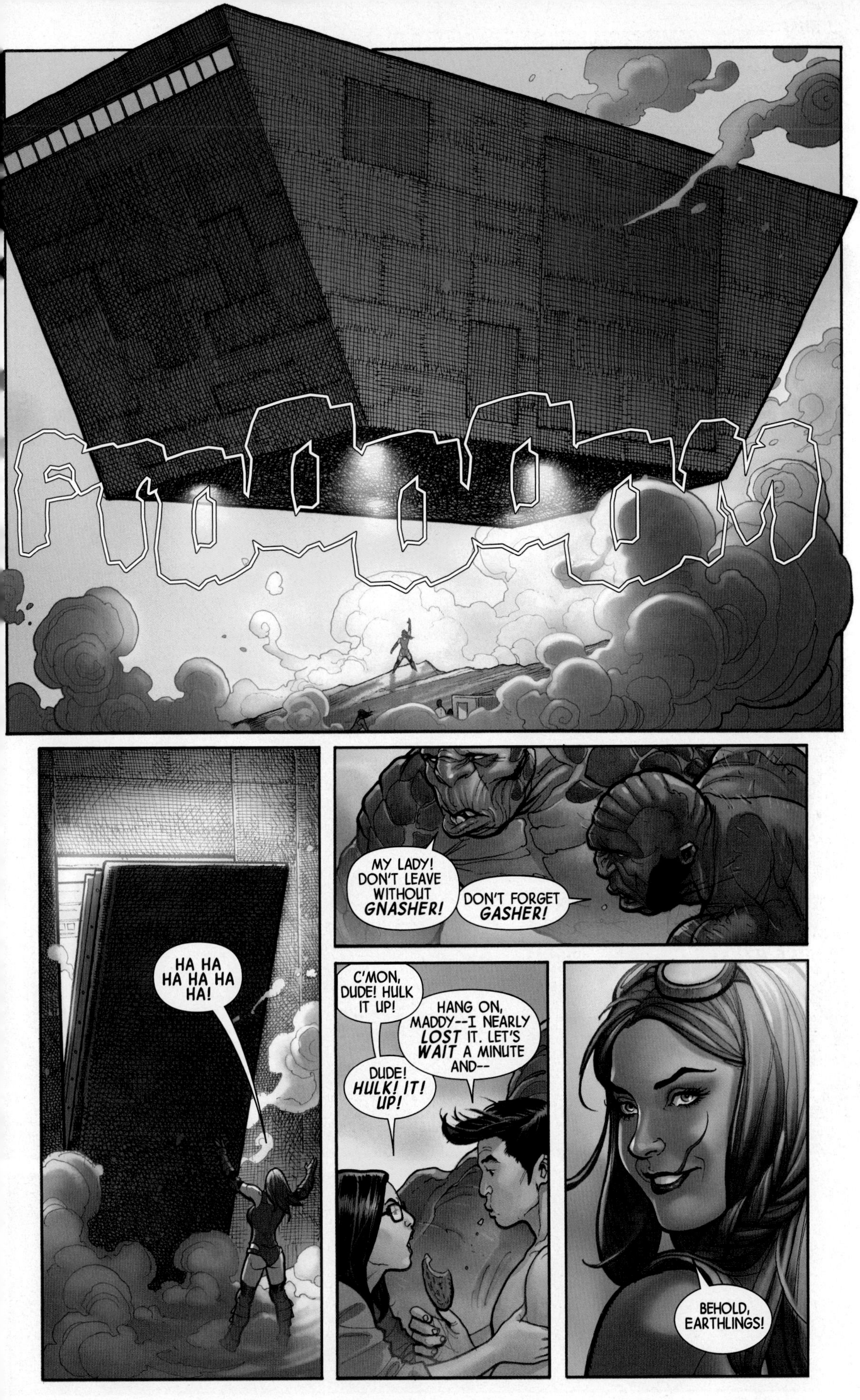
FWOOOOOM
HA HA HA HA HA HA!
MY LADY! DON'T LEAVE WITHOUT GNASHER!
DON'T FORGET GASHER!
C'MON, DUDE! HULK IT UP!
HANG ON, MADDY--I NEARLY LOST IT. LET'S WAIT A MINUTE AND--
DUDE! HULK! IT! UP!
BEHOLD, EARTHLINGS!

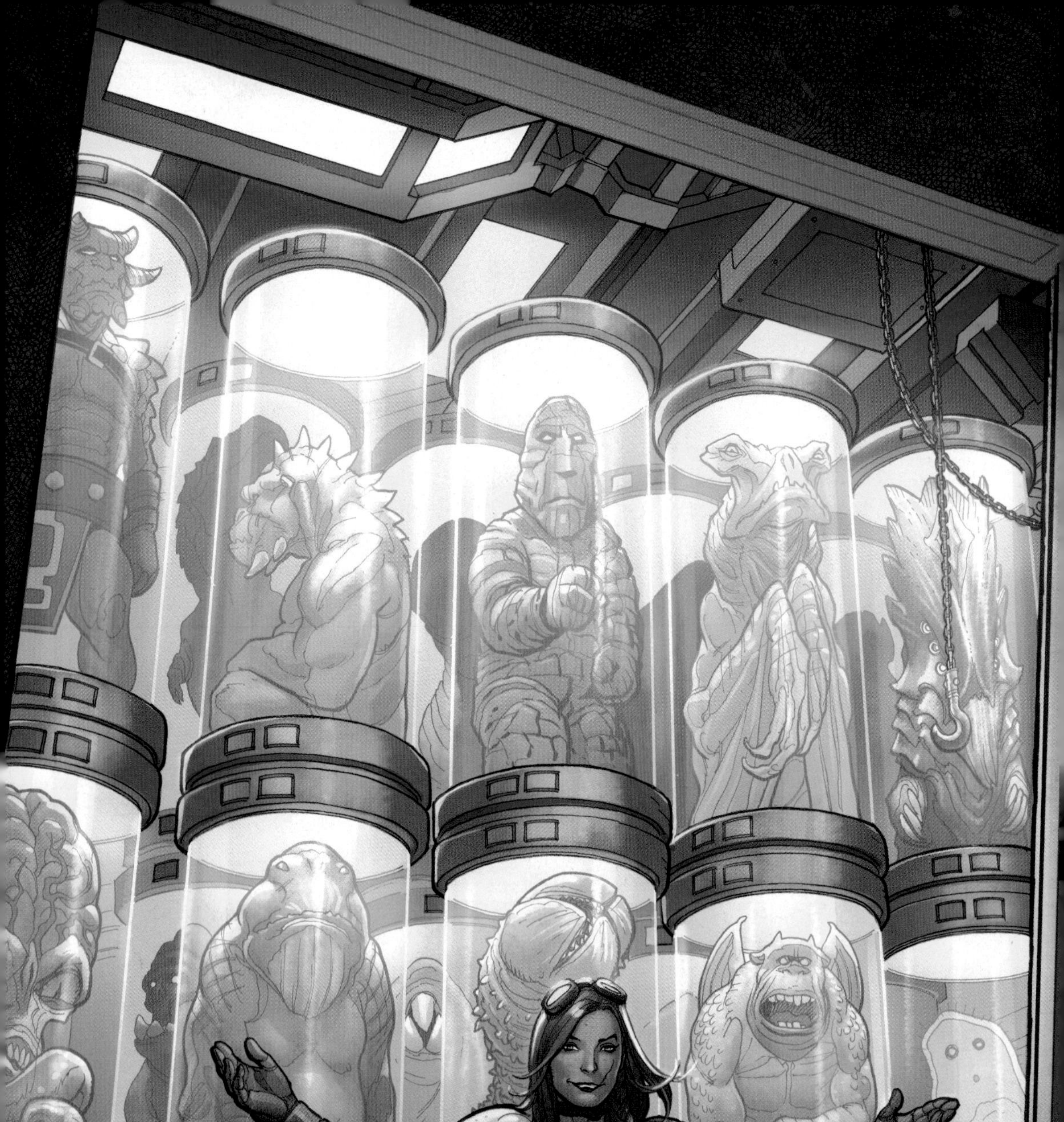

THIS IS *MY* COLLECTION.
AND SOON I'LL FLY THEM TO THE GREAT GARDENS OF SEKNARF NINE WHERE THEY WILL BE ADORED *FOR* THEIR GREAT, SAVAGE STRENGTH, NOT IN *SPITE* OF IT.
NOW JUST RESTORE THE BEASTS YOU'VE CAPTURED TO THEIR NATURAL SIZE AND WE'LL BE ON OUR WAY.
OH, *HELL* NO.

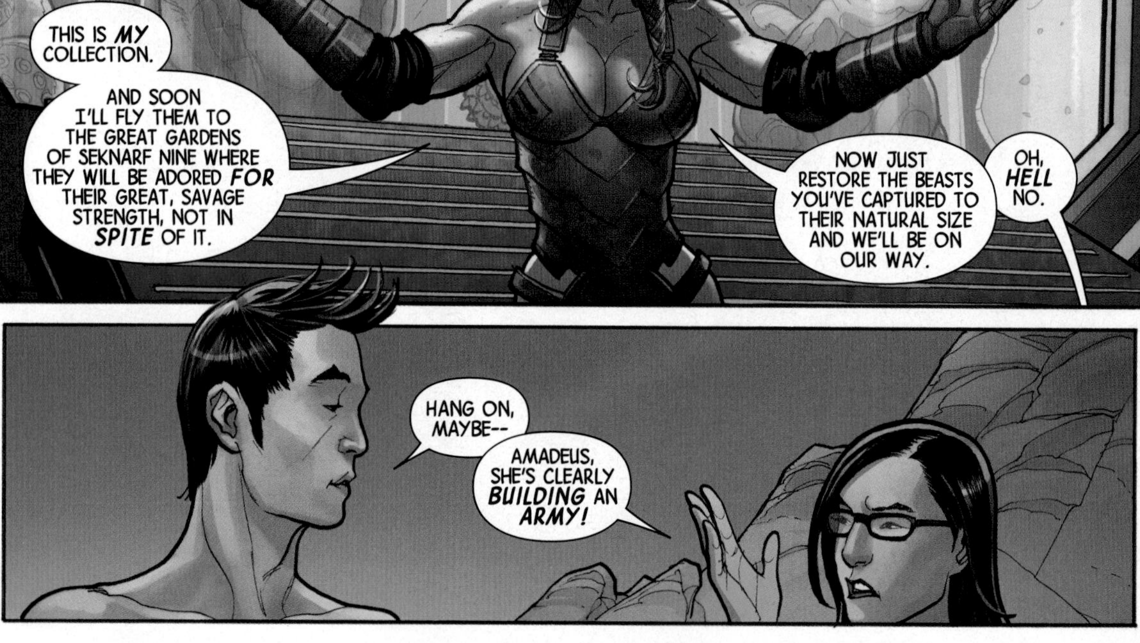

HANG ON, MAYBE--
AMADEUS, SHE'S CLEARLY *BUILDING* AN *ARMY*!

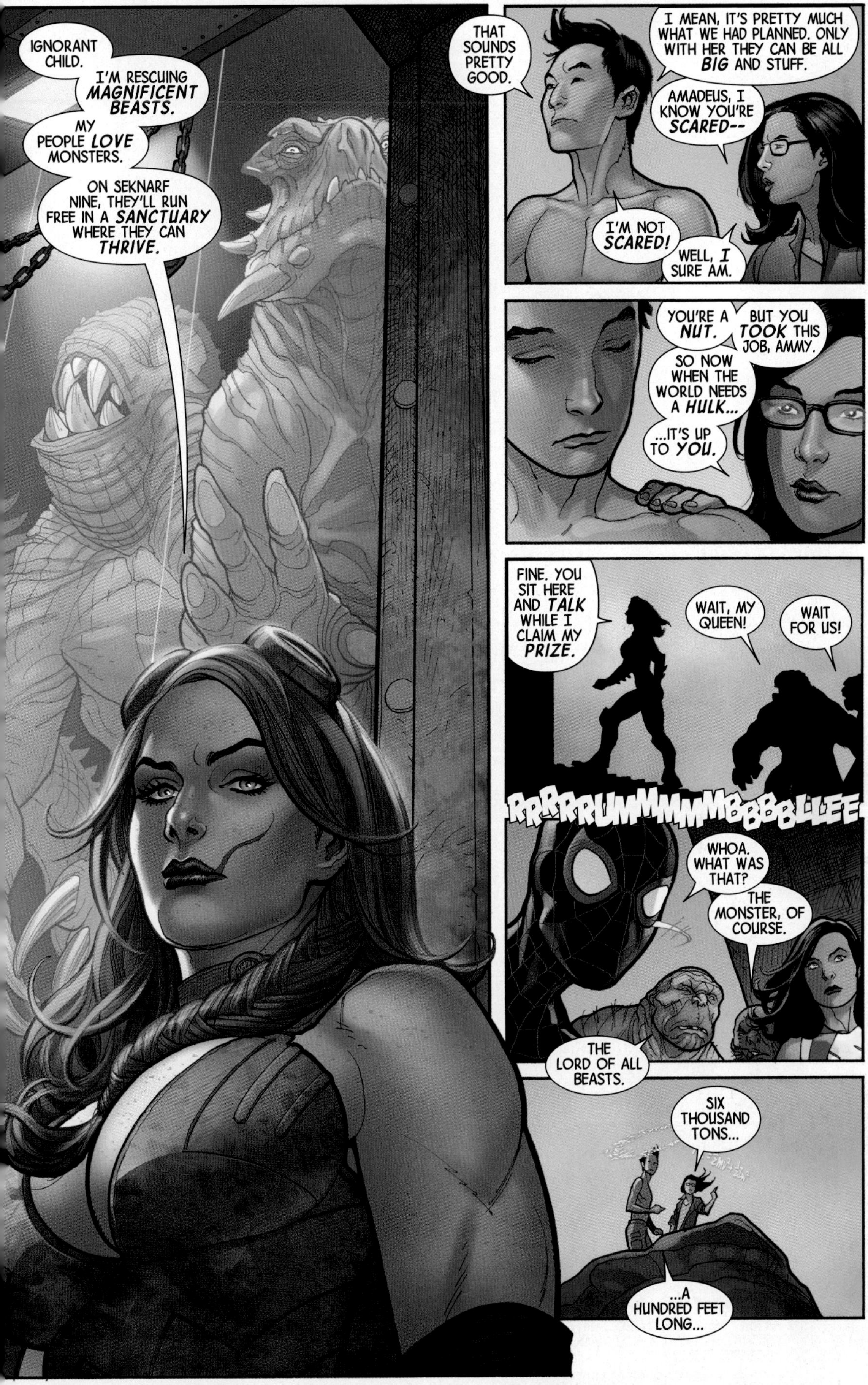
IGNORANT CHILD.
I'M RESCUING MAGNIFICENT BEASTS.
MY PEOPLE LOVE MONSTERS.
ON SEKNARF NINE, THEY'LL RUN FREE IN A SANCTUARY WHERE THEY CAN THRIVE.
THAT SOUNDS PRETTY GOOD.
I MEAN, IT'S PRETTY MUCH WHAT WE HAD PLANNED. ONLY WITH HER THEY CAN BE ALL BIG AND STUFF.
AMADEUS, I KNOW YOU'RE SCARED--
I'M NOT SCARED!
WELL, I SURE AM.
YOU'RE A NUT.
BUT YOU TOOK THIS JOB, AMMY.
SO NOW WHEN THE WORLD NEEDS A HULK...
...IT'S UP TO YOU.
FINE. YOU SIT HERE AND TALK WHILE I CLAIM MY PRIZE.
WAIT, MY QUEEN!
WAIT FOR US!
RRRRRUMMMMMMBBBBLLEE
WHOA. WHAT WAS THAT?
THE MONSTER, OF COURSE.
THE LORD OF ALL BEASTS.
SIX THOUSAND TONS...
...A HUNDRED FEET LONG...

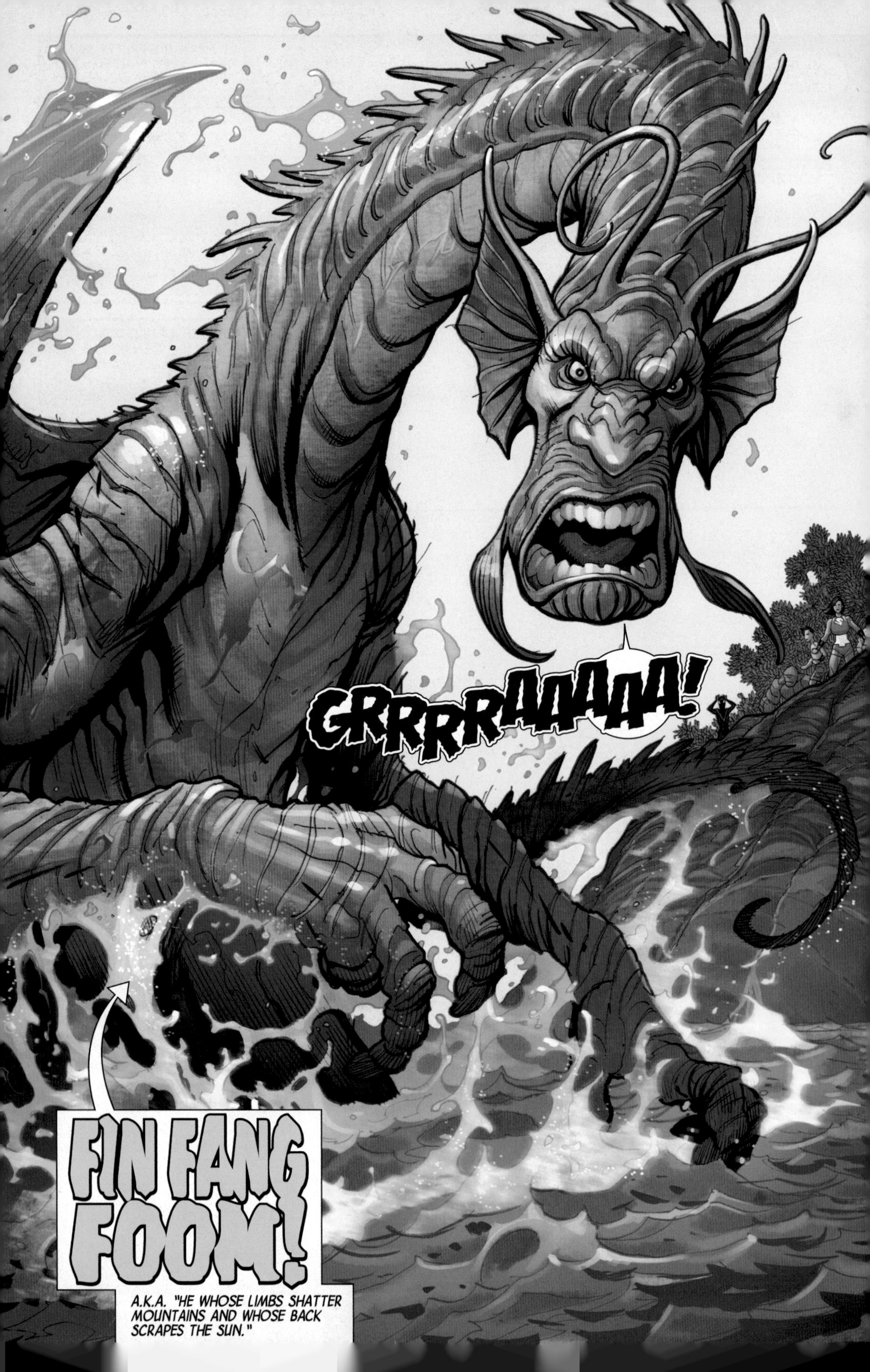
GRRRRAAAAAA!
FIN FANG FOOM!
A.K.A. "HE WHOSE LIMBS SHATTER MOUNTAINS AND WHOSE BACK SCRAPES THE SUN."

YAAAA!

NOW, LET ALL WHO WOULD WELCOME *DEATH* IF IT MEANT A CHANCE TO *BATTLE* THE GALAXY'S *FIERCEST* BEAST...

...JOIN ME NOW!

AMADEUS!

LIKE YOU SAID, MADDY...

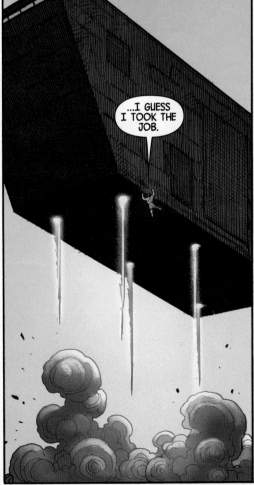

...I GUESS I TOOK THE JOB.

YEAH.

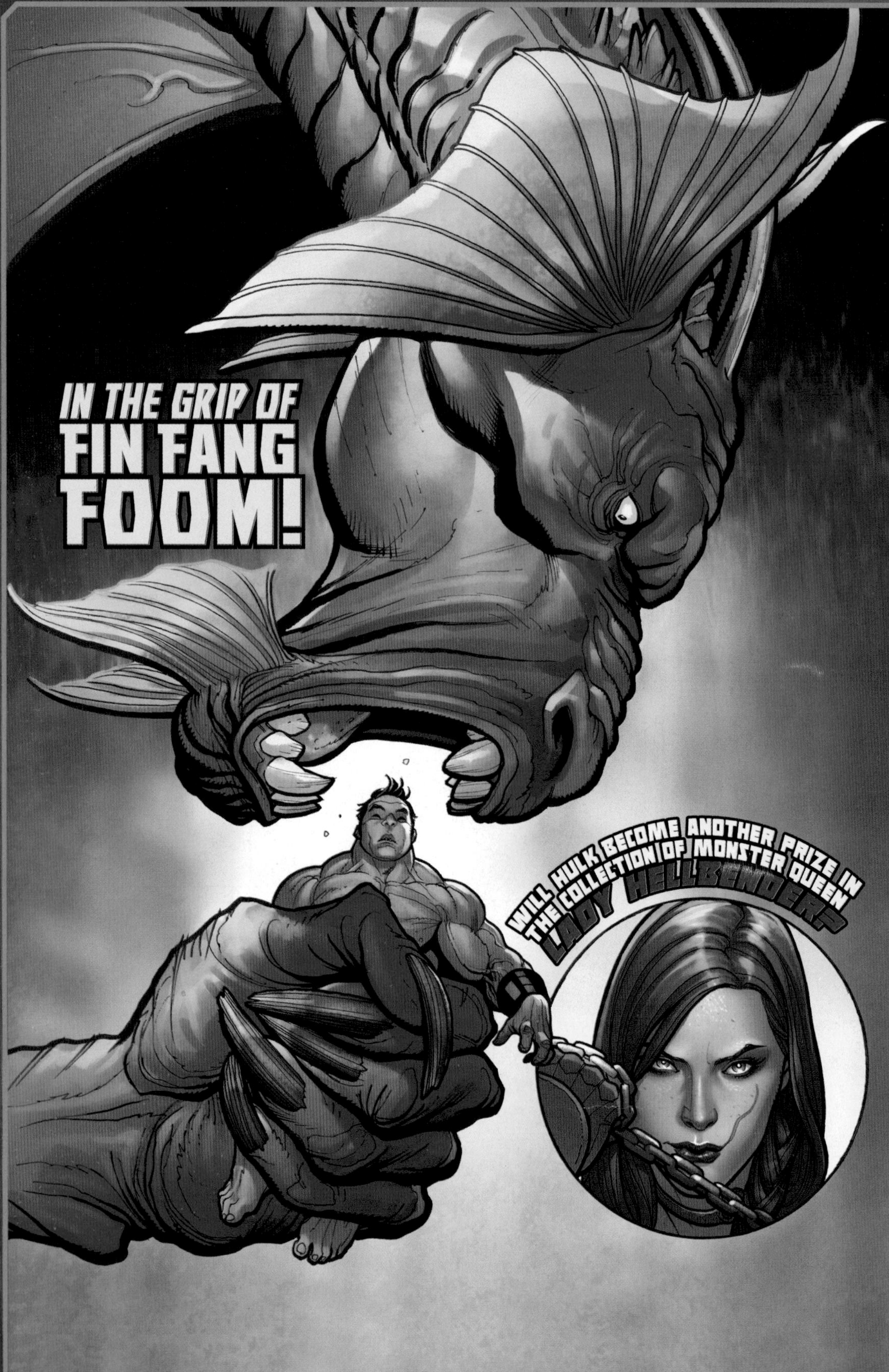
IN THE GRIP OF
FIN FANG
FOOM!
WILL HULK BECOME ANOTHER PRIZE IN THE COLLECTION OF MONSTER QUEEN
LADY HELLBENDER?

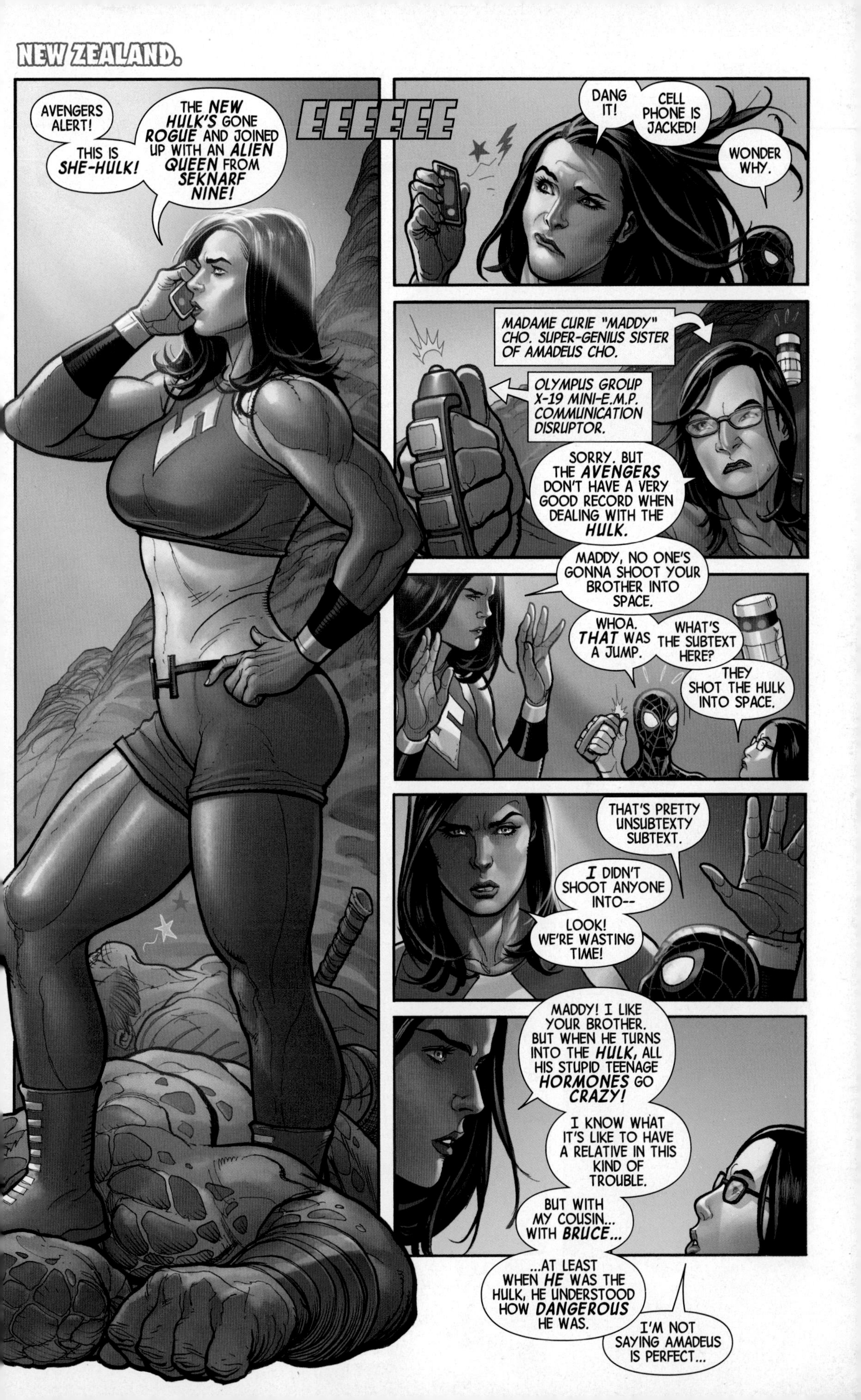
NEW ZEALAND.
AVENGERS ALERT!
THIS IS SHE-HULK!
THE NEW HULK'S GONE ROGUE AND JOINED UP WITH AN ALIEN QUEEN FROM SEKNARF NINE!
EEEEEE
DANG IT!
CELL PHONE IS JACKED!
WONDER WHY.
MADAME CURIE "MADDY" CHO. SUPER-GENIUS SISTER OF AMADEUS CHO.
OLYMPUS GROUP X-19 MINI-E.M.P. COMMUNICATION DISRUPTOR.
SORRY. BUT THE AVENGERS DON'T HAVE A VERY GOOD RECORD WHEN DEALING WITH THE HULK.
MADDY, NO ONE'S GONNA SHOOT YOUR BROTHER INTO SPACE.
WHOA. THAT WAS A JUMP.
WHAT'S THE SUBTEXT HERE?
THEY SHOT THE HULK INTO SPACE.
THAT'S PRETTY UNSUBTEXTY SUBTEXT.
I DIDN'T SHOOT ANYONE INTO--
LOOK! WE'RE WASTING TIME!
MADDY! I LIKE YOUR BROTHER. BUT WHEN HE TURNS INTO THE HULK, ALL HIS STUPID TEENAGE HORMONES GO CRAZY!
I KNOW WHAT IT'S LIKE TO HAVE A RELATIVE IN THIS KIND OF TROUBLE.
BUT WITH MY COUSIN... WITH BRUCE...
...AT LEAST WHEN HE WAS THE HULK, HE UNDERSTOOD HOW DANGEROUS HE WAS.
I'M NOT SAYING AMADEUS IS PERFECT...

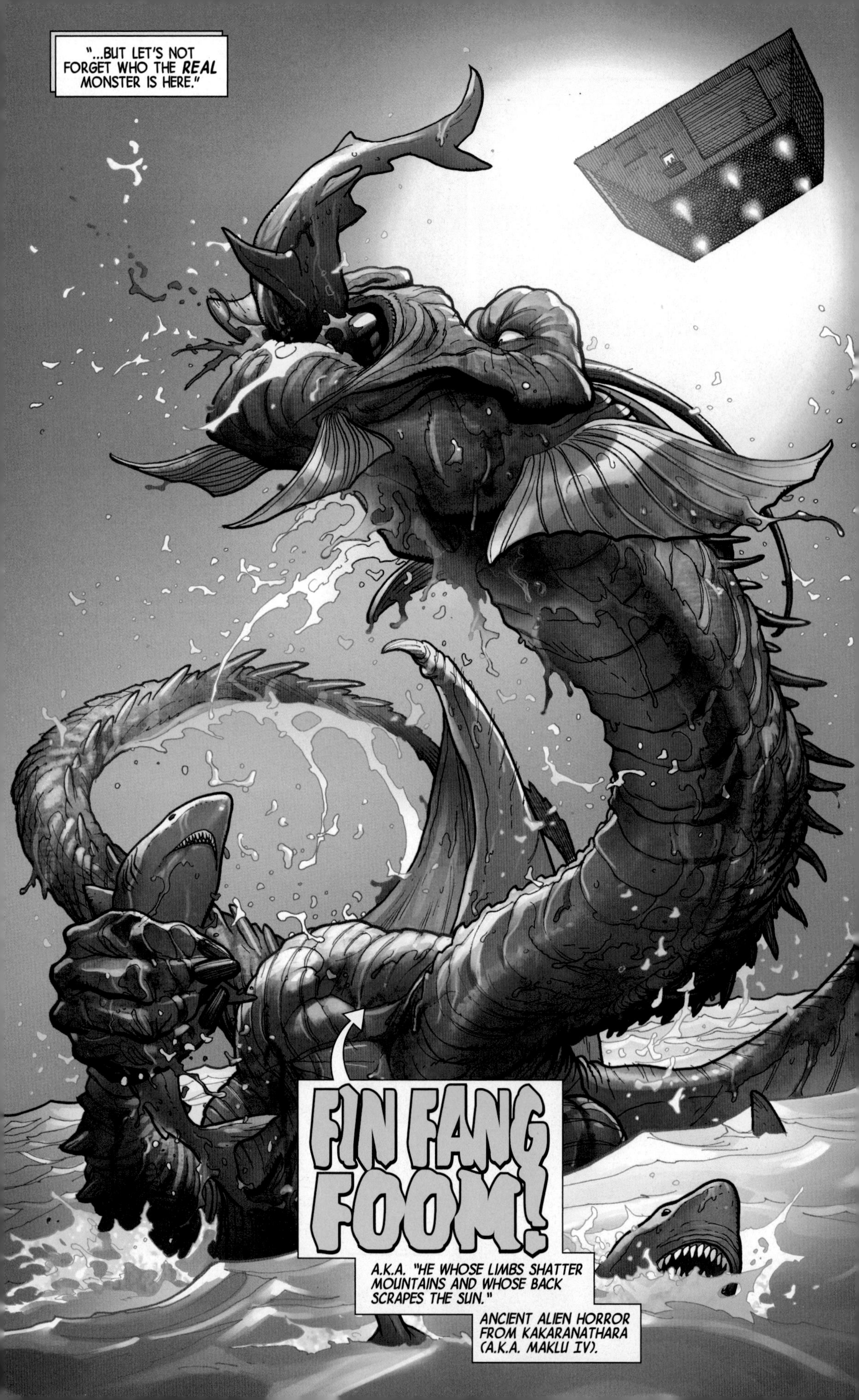
"...BUT LET'S NOT FORGET WHO THE *REAL* MONSTER IS HERE."
FIN FANG FOOM!
A.K.A. "HE WHOSE LIMBS SHATTER MOUNTAINS AND WHOSE BACK SCRAPES THE SUN."
ANCIENT ALIEN HORROR FROM KAKARANATHARA (A.K.A. MAKLU IV).

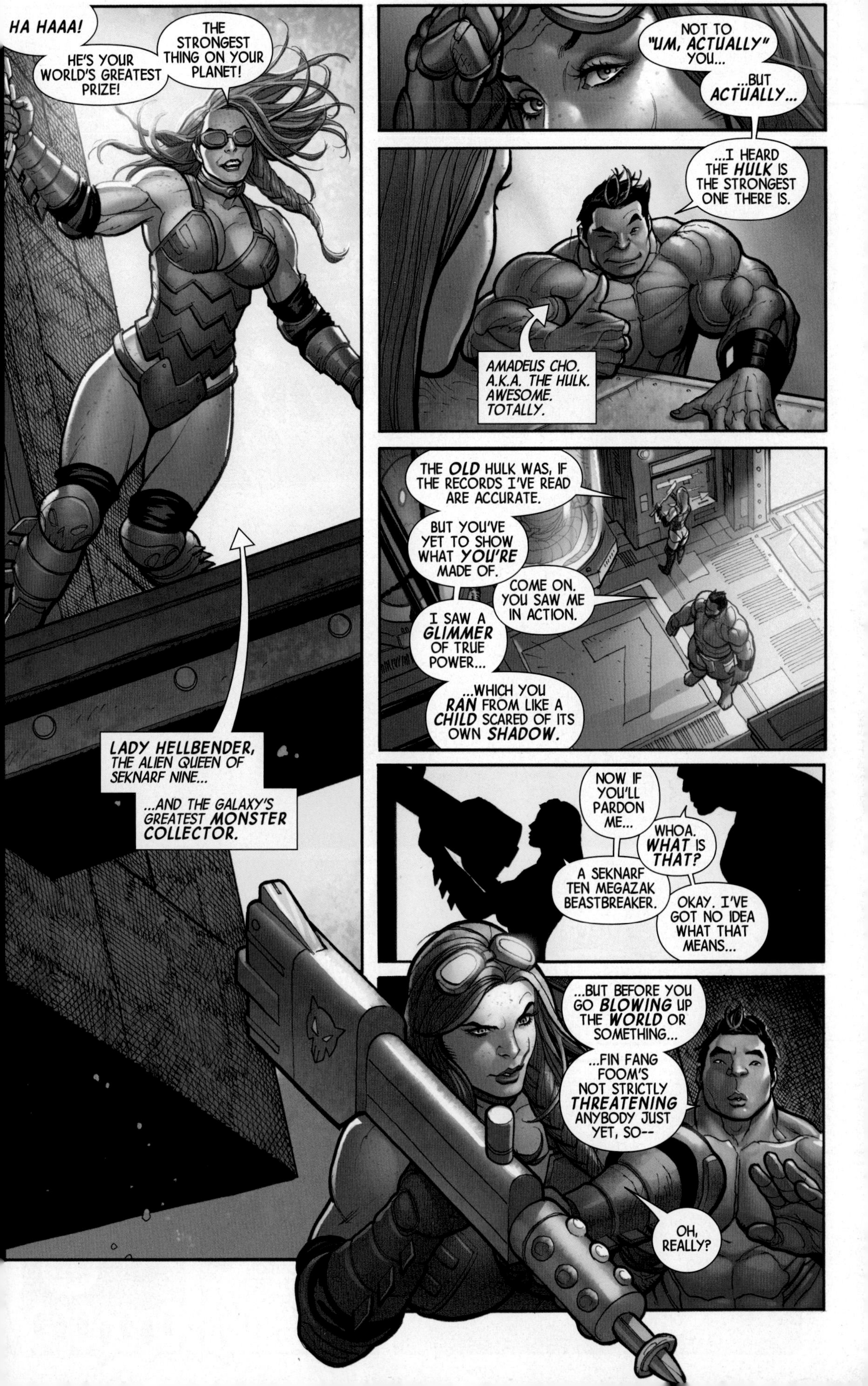
HA HAAA!
HE'S YOUR WORLD'S GREATEST PRIZE!
THE STRONGEST THING ON YOUR PLANET!
LADY HELLBENDER, THE ALIEN QUEEN OF SEKNARF NINE...
...AND THE GALAXY'S GREATEST MONSTER COLLECTOR.
NOT TO "UM, ACTUALLY" YOU...
...BUT ACTUALLY...
...I HEARD THE HULK IS THE STRONGEST ONE THERE IS.
AMADEUS CHO. A.K.A. THE HULK. AWESOME. TOTALLY.
THE OLD HULK WAS, IF THE RECORDS I'VE READ ARE ACCURATE.
BUT YOU'VE YET TO SHOW WHAT YOU'RE MADE OF.
COME ON. YOU SAW ME IN ACTION.
I SAW A GLIMMER OF TRUE POWER...
...WHICH YOU RAN FROM LIKE A CHILD SCARED OF ITS OWN SHADOW.
NOW IF YOU'LL PARDON ME...
WHOA. WHAT IS THAT?
A SEKNARF TEN MEGAZAK BEASTBREAKER.
OKAY. I'VE GOT NO IDEA WHAT THAT MEANS...
...BUT BEFORE YOU GO BLOWING UP THE WORLD OR SOMETHING...
...FIN FANG FOOM'S NOT STRICTLY THREATENING ANYBODY JUST YET, SO--
OH, REALLY?

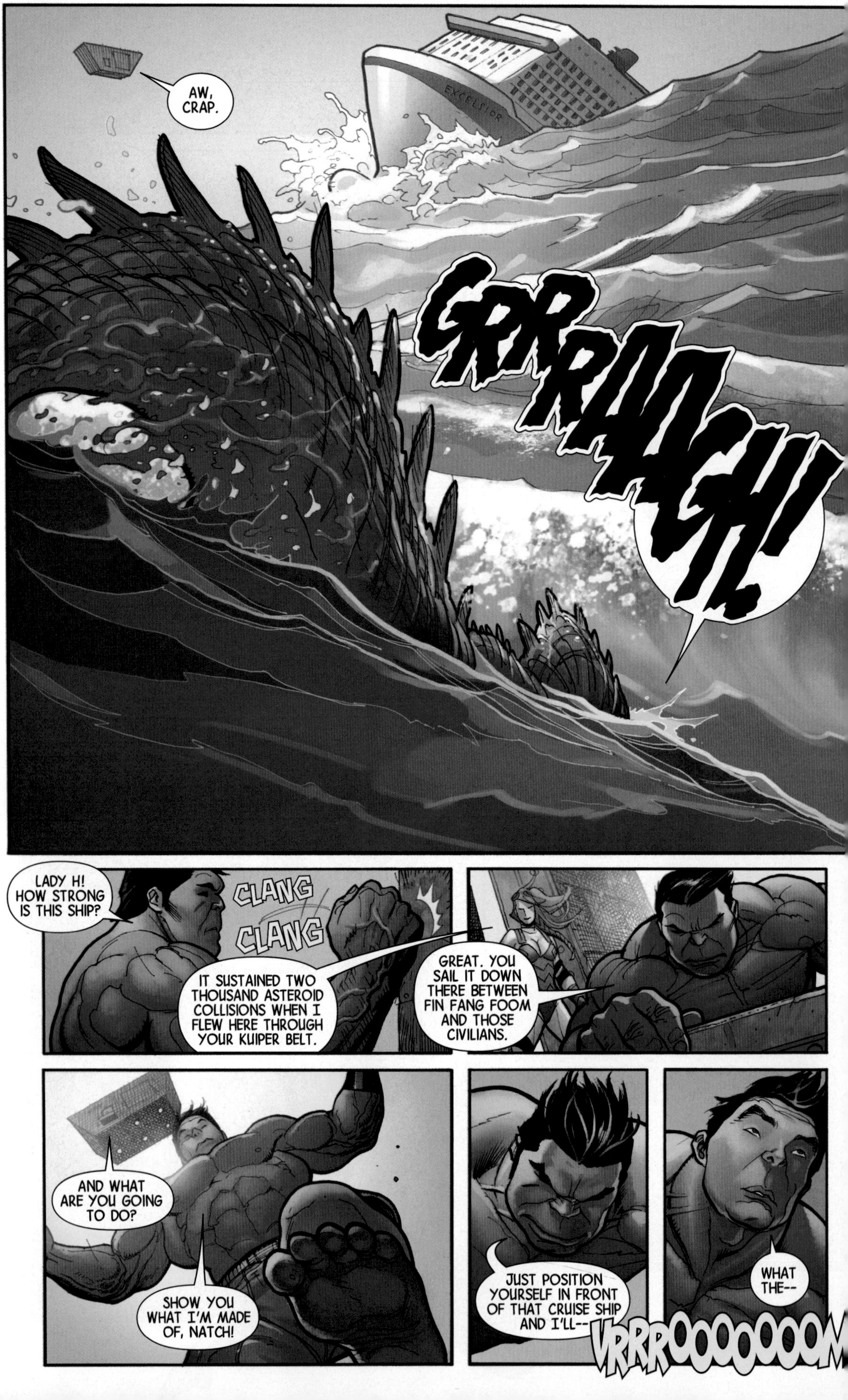
AW, CRAP.
EXCELSIOR
GRRRAAGH!
LADY H! HOW STRONG IS THIS SHIP?
CLANG
CLANG
IT SUSTAINED TWO THOUSAND ASTEROID COLLISIONS WHEN I FLEW HERE THROUGH YOUR KUIPER BELT.
GREAT. YOU SAIL IT DOWN THERE BETWEEN FIN FANG FOOM AND THOSE CIVILIANS.
AND WHAT ARE YOU GOING TO DO?
SHOW YOU WHAT I'M MADE OF, NATCH!
JUST POSITION YOURSELF IN FRONT OF THAT CRUISE SHIP AND I'LL--
WHAT THE--
VRRROOOOOOOM

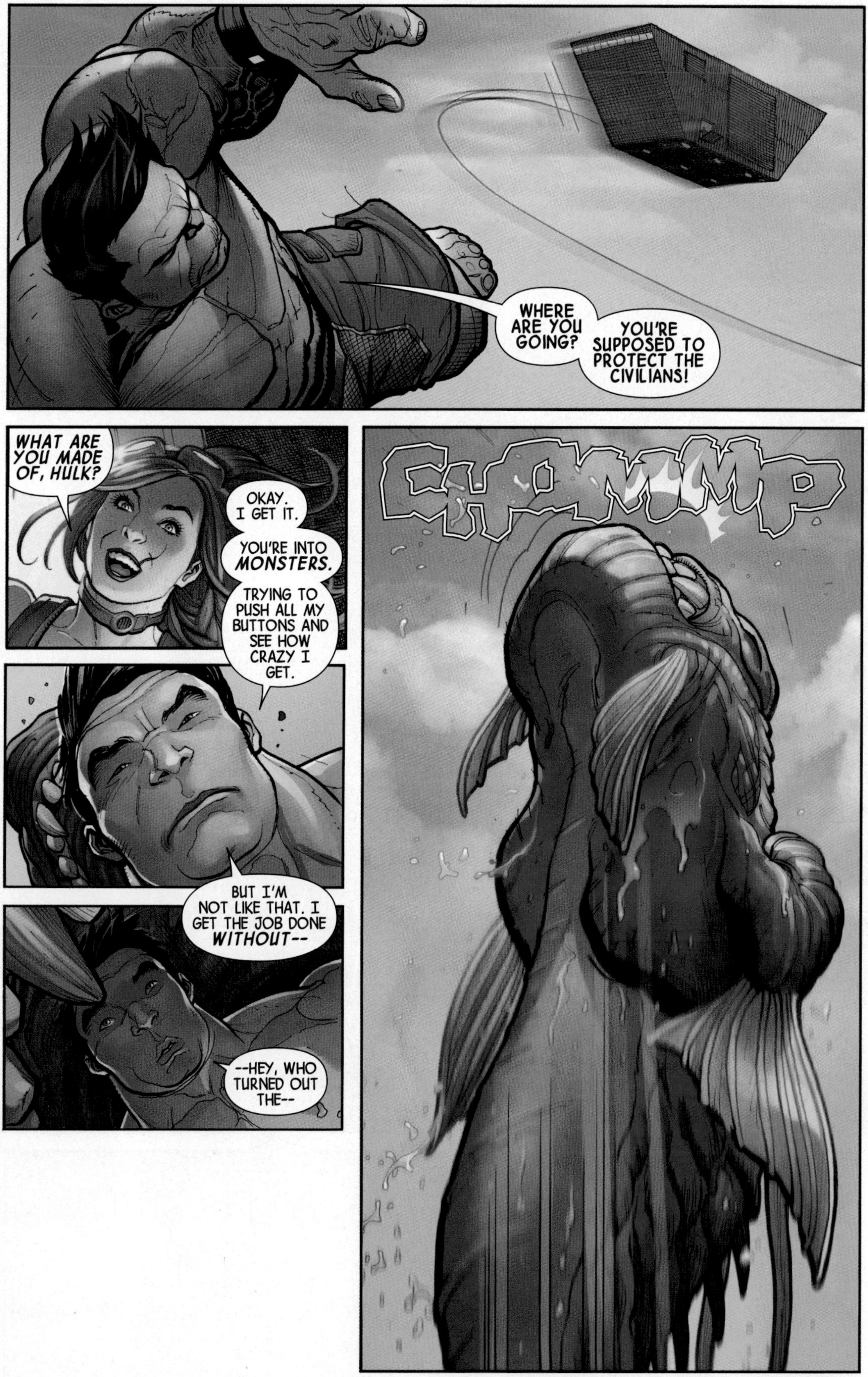
WHERE ARE YOU GOING?
YOU'RE SUPPOSED TO PROTECT THE CIVILIANS!
WHAT ARE YOU MADE OF, HULK?
OKAY. I GET IT.
YOU'RE INTO MONSTERS.
TRYING TO PUSH ALL MY BUTTONS AND SEE HOW CRAZY I GET.
BUT I'M NOT LIKE THAT. I GET THE JOB DONE WITHOUT--
--HEY, WHO TURNED OUT THE--
CHOMMP

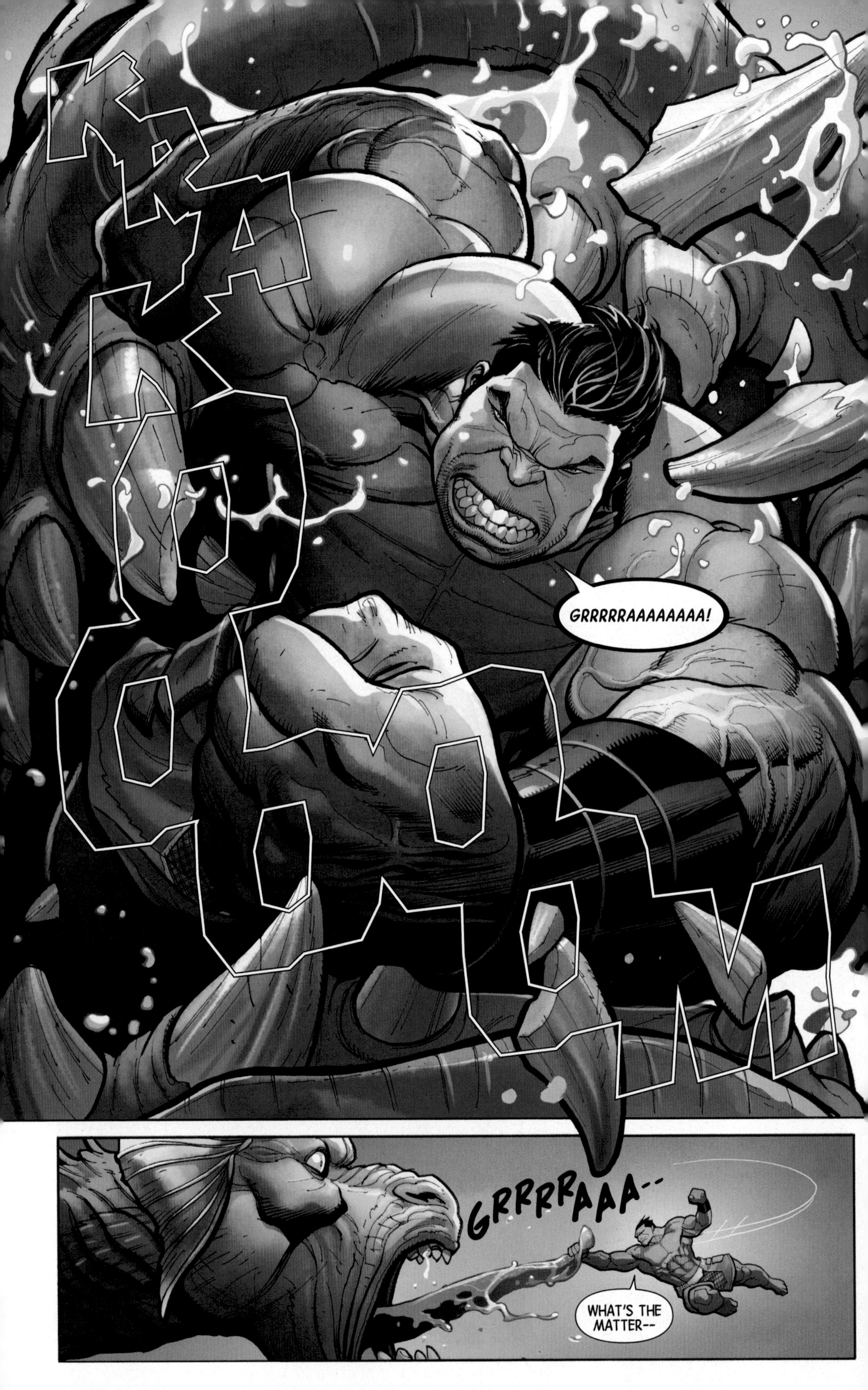
KRAKOOOOOM
GRRRRRAAAAAAAA!
GRRRRAAA--
WHAT'S THE MATTER--

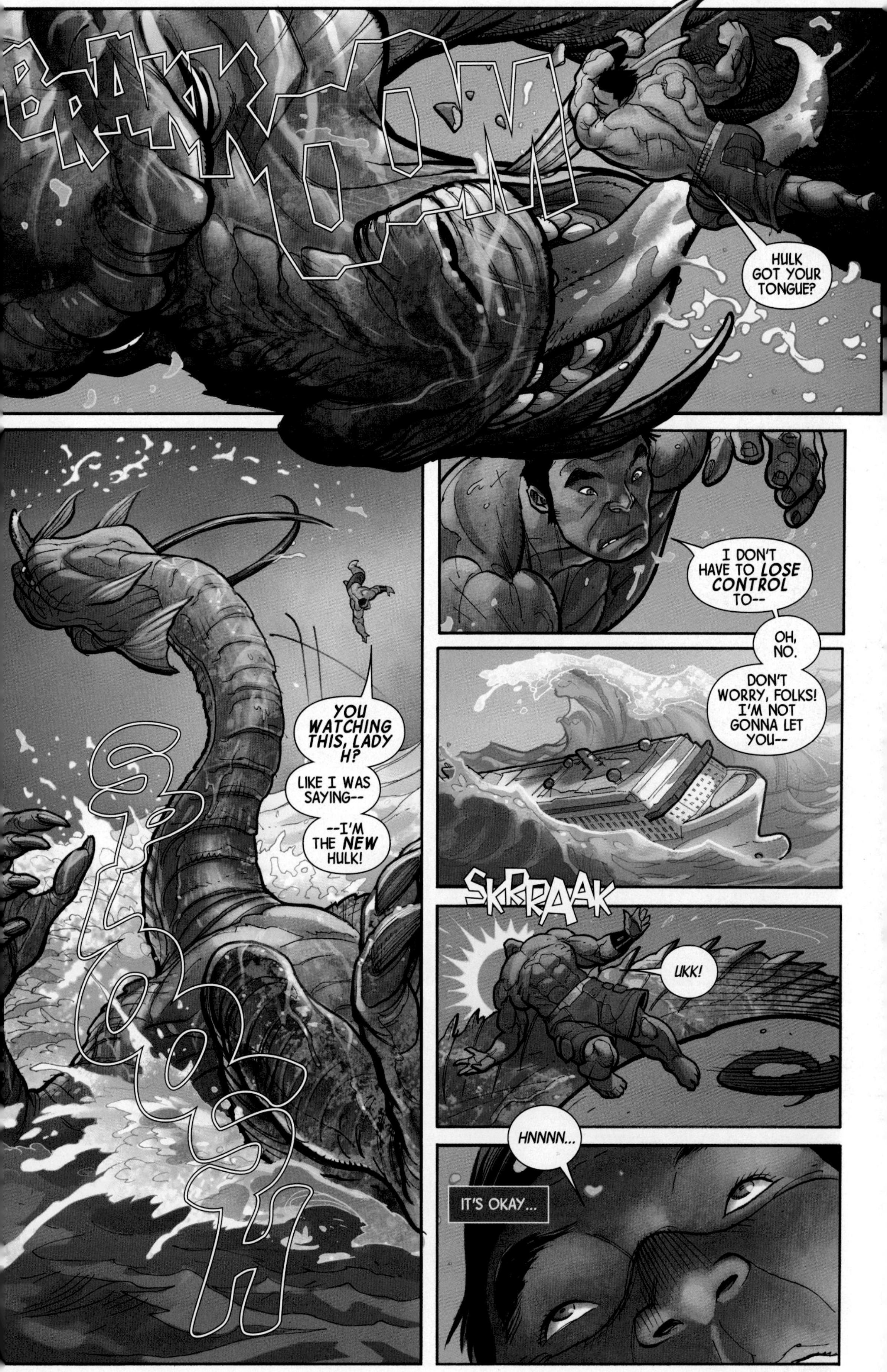

HULK GOT YOUR TONGUE?
YOU WATCHING THIS, LADY H?
LIKE I WAS SAYING--
--I'M THE NEW HULK!
I DON'T HAVE TO LOSE CONTROL TO--
OH, NO.
DON'T WORRY, FOLKS! I'M NOT GONNA LET YOU--
SKRRAAK
UKK!
HNNNN...
IT'S OKAY...

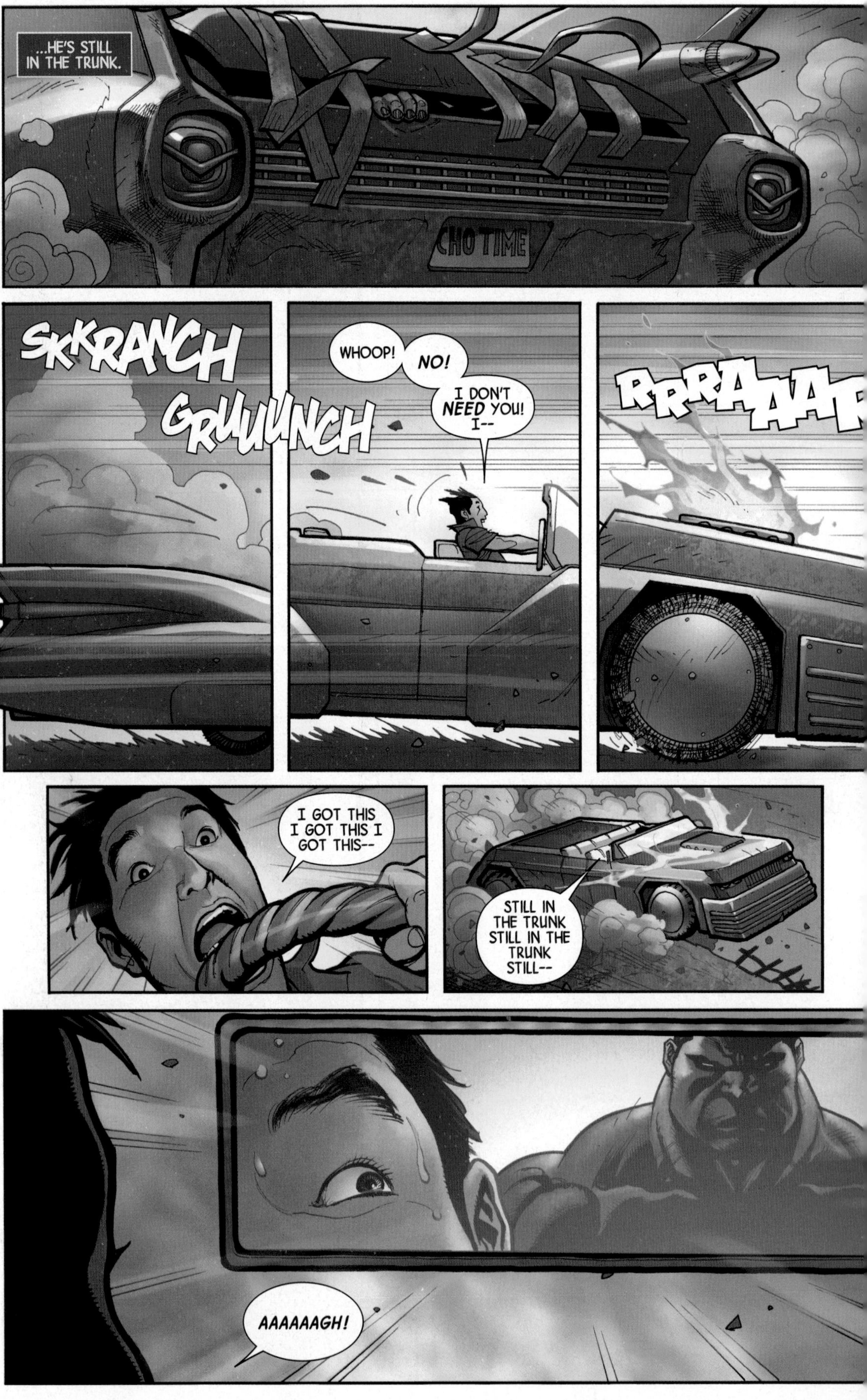

...HE'S STILL IN THE TRUNK.
CHO TIME
SKKRANCH
GRUUUNCH
WHOOP!
NO!
I DON'T NEED YOU! I--
RRRAAAAR
I GOT THIS I GOT THIS I GOT THIS--
STILL IN THE TRUNK STILL IN THE TRUNK STILL--
AAAAAAGH!

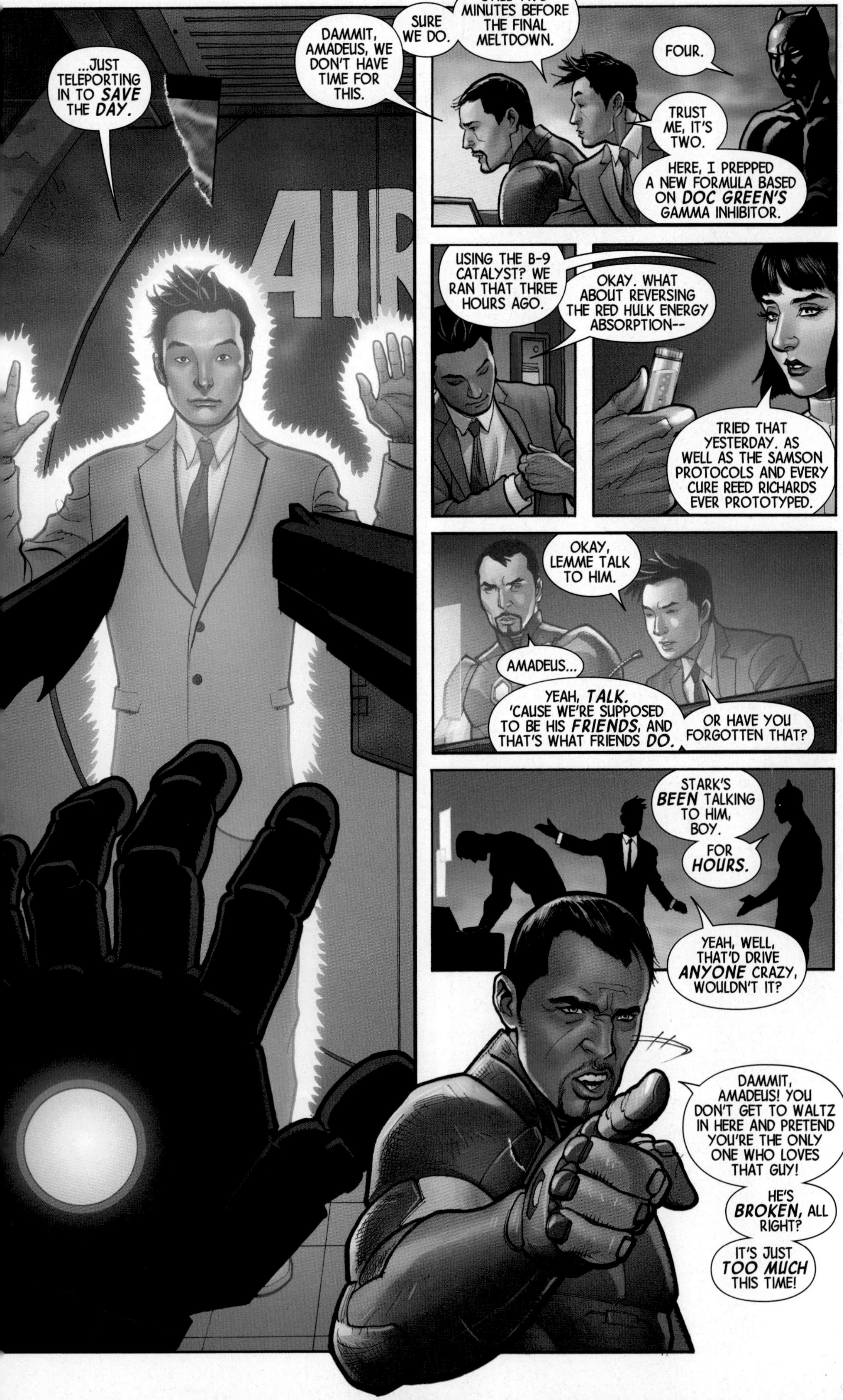
...JUST TELEPORTING IN TO SAVE THE DAY.
DAMMIT, AMADEUS, WE DON'T HAVE TIME FOR THIS.
SURE WE DO.
STILL TWO MINUTES BEFORE THE FINAL MELTDOWN.
FOUR.
TRUST ME, IT'S TWO.
HERE, I PREPPED A NEW FORMULA BASED ON DOC GREEN'S GAMMA INHIBITOR.
USING THE B-9 CATALYST? WE RAN THAT THREE HOURS AGO.
OKAY. WHAT ABOUT REVERSING THE RED HULK ENERGY ABSORPTION--
TRIED THAT YESTERDAY. AS WELL AS THE SAMSON PROTOCOLS AND EVERY CURE REED RICHARDS EVER PROTOTYPED.
OKAY, LEMME TALK TO HIM.
AMADEUS...
YEAH, TALK. 'CAUSE WE'RE SUPPOSED TO BE HIS FRIENDS, AND THAT'S WHAT FRIENDS DO.
OR HAVE YOU FORGOTTEN THAT?
STARK'S BEEN TALKING TO HIM, BOY.
FOR HOURS.
YEAH, WELL, THAT'D DRIVE ANYONE CRAZY, WOULDN'T IT?
DAMMIT, AMADEUS! YOU DON'T GET TO WALTZ IN HERE AND PRETEND YOU'RE THE ONLY ONE WHO LOVES THAT GUY!
HE'S BROKEN, ALL RIGHT?
IT'S JUST TOO MUCH THIS TIME!

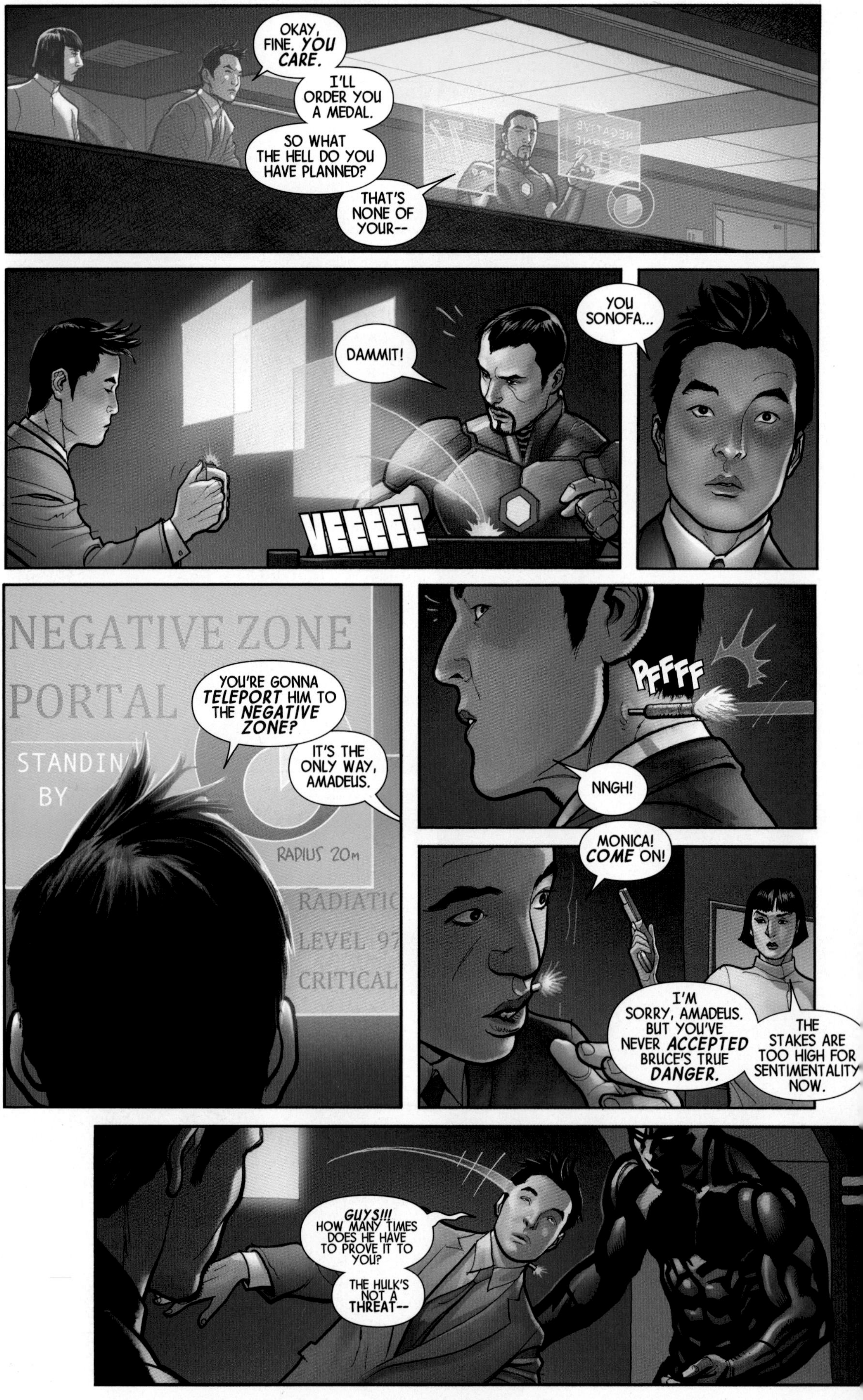

OKAY, FINE. YOU CARE.
I'LL ORDER YOU A MEDAL.
SO WHAT THE HELL DO YOU HAVE PLANNED?
THAT'S NONE OF YOUR--
NEGATIVE ZONE
DAMMIT!
VEEEEE
YOU SONOFA...
NEGATIVE ZONE PORTAL
STANDING BY
RADIUS 20m
RADIATION LEVEL 97
CRITICAL
YOU'RE GONNA TELEPORT HIM TO THE NEGATIVE ZONE?
IT'S THE ONLY WAY, AMADEUS.
PFFFF
NNGH!
MONICA! COME ON!
I'M SORRY, AMADEUS. BUT YOU'VE NEVER ACCEPTED BRUCE'S TRUE DANGER.
THE STAKES ARE TOO HIGH FOR SENTIMENTALITY NOW.
GUYS!!! HOW MANY TIMES DOES HE HAVE TO PROVE IT TO YOU?
THE HULK'S NOT A THREAT--

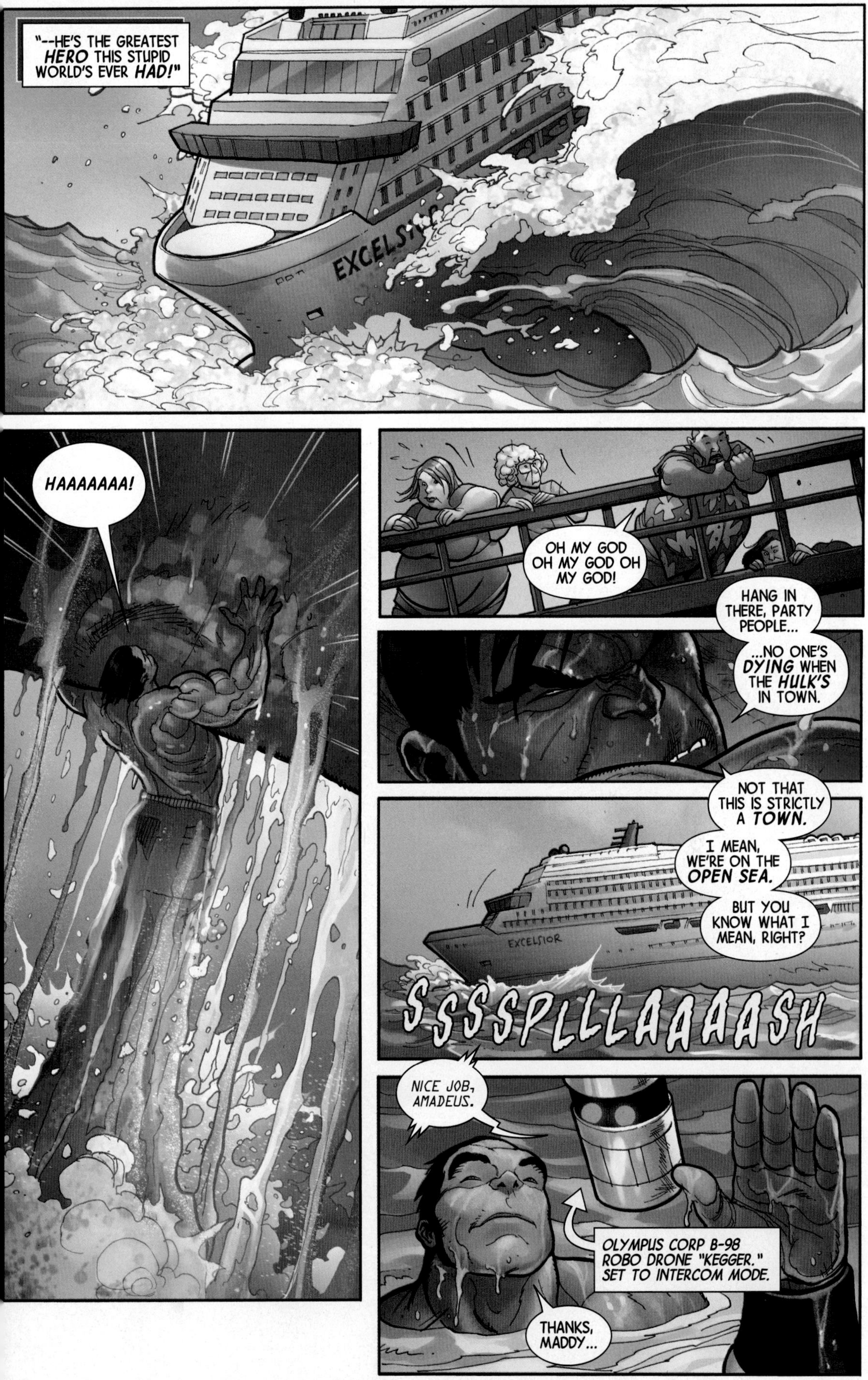
"--HE'S THE GREATEST HERO THIS STUPID WORLD'S EVER HAD!"
EXCELSIOR
HAAAAAAA!
OH MY GOD OH MY GOD OH MY GOD!
HANG IN THERE, PARTY PEOPLE...
...NO ONE'S DYING WHEN THE HULK'S IN TOWN.
NOT THAT THIS IS STRICTLY A TOWN.
I MEAN, WE'RE ON THE OPEN SEA.
BUT YOU KNOW WHAT I MEAN, RIGHT?
EXCELSIOR
SSSSPLLLAAAAASH
NICE JOB, AMADEUS.
OLYMPUS CORP B-98 ROBO DRONE "KEGGER." SET TO INTERCOM MODE.
THANKS, MADDY...

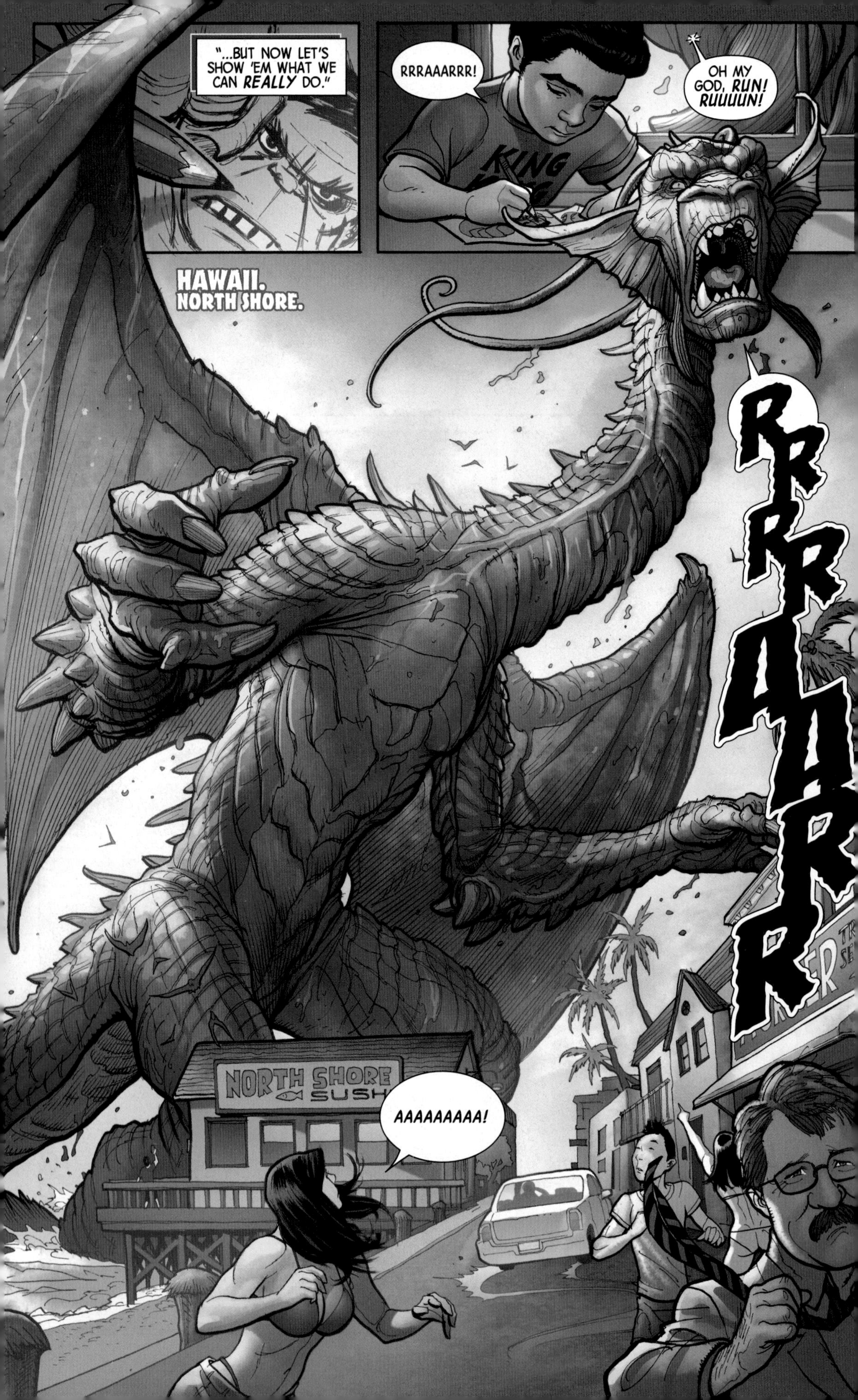
"...BUT NOW LET'S SHOW 'EM WHAT WE CAN *REALLY* DO."
RRRAAARRR!
KING
OH MY GOD, *RUN!* RUUUUN!
HAWAII.
NORTH SHORE.
RRRRAARR
NORTH SHORE
SUSH
AAAAAAAAA!

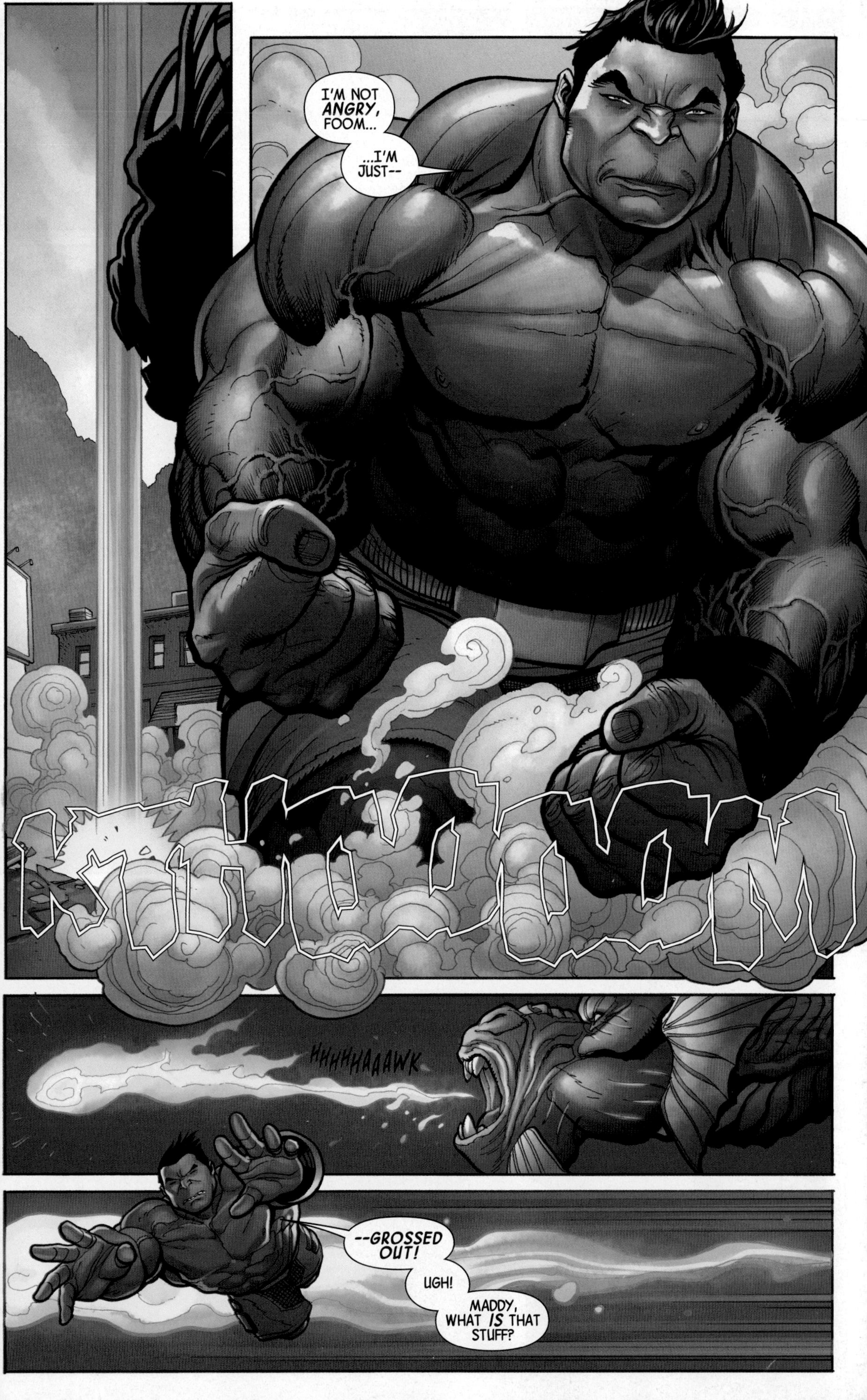

I'M NOT ANGRY, FOOM...
...I'M JUST--
KRAKOOOOOM
HHHHHHAAAWK
--GROSSED OUT!
UGH!
MADDY, WHAT IS THAT STUFF?

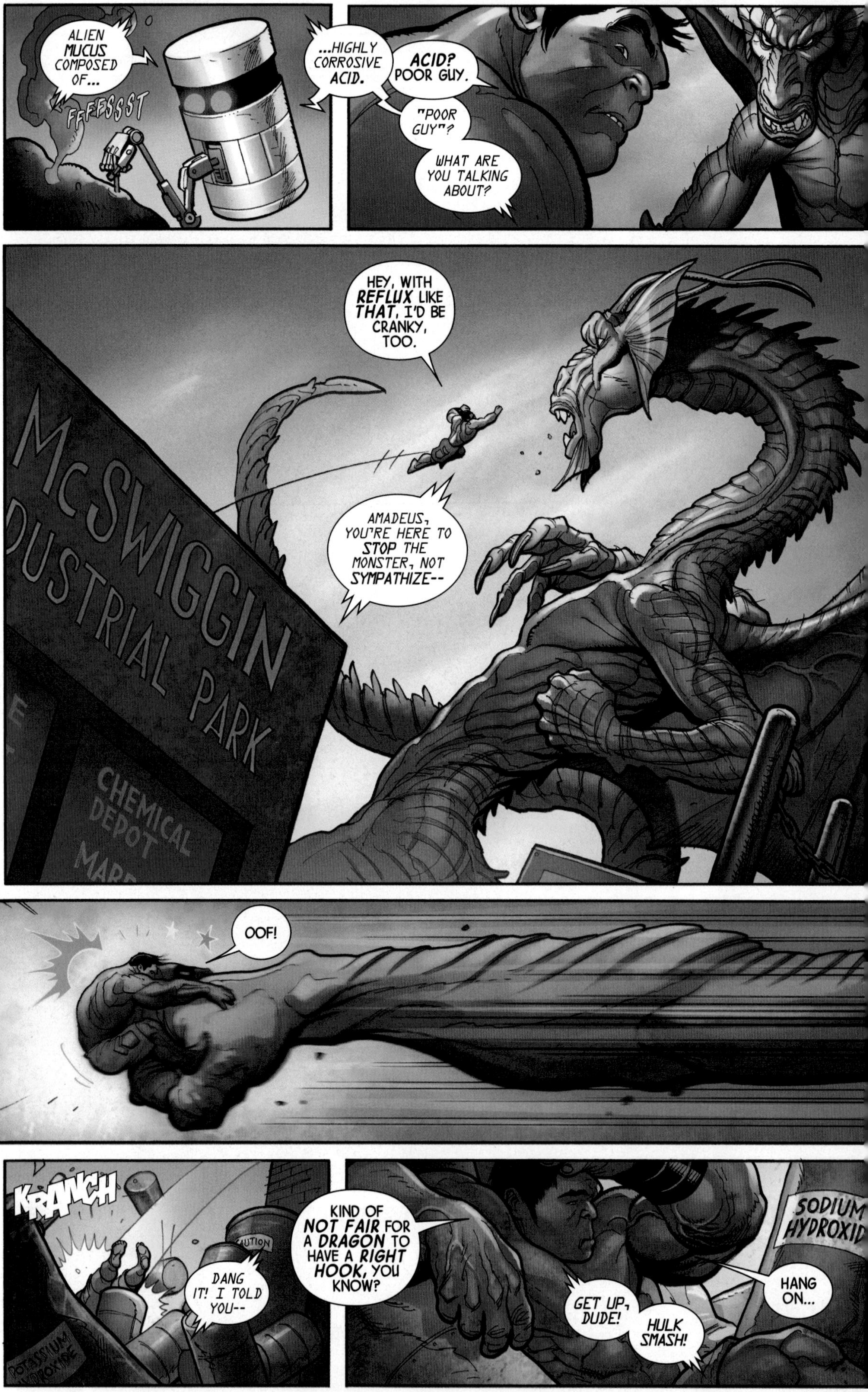
ALIEN MUCUS COMPOSED OF...
FFFFSSST
...HIGHLY CORROSIVE ACID.
ACID? POOR GUY.
"POOR GUY"?
WHAT ARE YOU TALKING ABOUT?
McSWIGGIN
DUSTRIAL PARK
CHEMICAL DEPOT
HEY, WITH REFLUX LIKE THAT, I'D BE CRANKY, TOO.
AMADEUS, YOU'RE HERE TO STOP THE MONSTER, NOT SYMPATHIZE--
OOF!
KRANCH
CAUTION
DANG IT! I TOLD YOU--
POTASSIUM HYDROXIDE
KIND OF NOT FAIR FOR A DRAGON TO HAVE A RIGHT HOOK, YOU KNOW?
SODIUM HYDROXID
GET UP, DUDE!
HULK SMASH!
HANG ON...

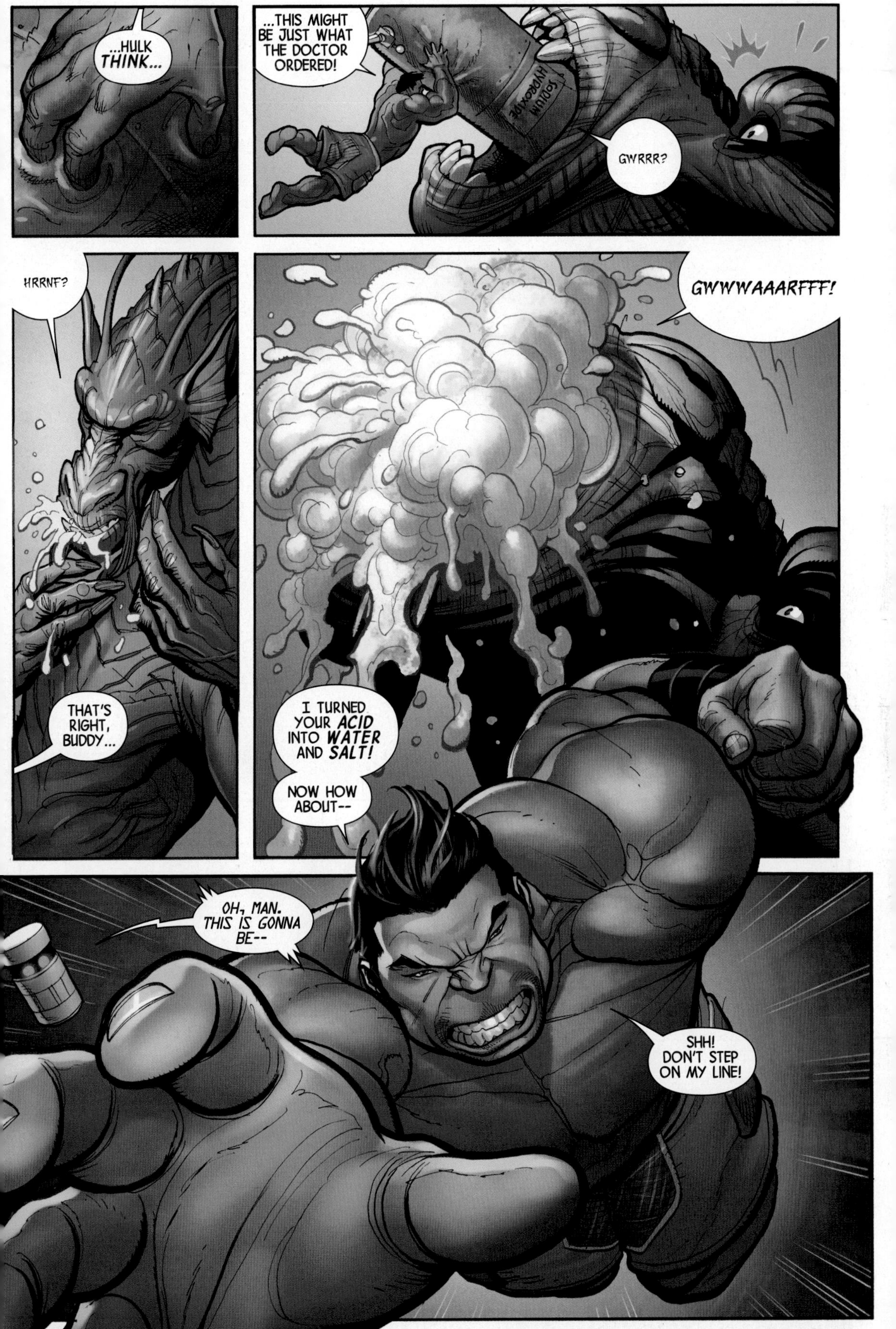
...HULK THINK...
...THIS MIGHT BE JUST WHAT THE DOCTOR ORDERED!
SODIUM HYDROXIDE
GWRRR?
HRRNF?
GWWWAAARFFF!
THAT'S RIGHT, BUDDY...
I TURNED YOUR ACID INTO WATER AND SALT!
NOW HOW ABOUT--
OH, MAN. THIS IS GONNA BE--
SHH! DON'T STEP ON MY LINE!

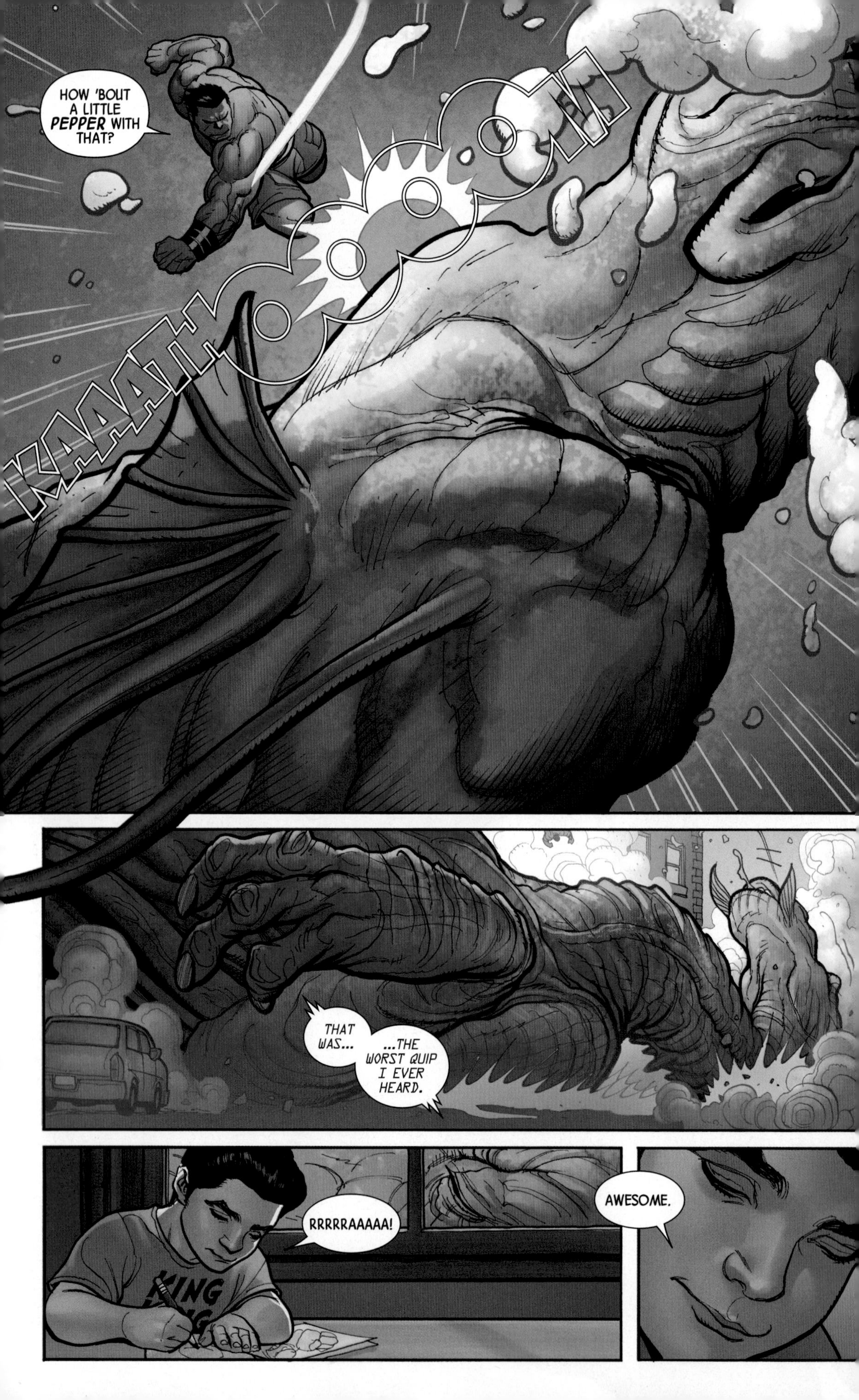
HOW 'BOUT A LITTLE PEPPER WITH THAT?
KAAATHOOOOOM
THAT WAS...
...THE WORST QUIP I EVER HEARD.
RRRRRAAAAAA!
AWESOME.

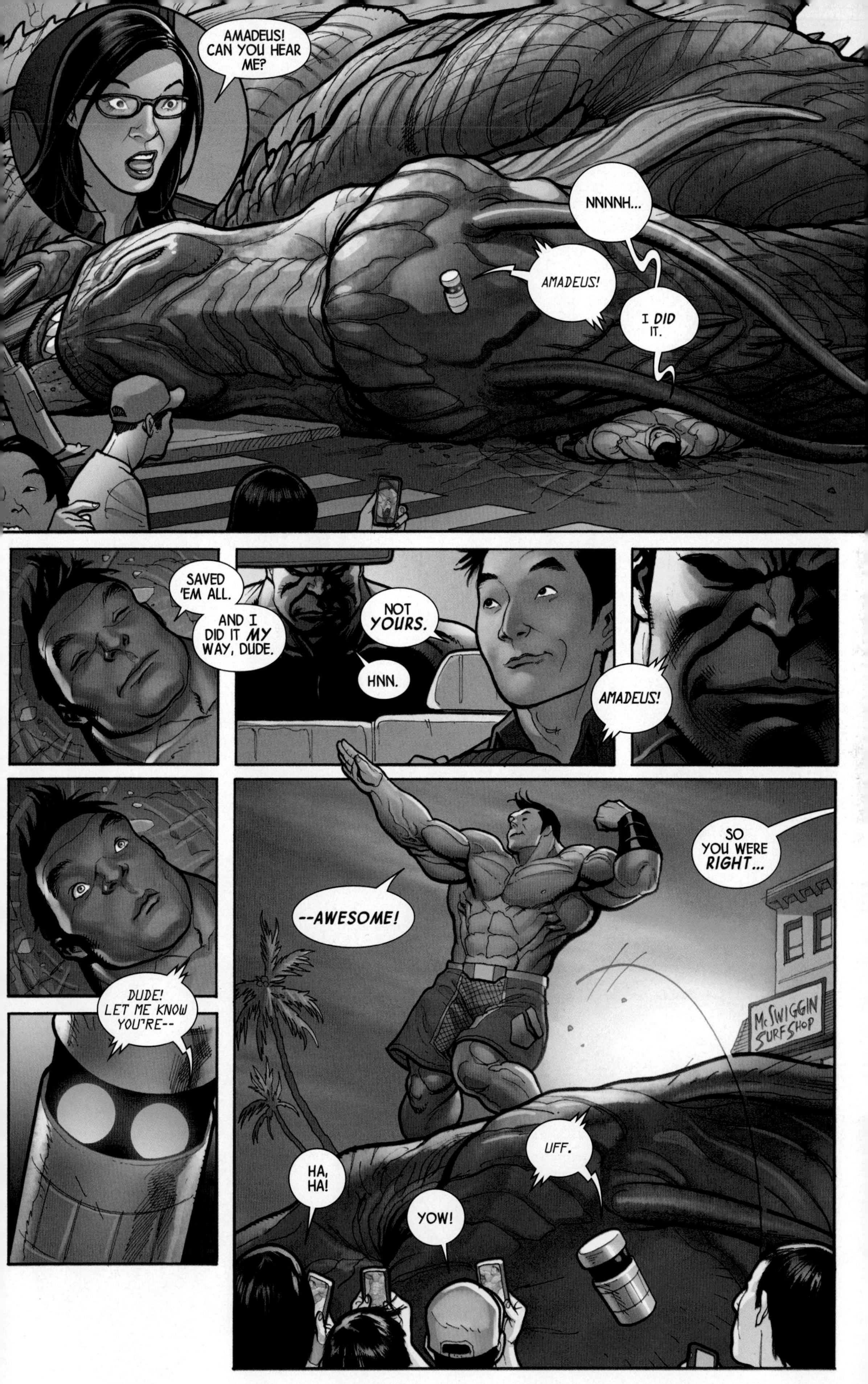
AMADEUS! CAN YOU HEAR ME?
NNNNH...
AMADEUS!
I DID IT.
SAVED 'EM ALL.
AND I DID IT MY WAY, DUDE.
NOT YOURS.
HNN.
AMADEUS!
DUDE! LET ME KNOW YOU'RE--
--AWESOME!
SO YOU WERE RIGHT...
McSWIGGIN SURF SHOP
UFF.
HA, HA!
YOW!

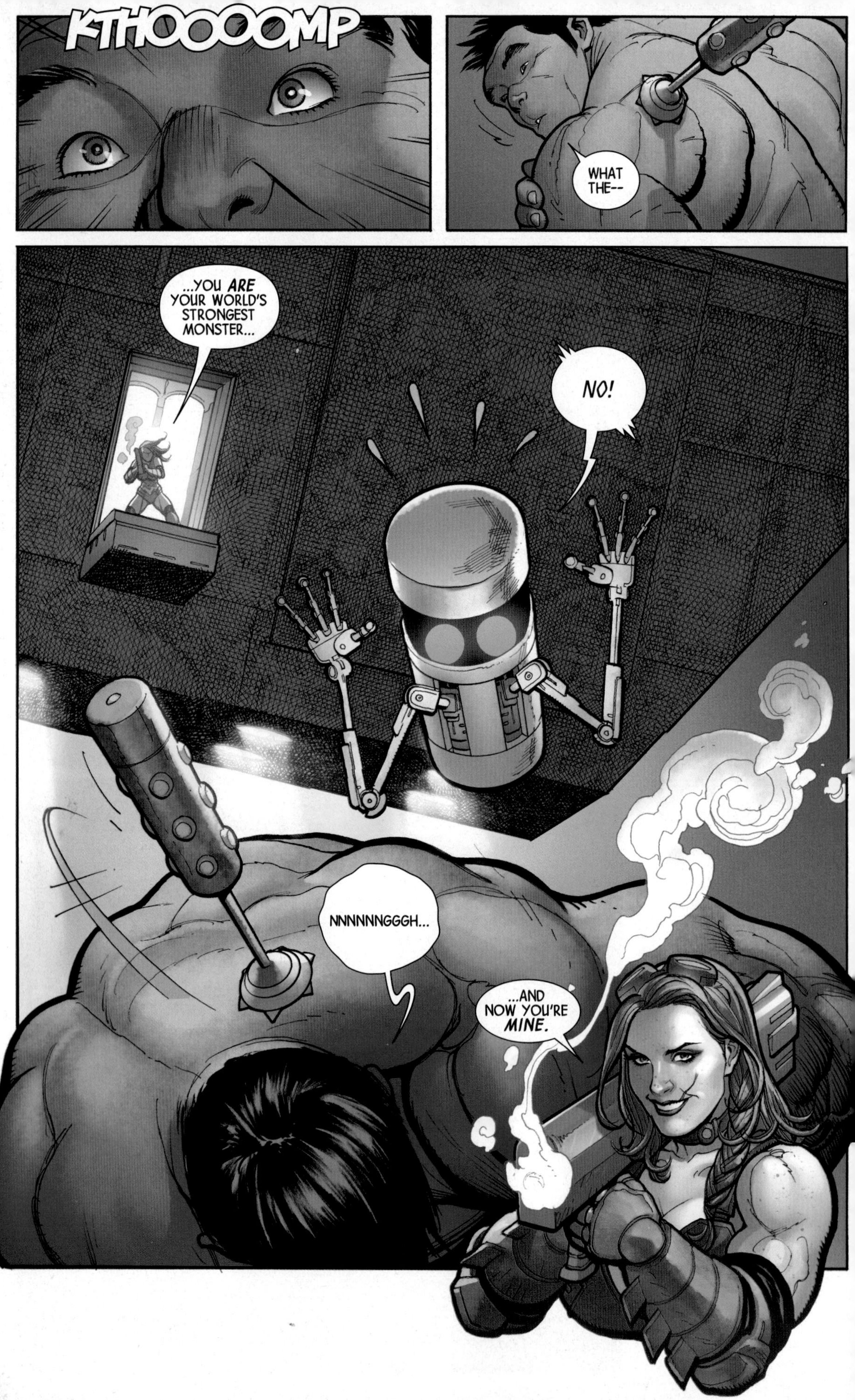
KTHOOOOMP
WHAT THE--
...YOU ARE YOUR WORLD'S STRONGEST MONSTER...
NO!
NNNNNNGGGH...
...AND NOW YOU'RE MINE.

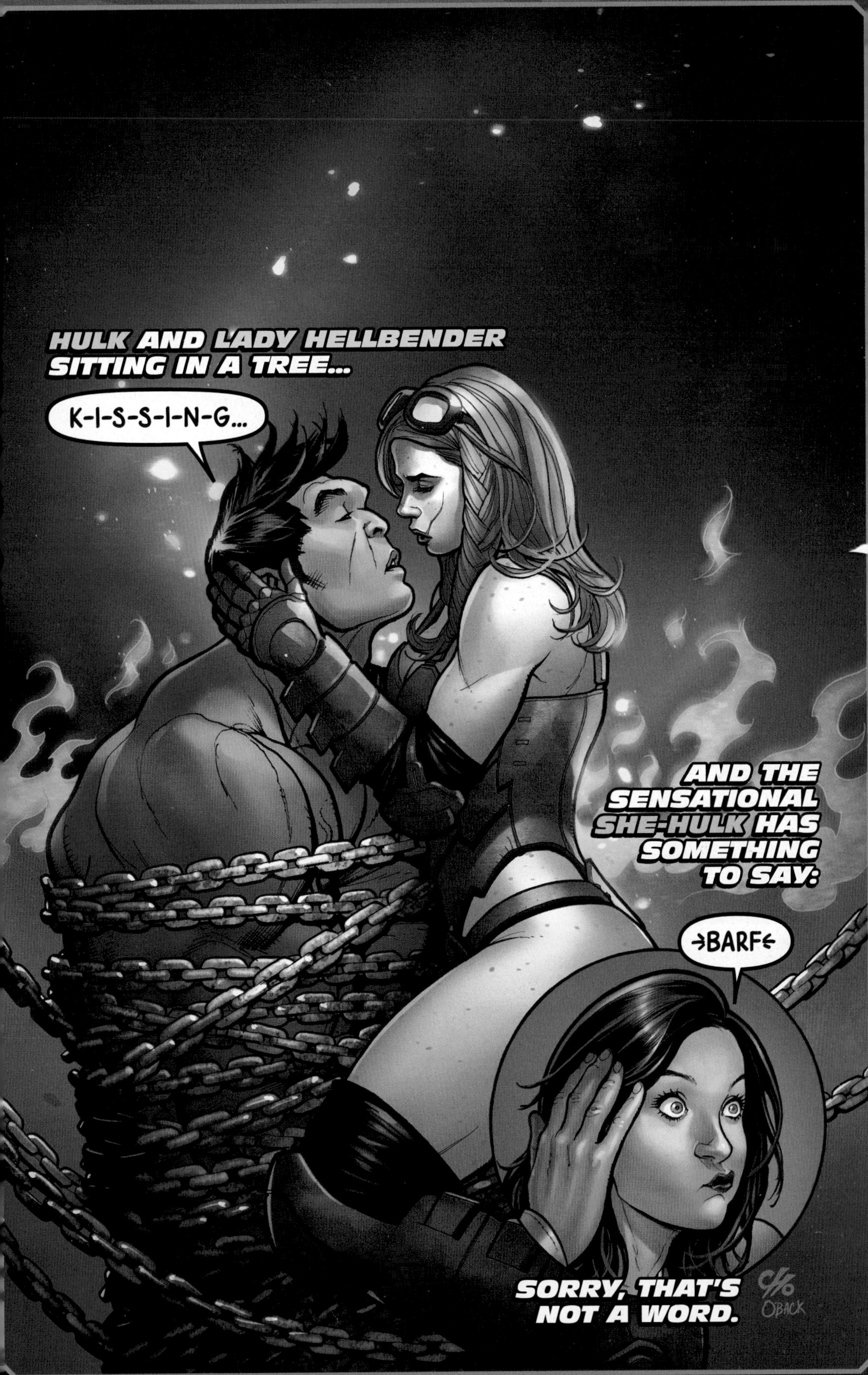
HULK AND LADY HELLBENDER SITTING IN A TREE...
K-I-S-S-I-N-G...
AND THE SENSATIONAL SHE-HULK HAS SOMETHING TO SAY:
»BARF«
SORRY, THAT'S NOT A WORD.

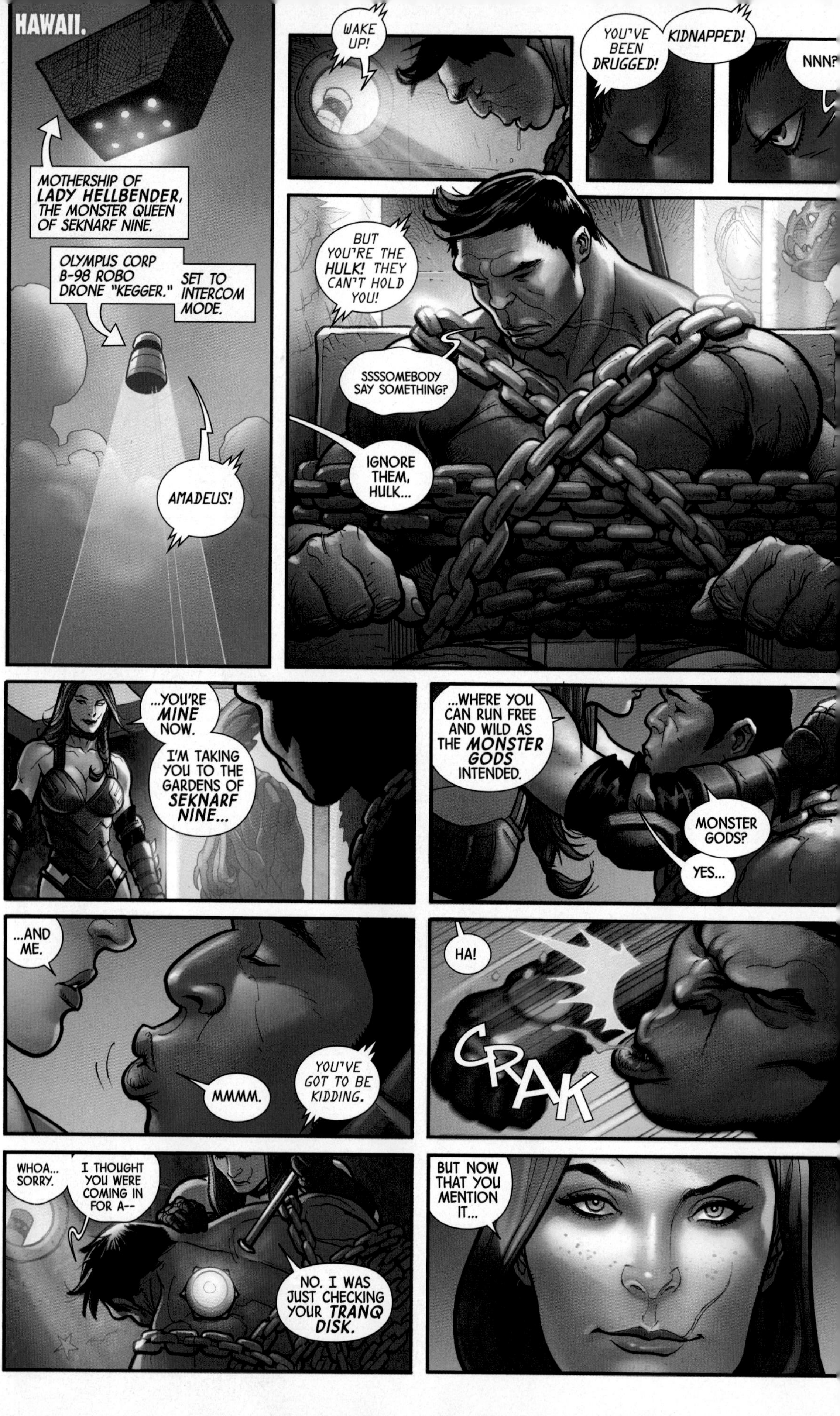

HAWAII.
MOTHERSHIP OF LADY HELLBENDER, THE MONSTER QUEEN OF SEKNARF NINE.
OLYMPUS CORP B-98 ROBO DRONE "KEGGER."
SET TO INTERCOM MODE.
AMADEUS!
WAKE UP!
YOU'VE BEEN DRUGGED!
KIDNAPPED!
NNN?
BUT YOU'RE THE HULK! THEY CAN'T HOLD YOU!
SSSSOMEBODY SAY SOMETHING?
IGNORE THEM, HULK...
...YOU'RE MINE NOW.
I'M TAKING YOU TO THE GARDENS OF SEKNARF NINE...
...WHERE YOU CAN RUN FREE AND WILD AS THE MONSTER GODS INTENDED.
MONSTER GODS?
YES...
...AND ME.
MMMM.
YOU'VE GOT TO BE KIDDING.
HA!
CRAK
WHOA... SORRY.
I THOUGHT YOU WERE COMING IN FOR A--
NO. I WAS JUST CHECKING YOUR TRANQ DISK.
BUT NOW THAT YOU MENTION IT...

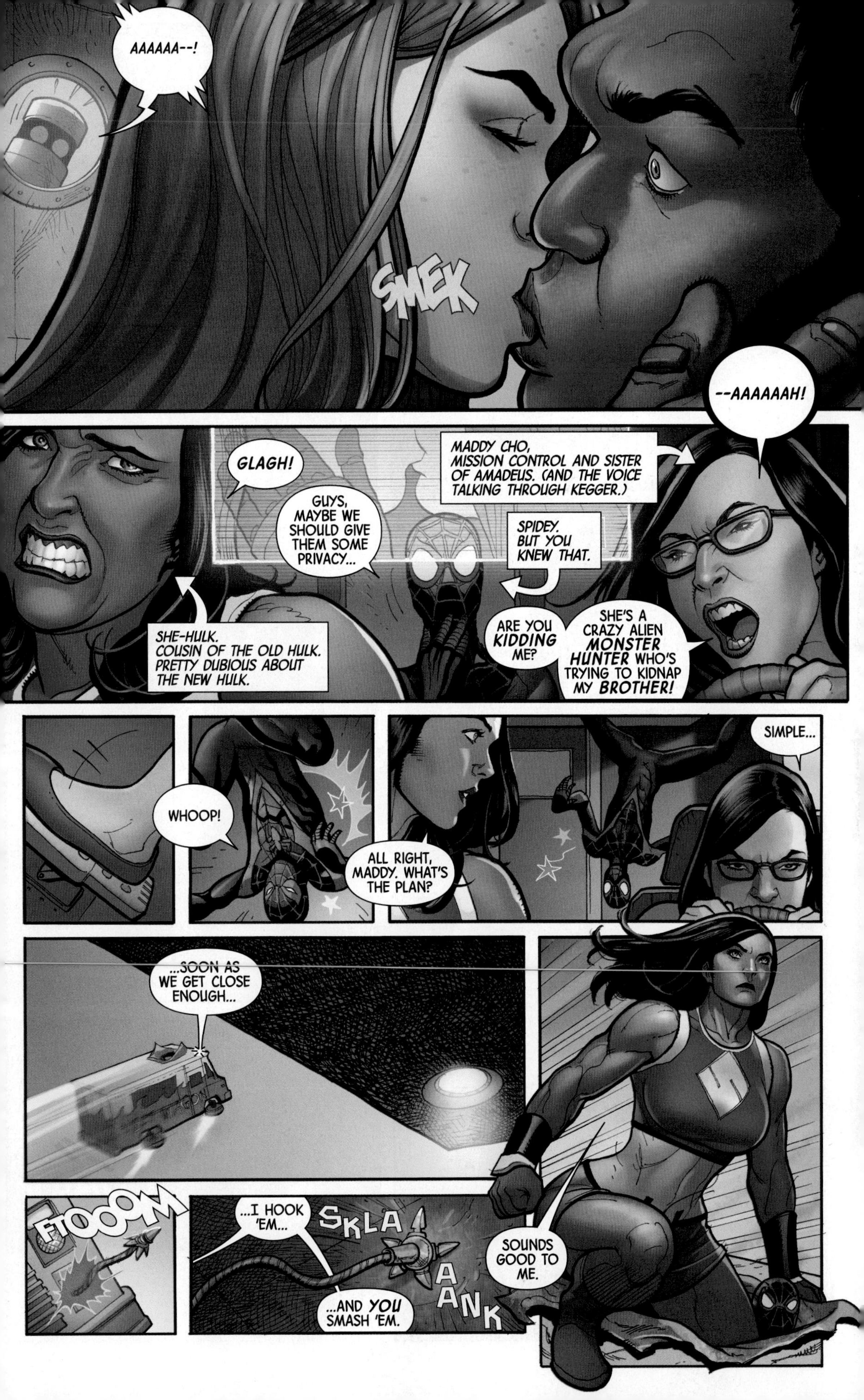
AAAAAA--!
SMEK
--AAAAAAH!
GLAGH!
GUYS, MAYBE WE SHOULD GIVE THEM SOME PRIVACY...
MADDY CHO, MISSION CONTROL AND SISTER OF AMADEUS. (AND THE VOICE TALKING THROUGH KEGGER.)
SPIDEY. BUT YOU KNEW THAT.
SHE-HULK. COUSIN OF THE OLD HULK. PRETTY DUBIOUS ABOUT THE NEW HULK.
ARE YOU KIDDING ME?
SHE'S A CRAZY ALIEN MONSTER HUNTER WHO'S TRYING TO KIDNAP MY BROTHER!
WHOOP!
ALL RIGHT, MADDY. WHAT'S THE PLAN?
SIMPLE...
...SOON AS WE GET CLOSE ENOUGH...
FTOOOM
...I HOOK 'EM...
SKLA AANK
...AND YOU SMASH 'EM.
SOUNDS GOOD TO ME.

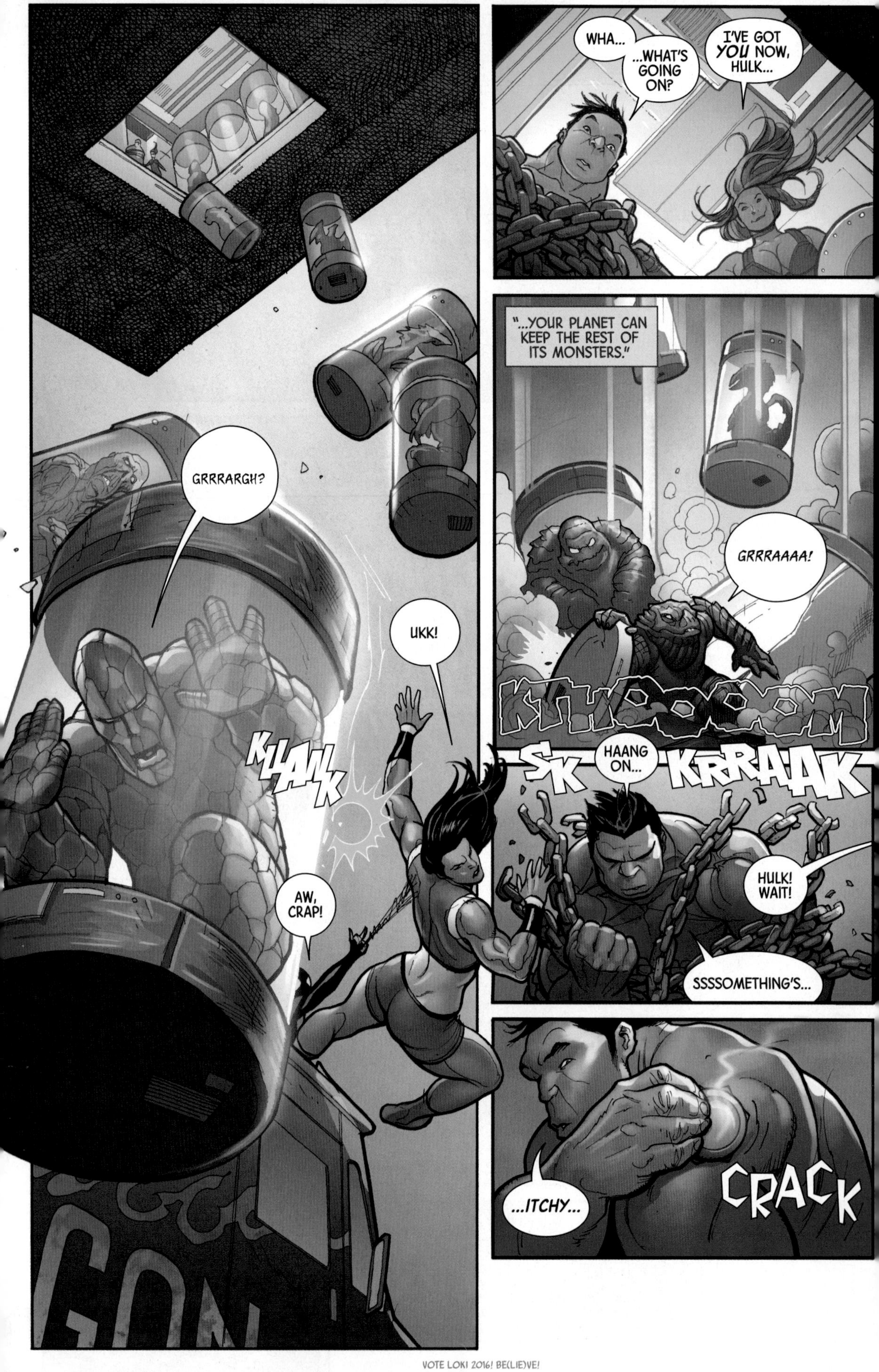
GRRRARGH?
KLLANK
UKK!
AW, CRAP!
WHA...
...WHAT'S GOING ON?
I'VE GOT *YOU* NOW, HULK...
"...YOUR PLANET CAN KEEP THE REST OF ITS MONSTERS."
GRRRAAAA!
KTHOOOOOM
SK
HAANG ON...
KRRAAAK
HULK! WAIT!
SSSSOMETHING'S...
...ITCHY...
CRACK

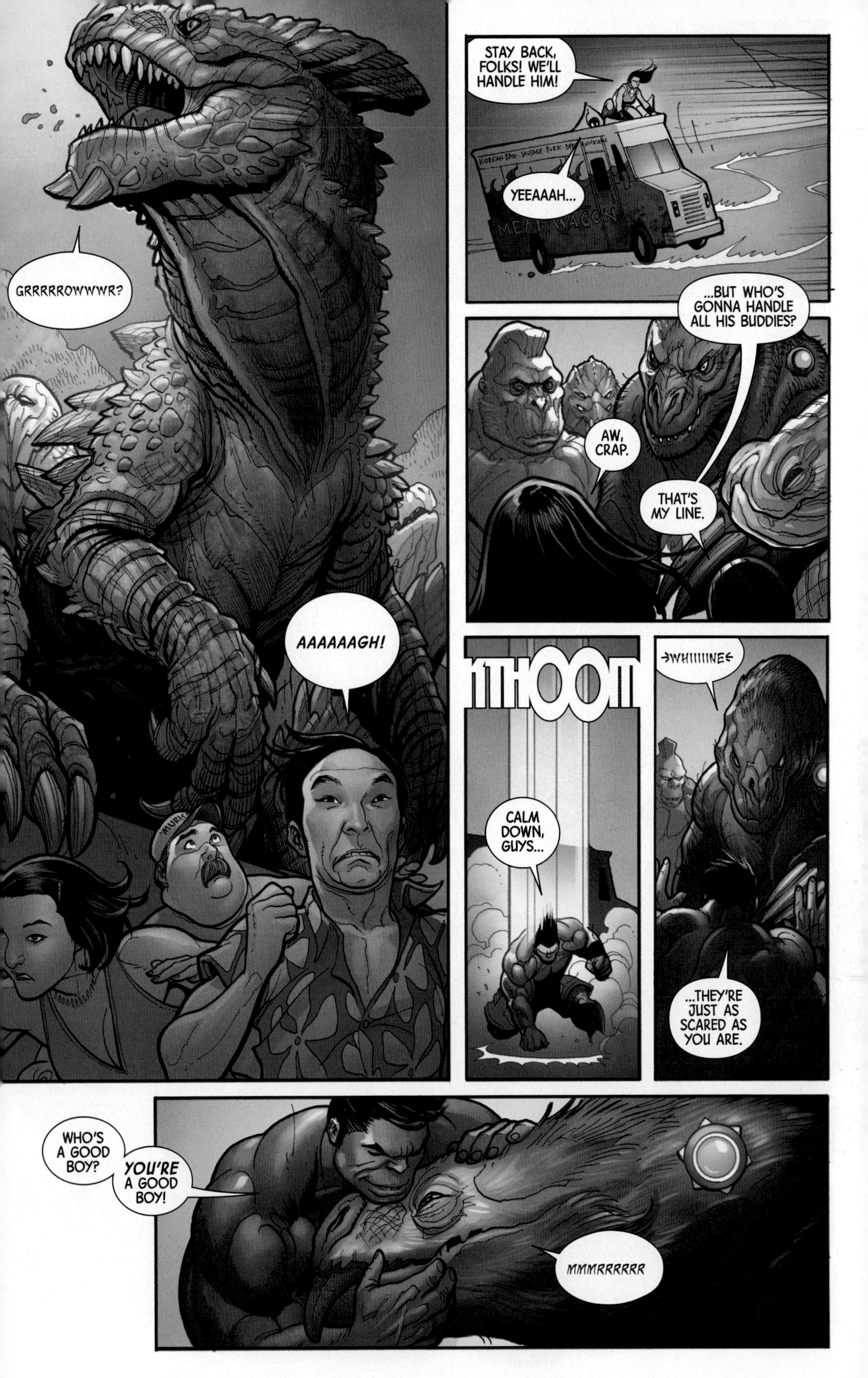
GRRRRROWWWR?
AAAAAAGH!
STAY BACK, FOLKS! WE'LL HANDLE HIM!
YEEAAAH...
MEAT WAGON
...BUT WHO'S GONNA HANDLE ALL HIS BUDDIES?
AW, CRAP.
THAT'S MY LINE.
K'THOOM
CALM DOWN, GUYS...
WHIIIIINE
...THEY'RE JUST AS SCARED AS YOU ARE.
WHO'S A GOOD BOY?
YOU'RE A GOOD BOY!
MMMRRRRRR

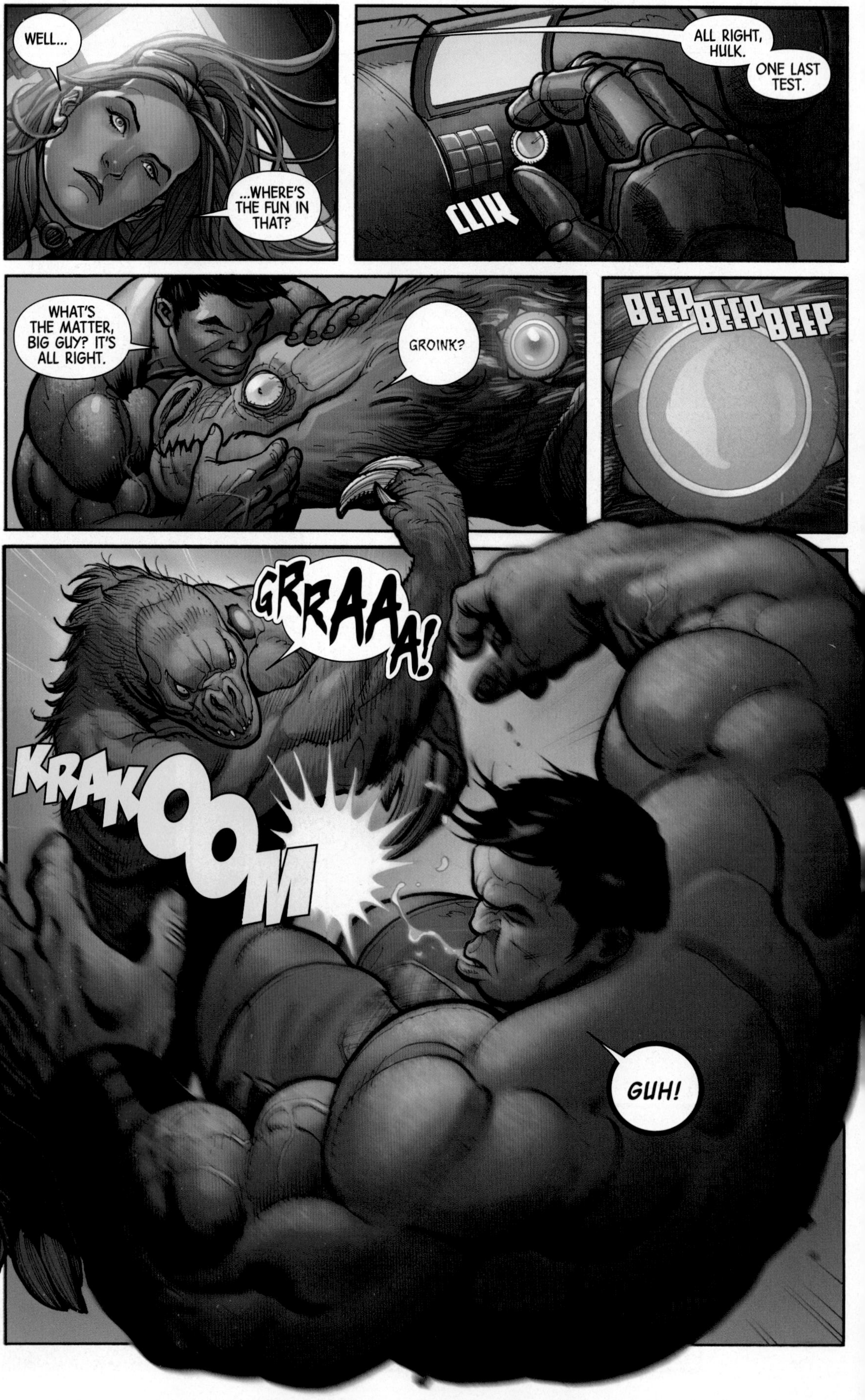
WELL...
...WHERE'S THE FUN IN THAT?
ALL RIGHT, HULK.
ONE LAST TEST.
CLIK
WHAT'S THE MATTER, BIG GUY? IT'S ALL RIGHT.
GROINK?
BEEP BEEP BEEP
GRRAAAA!
KRAKOOOM
GUH!

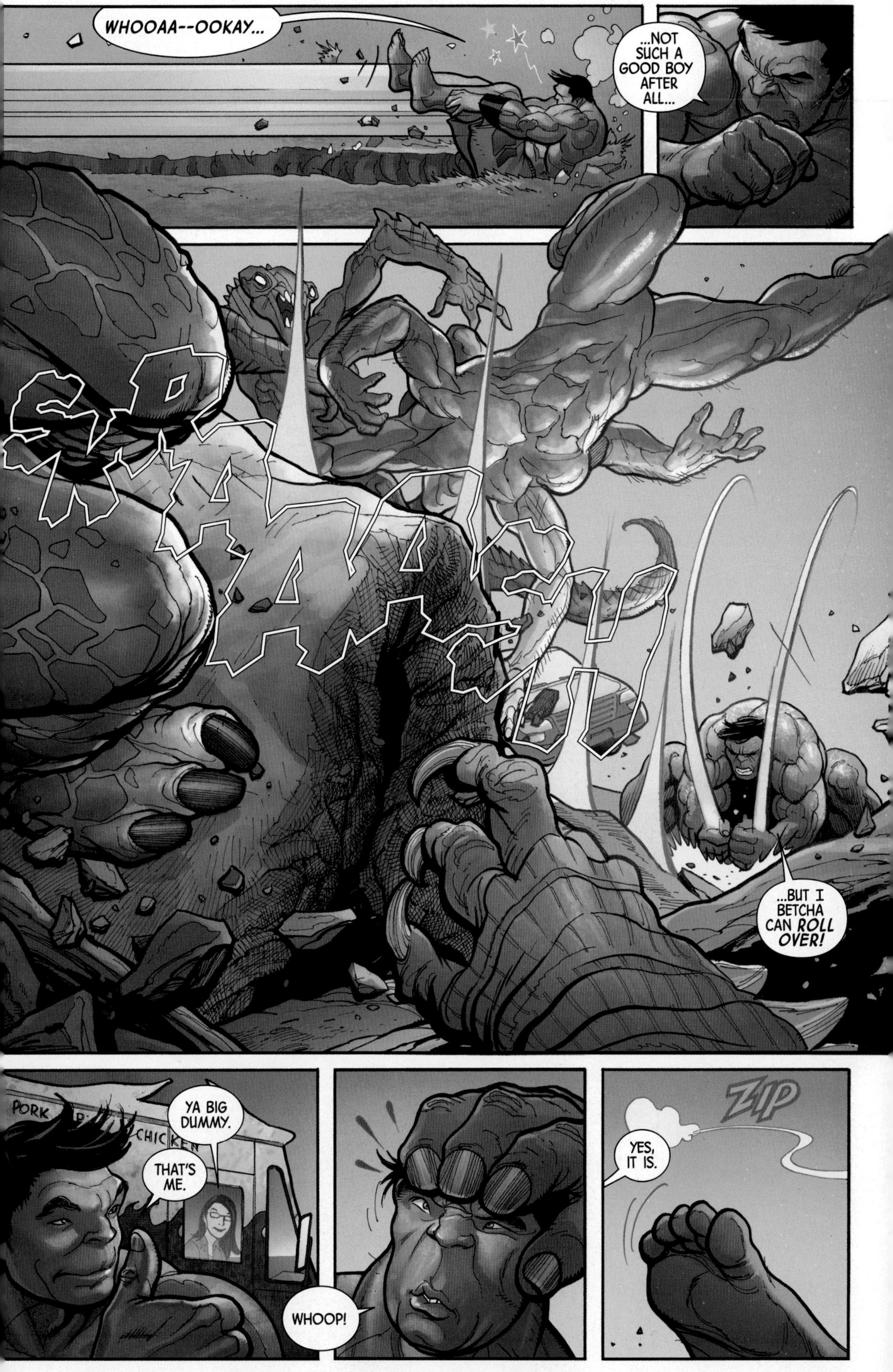
WHOOAA--OOKAY...
...NOT SUCH A GOOD BOY AFTER ALL...
...BUT I BETCHA CAN *ROLL OVER!*
PORK
CHICKEN
YA BIG DUMMY.
THAT'S ME.
WHOOP!
ZIP
YES, IT IS.

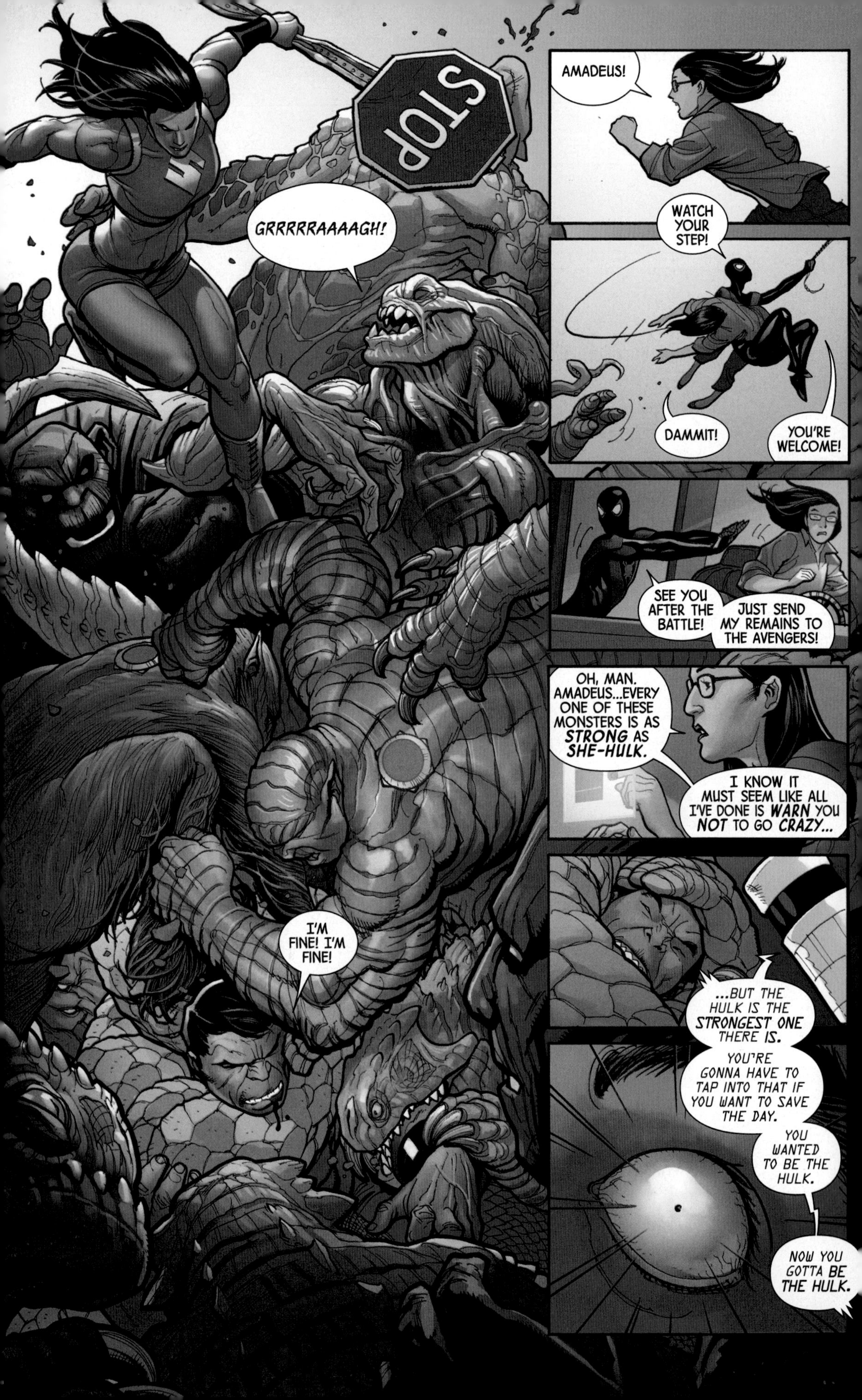
STOP
GRRRRRAAAAGH!
I'M FINE! I'M FINE!
AMADEUS!
WATCH YOUR STEP!
DAMMIT!
YOU'RE WELCOME!
SEE YOU AFTER THE BATTLE!
JUST SEND MY REMAINS TO THE AVENGERS!
OH, MAN. AMADEUS...EVERY ONE OF THESE MONSTERS IS AS STRONG AS SHE-HULK.
I KNOW IT MUST SEEM LIKE ALL I'VE DONE IS WARN YOU NOT TO GO CRAZY...
...BUT THE HULK IS THE STRONGEST ONE THERE IS.
YOU'RE GONNA HAVE TO TAP INTO THAT IF YOU WANT TO SAVE THE DAY.
YOU WANTED TO BE THE HULK.
NOW YOU GOTTA BE THE HULK.

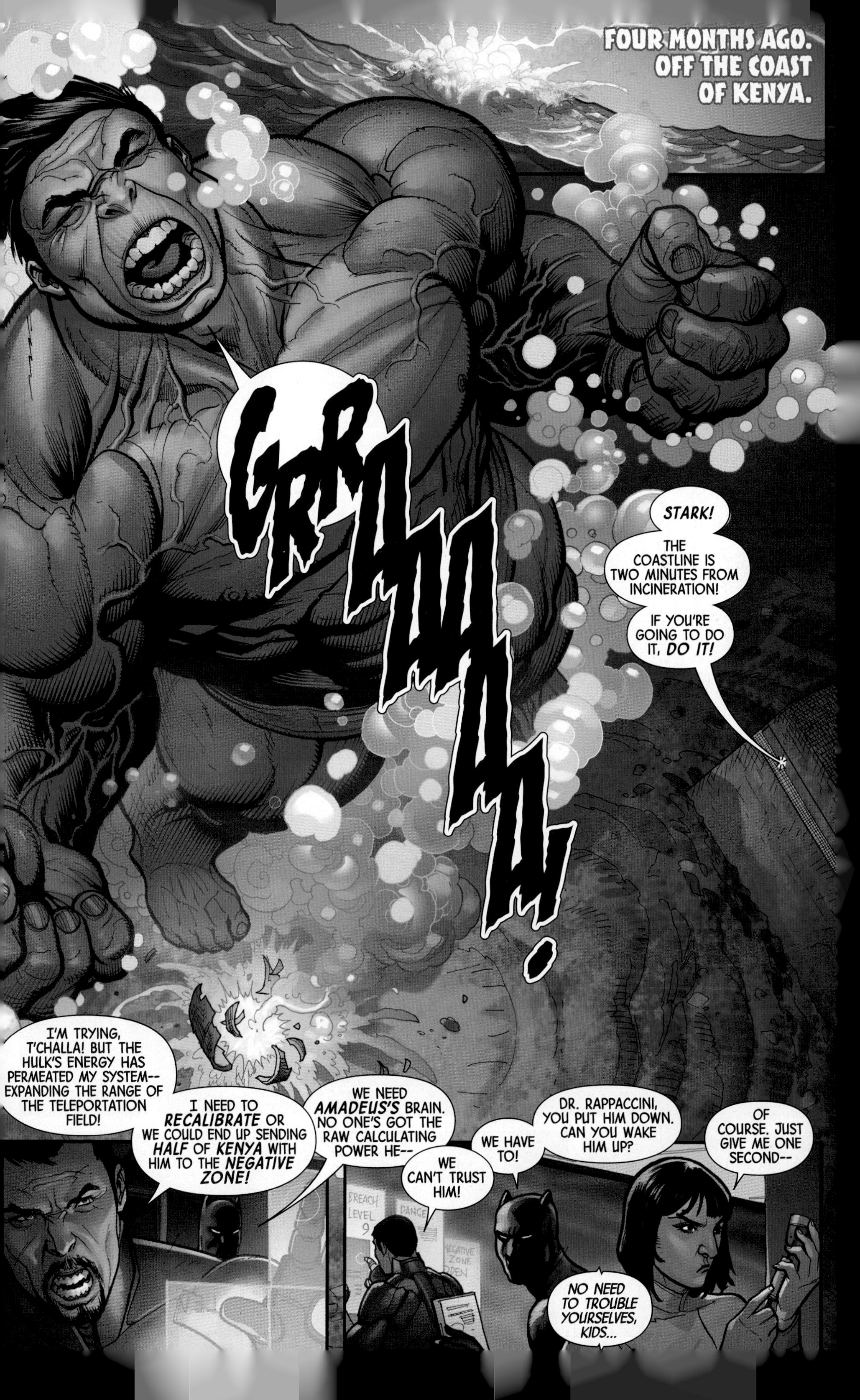
FOUR MONTHS AGO. OFF THE COAST OF KENYA.
GRRAAAAA!
STARK!
THE COASTLINE IS TWO MINUTES FROM INCINERATION!
IF YOU'RE GOING TO DO IT, DO IT!
I'M TRYING, T'CHALLA! BUT THE HULK'S ENERGY HAS PERMEATED MY SYSTEM-- EXPANDING THE RANGE OF THE TELEPORTATION FIELD!
I NEED TO RECALIBRATE OR WE COULD END UP SENDING HALF OF KENYA WITH HIM TO THE NEGATIVE ZONE!
WE NEED AMADEUS'S BRAIN. NO ONE'S GOT THE RAW CALCULATING POWER HE--
WE CAN'T TRUST HIM!
WE HAVE TO!
DR. RAPPACCINI, YOU PUT HIM DOWN. CAN YOU WAKE HIM UP?
OF COURSE. JUST GIVE ME ONE SECOND--
NO NEED TO TROUBLE YOURSELVES, KIDS...
BREACH LEVEL 9
DANGE
NEGATIVE ZONE OPEN

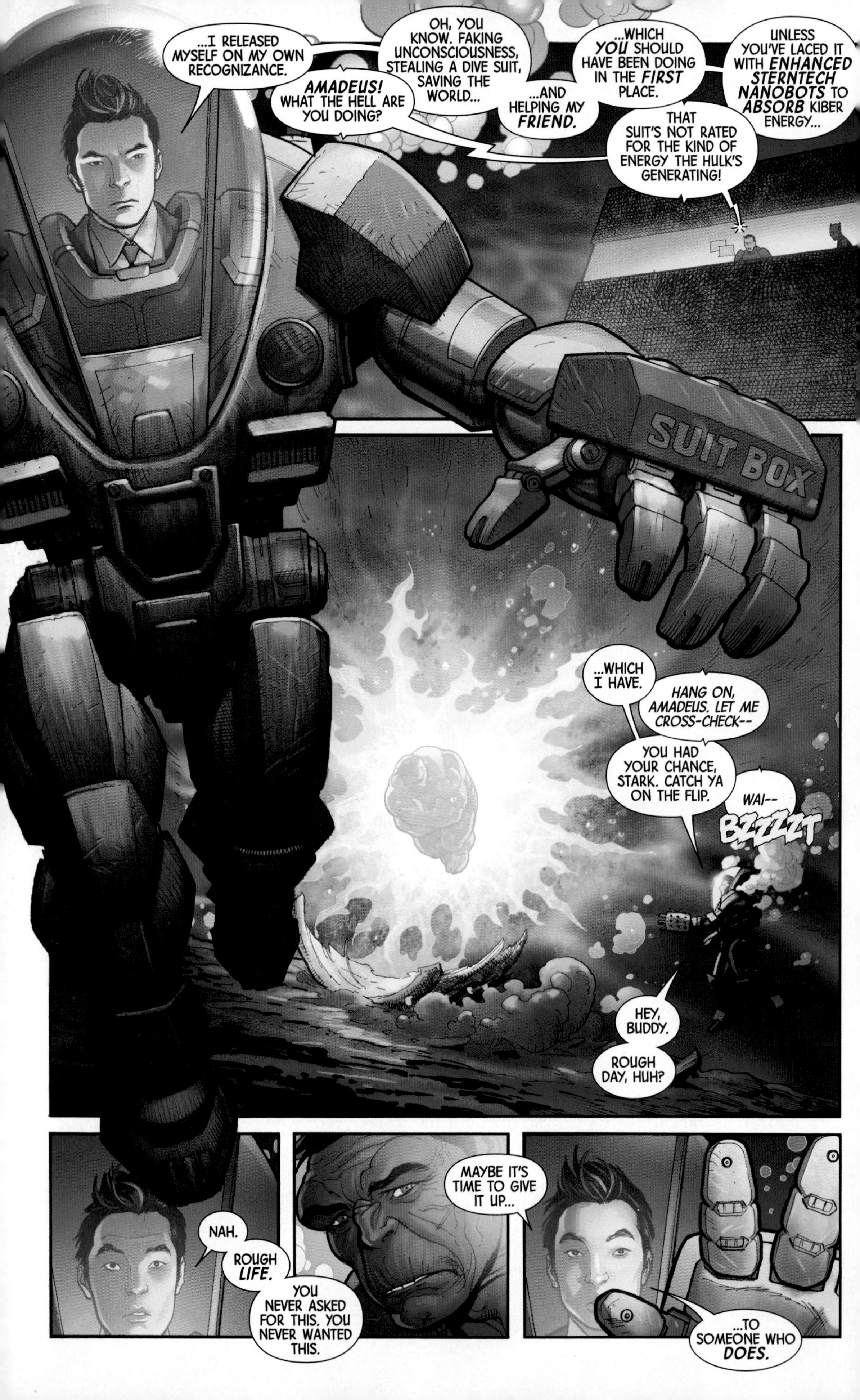
...I RELEASED MYSELF ON MY OWN RECOGNIZANCE.
AMADEUS! WHAT THE HELL ARE YOU DOING?
OH, YOU KNOW. FAKING UNCONSCIOUSNESS, STEALING A DIVE SUIT, SAVING THE WORLD...
...AND HELPING MY FRIEND.
...WHICH YOU SHOULD HAVE BEEN DOING IN THE FIRST PLACE.
THAT SUIT'S NOT RATED FOR THE KIND OF ENERGY THE HULK'S GENERATING!
UNLESS YOU'VE LACED IT WITH ENHANCED STERNTECH NANOBOTS TO ABSORB KIBER ENERGY...
SUIT BOX
...WHICH I HAVE.
HANG ON, AMADEUS. LET ME CROSS-CHECK--
YOU HAD YOUR CHANCE, STARK. CATCH YA ON THE FLIP.
WAI--
BZZZZT
HEY, BUDDY.
ROUGH DAY, HUH?
NAH.
ROUGH LIFE.
YOU NEVER ASKED FOR THIS. YOU NEVER WANTED THIS.
MAYBE IT'S TIME TO GIVE IT UP...
...TO SOMEONE WHO DOES.

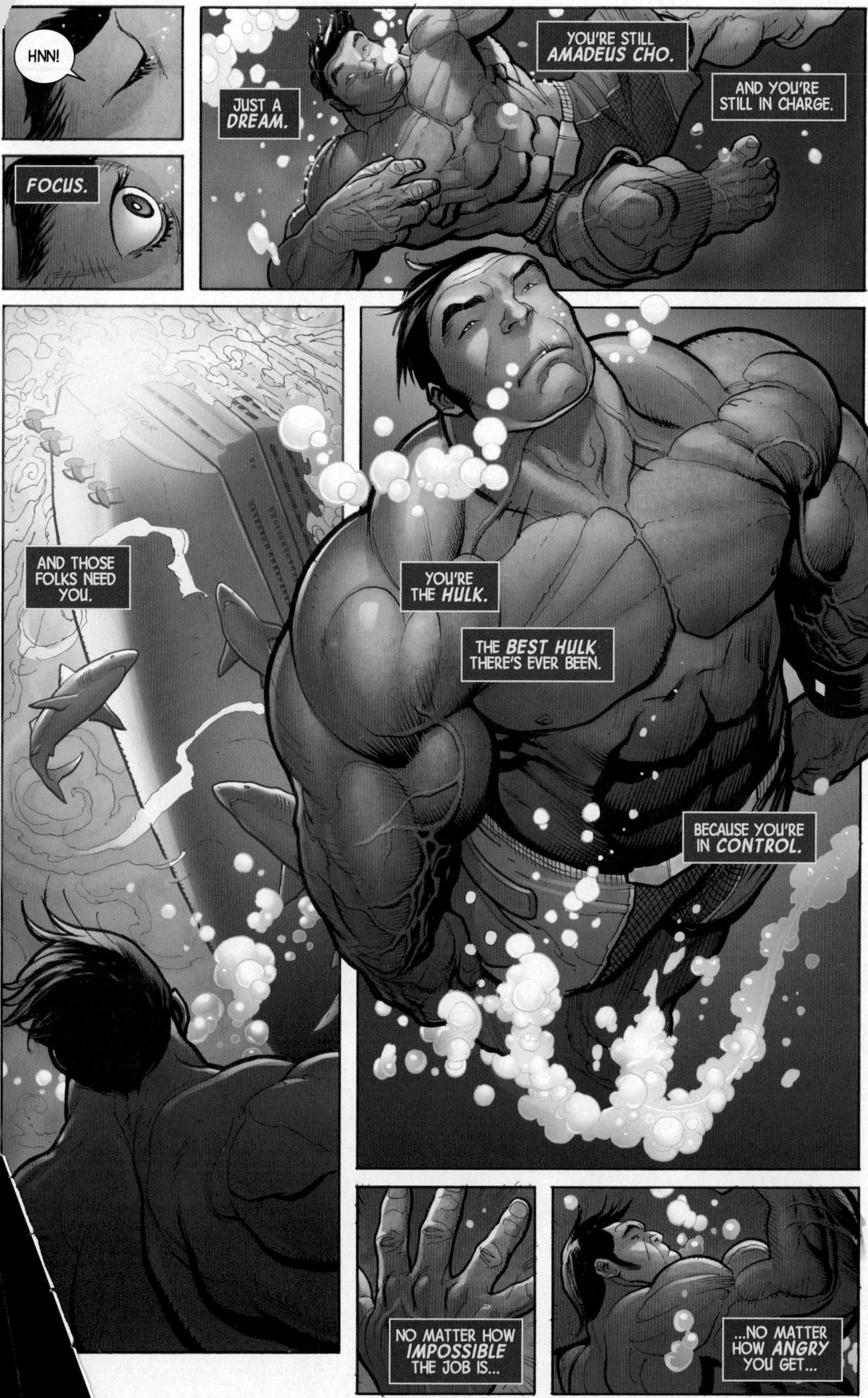
HNN!
FOCUS.
JUST A DREAM.
YOU'RE STILL AMADEUS CHO.
AND YOU'RE STILL IN CHARGE.
AND THOSE FOLKS NEED YOU.
YOU'RE THE HULK.
THE BEST HULK THERE'S EVER BEEN.
BECAUSE YOU'RE IN CONTROL.
NO MATTER HOW IMPOSSIBLE THE JOB IS...
...NO MATTER HOW ANGRY YOU GET...

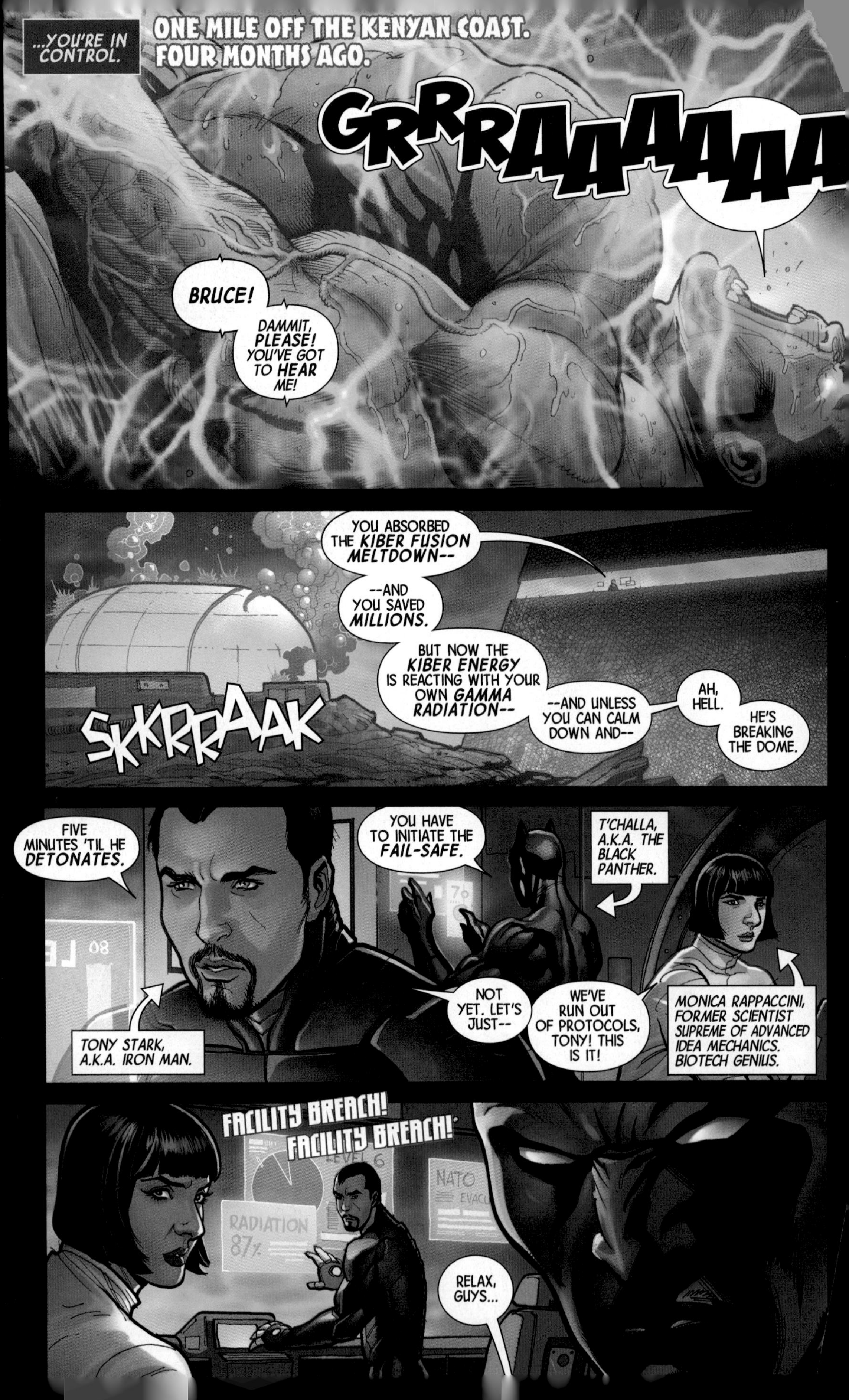

...YOU'RE IN CONTROL.
ONE MILE OFF THE KENYAN COAST. FOUR MONTHS AGO.
GRRRAAAAAA
BRUCE!
DAMMIT, PLEASE! YOU'VE GOT TO HEAR ME!
YOU ABSORBED THE KIBER FUSION MELTDOWN--
--AND YOU SAVED MILLIONS.
BUT NOW THE KIBER ENERGY IS REACTING WITH YOUR OWN GAMMA RADIATION--
SKKRRAAK
--AND UNLESS YOU CAN CALM DOWN AND--
AH, HELL.
HE'S BREAKING THE DOME.
FIVE MINUTES 'TIL HE DETONATES.
YOU HAVE TO INITIATE THE FAIL-SAFE.
T'CHALLA, A.K.A. THE BLACK PANTHER.
TONY STARK, A.K.A. IRON MAN.
NOT YET. LET'S JUST--
WE'VE RUN OUT OF PROTOCOLS, TONY! THIS IS IT!
MONICA RAPPACCINI, FORMER SCIENTIST SUPREME OF ADVANCED IDEA MECHANICS. BIOTECH GENIUS.
FACILITY BREACH!
FACILITY BREACH!
LEVEL 6
RADIATION 87%
NATO
RELAX, GUYS...

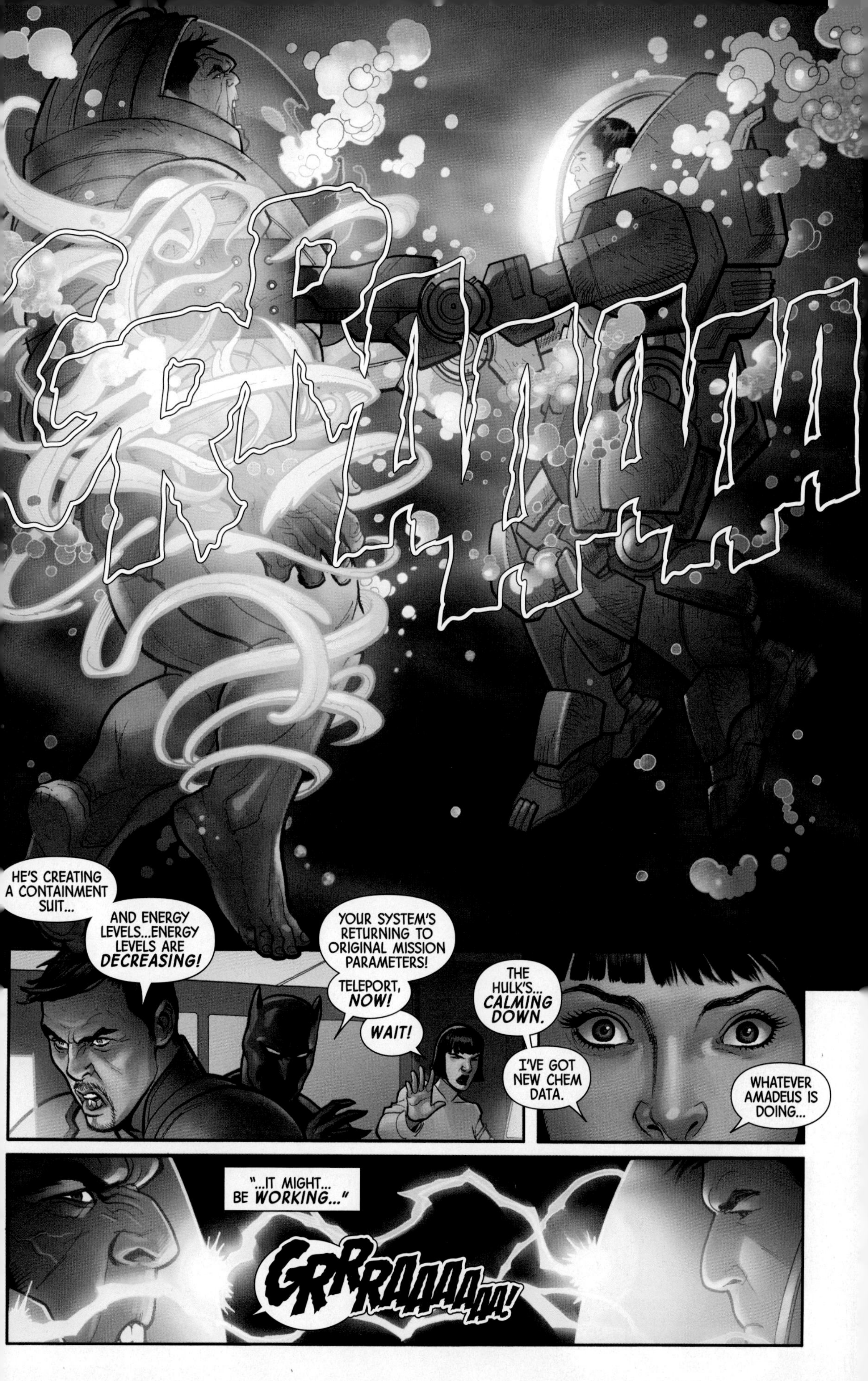

HE'S CREATING A CONTAINMENT SUIT...
AND ENERGY LEVELS...ENERGY LEVELS ARE DECREASING!
YOUR SYSTEM'S RETURNING TO ORIGINAL MISSION PARAMETERS!
TELEPORT, NOW!
WAIT!
THE HULK'S... CALMING DOWN.
I'VE GOT NEW CHEM DATA.
WHATEVER AMADEUS IS DOING...
"...IT MIGHT... BE WORKING..."
GRRRAAAAAA!

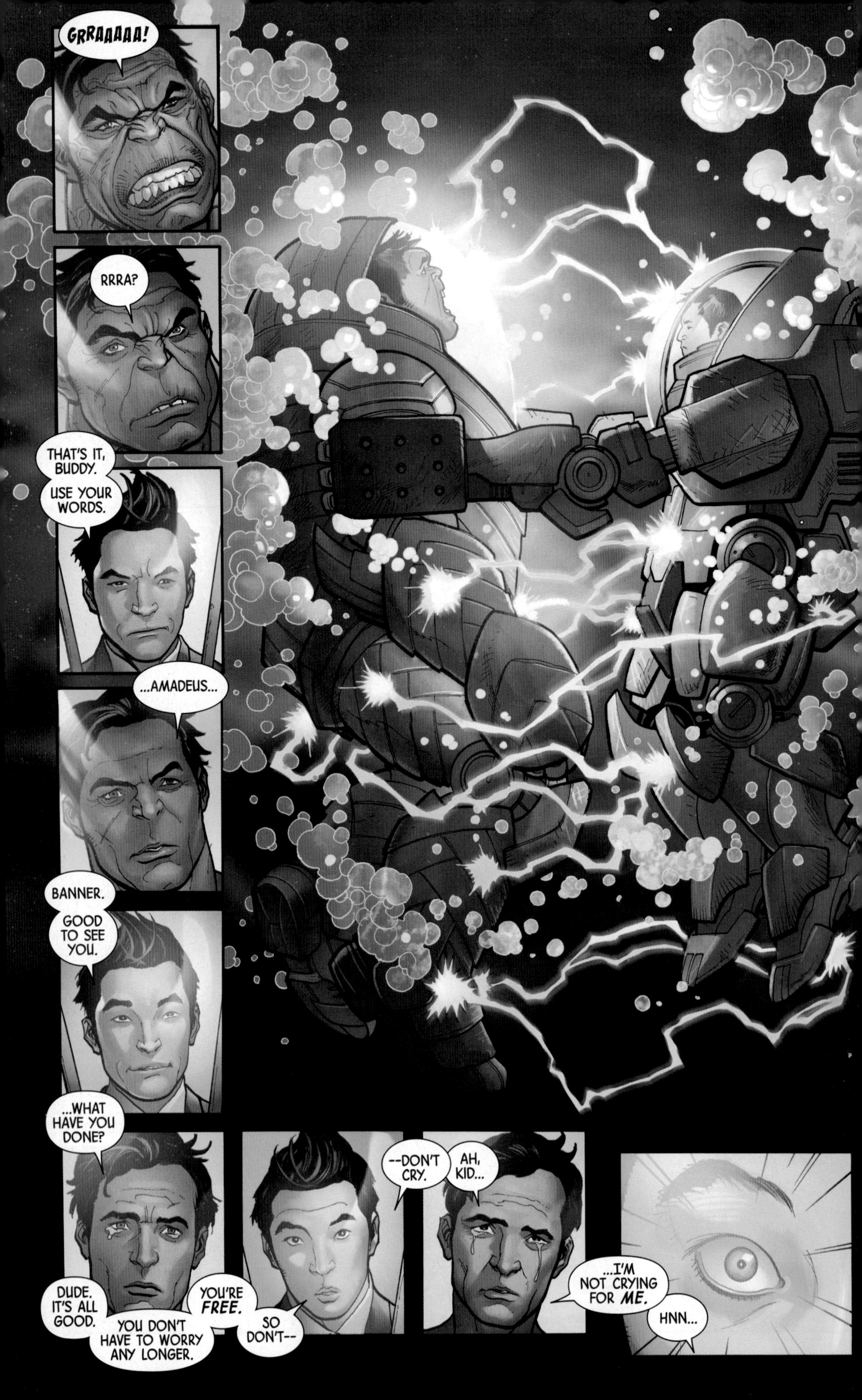
GRRAAAAA!
RRRA?
THAT'S IT, BUDDY.
USE YOUR WORDS.
...AMADEUS...
BANNER.
GOOD TO SEE YOU.
...WHAT HAVE YOU DONE?
DUDE. IT'S ALL GOOD.
YOU DON'T HAVE TO WORRY ANY LONGER.
YOU'RE FREE.
SO DON'T--
--DON'T CRY.
AH, KID...
...I'M NOT CRYING FOR ME.
HNN...

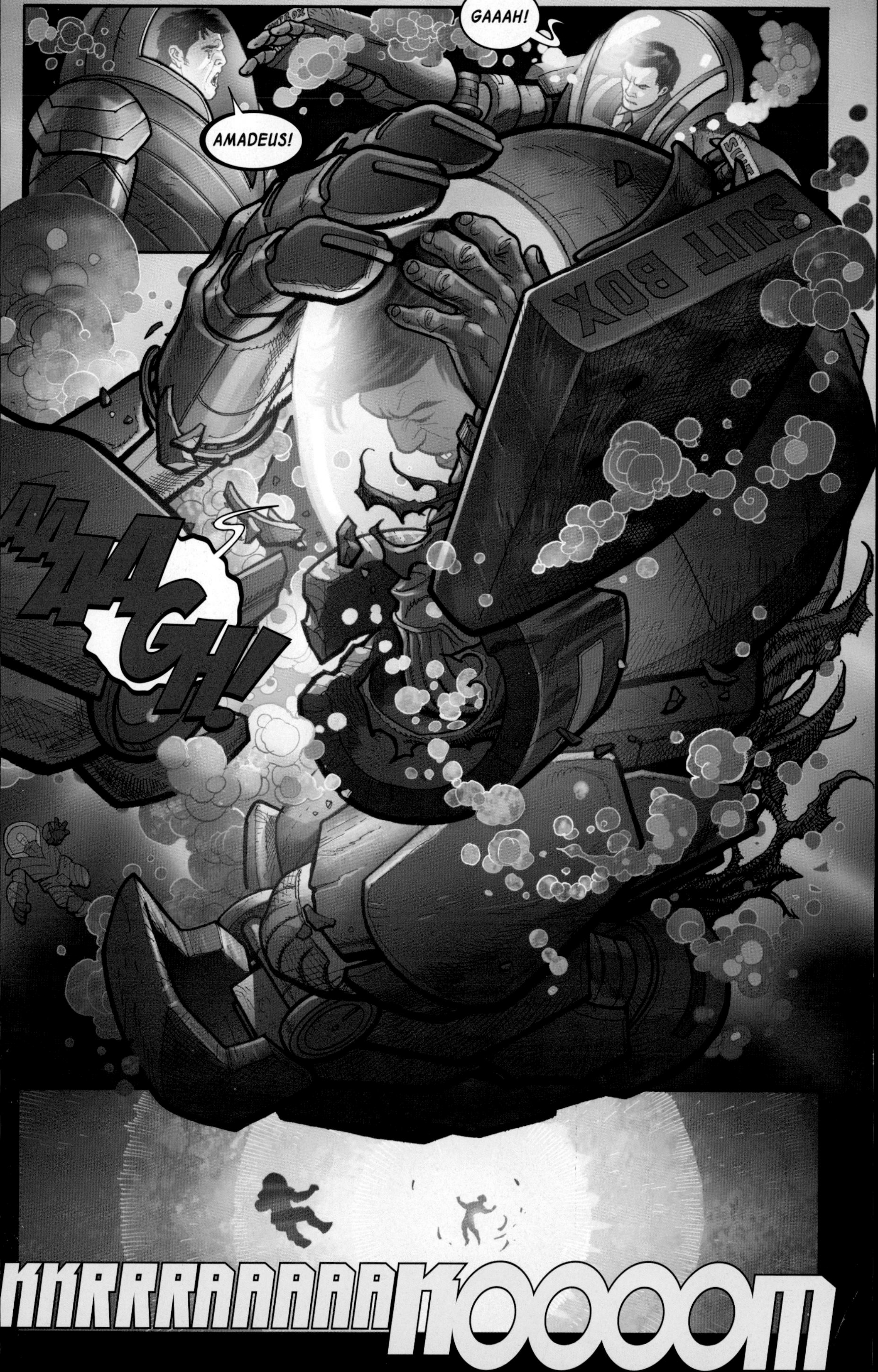

AMADEUS!
GAAAH!
SUIT BOX
AAAAGH!
KKRRRRAAAAAAKOOOOOM

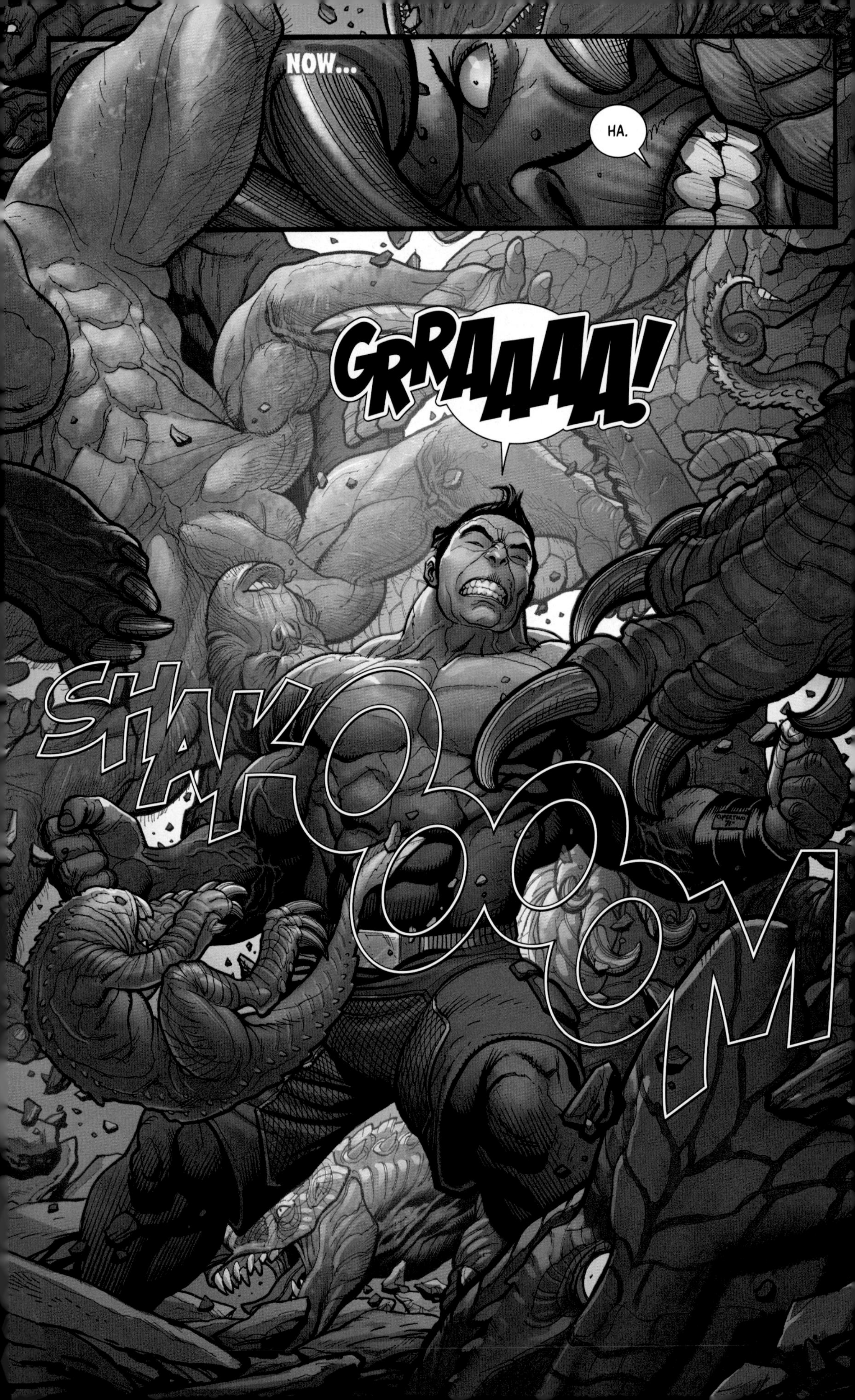
NOW...
HA.
GRRAAAAA!
SHAKOOOOM

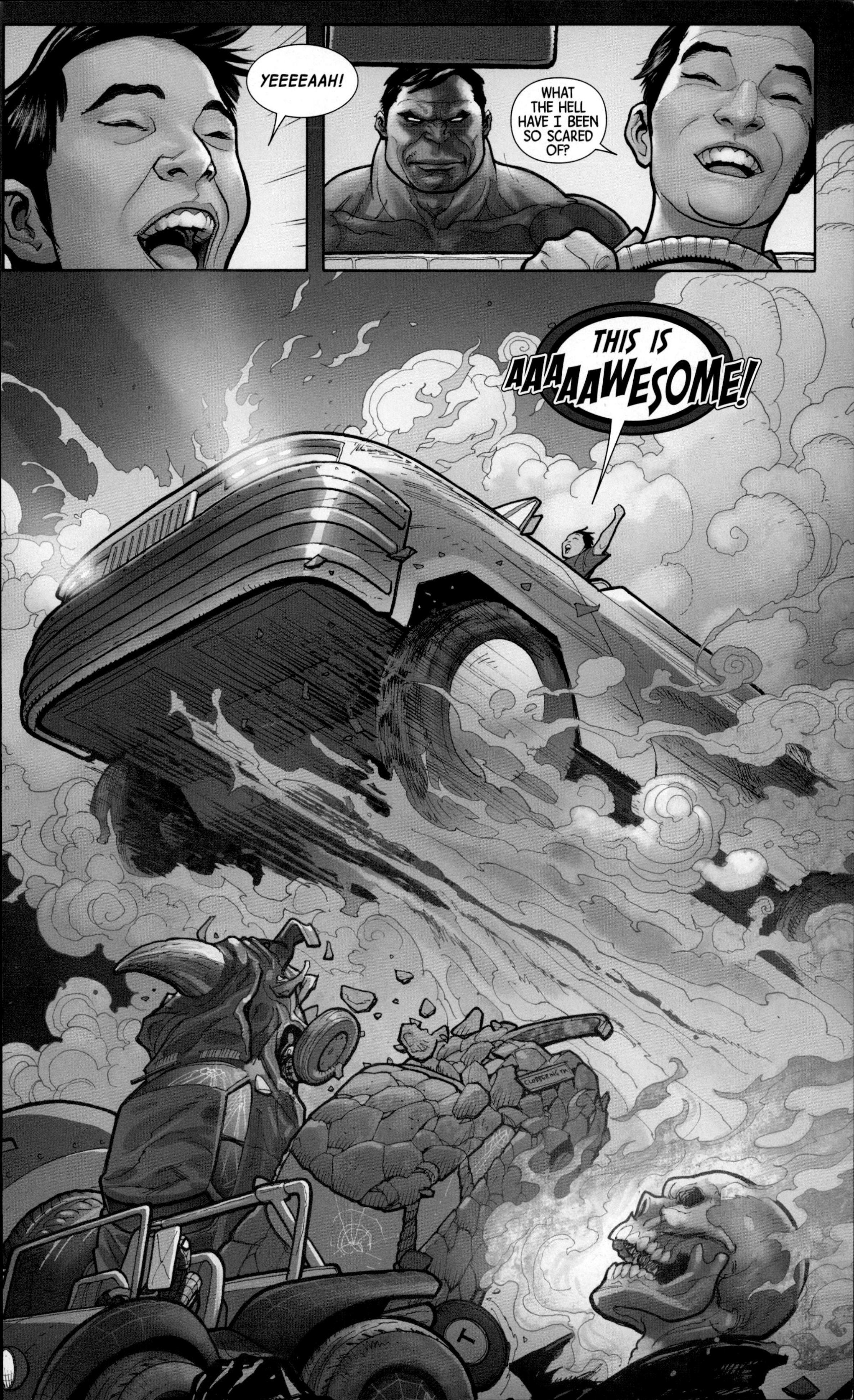
YEEEEAAH!
WHAT THE HELL HAVE I BEEN SO SCARED OF?
THIS IS AAAAAWESOME!

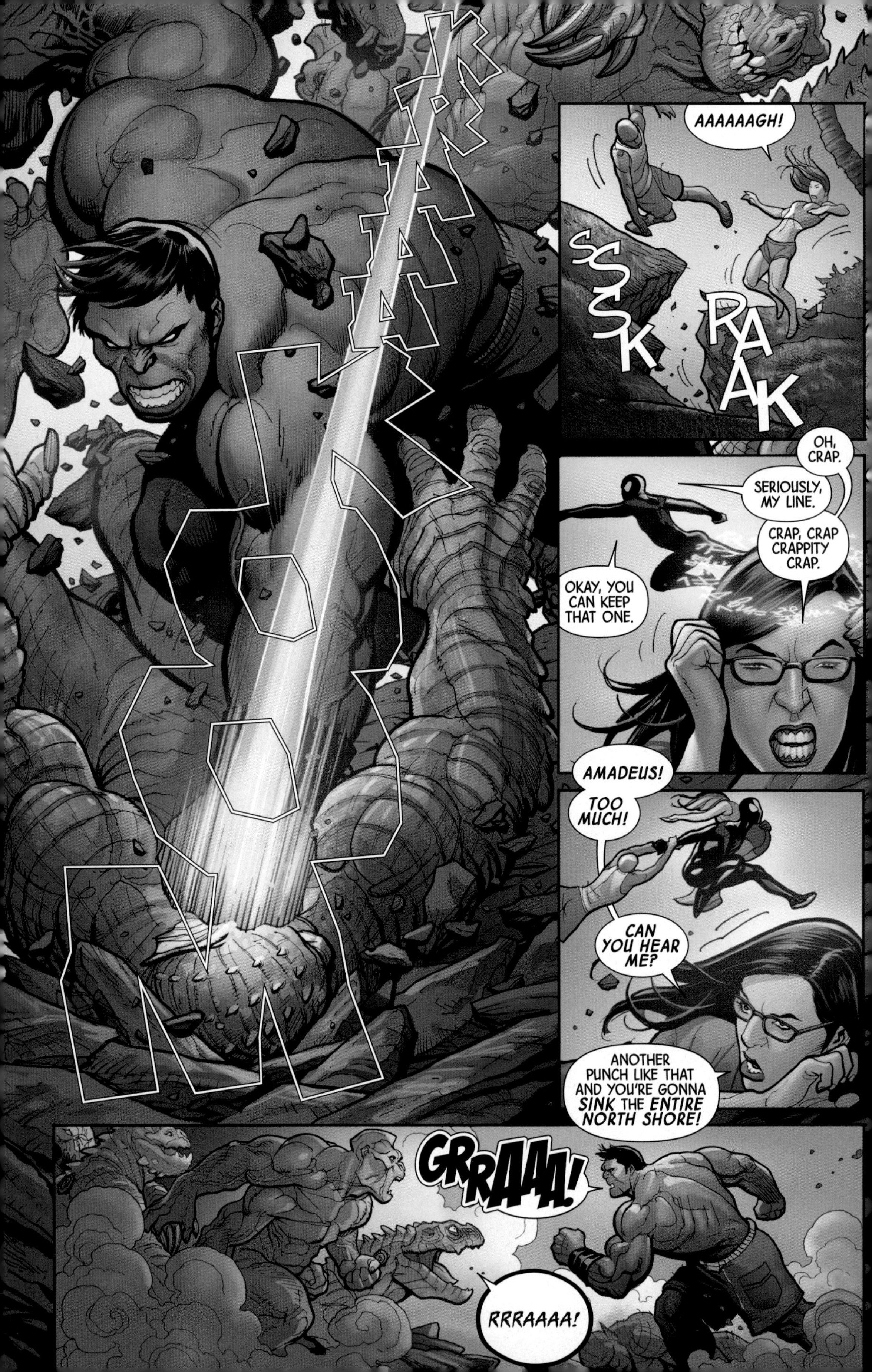
KA-THOOOM
AAAAAAGH!
SSSK
RAAAK
OH, CRAP.
SERIOUSLY, MY LINE.
CRAP, CRAP CRAPPITY CRAP.
OKAY, YOU CAN KEEP THAT ONE.
AMADEUS!
TOO MUCH!
CAN YOU HEAR ME?
ANOTHER PUNCH LIKE THAT AND YOU'RE GONNA SINK THE ENTIRE NORTH SHORE!
GRRAAAA!
RRRAAAA!

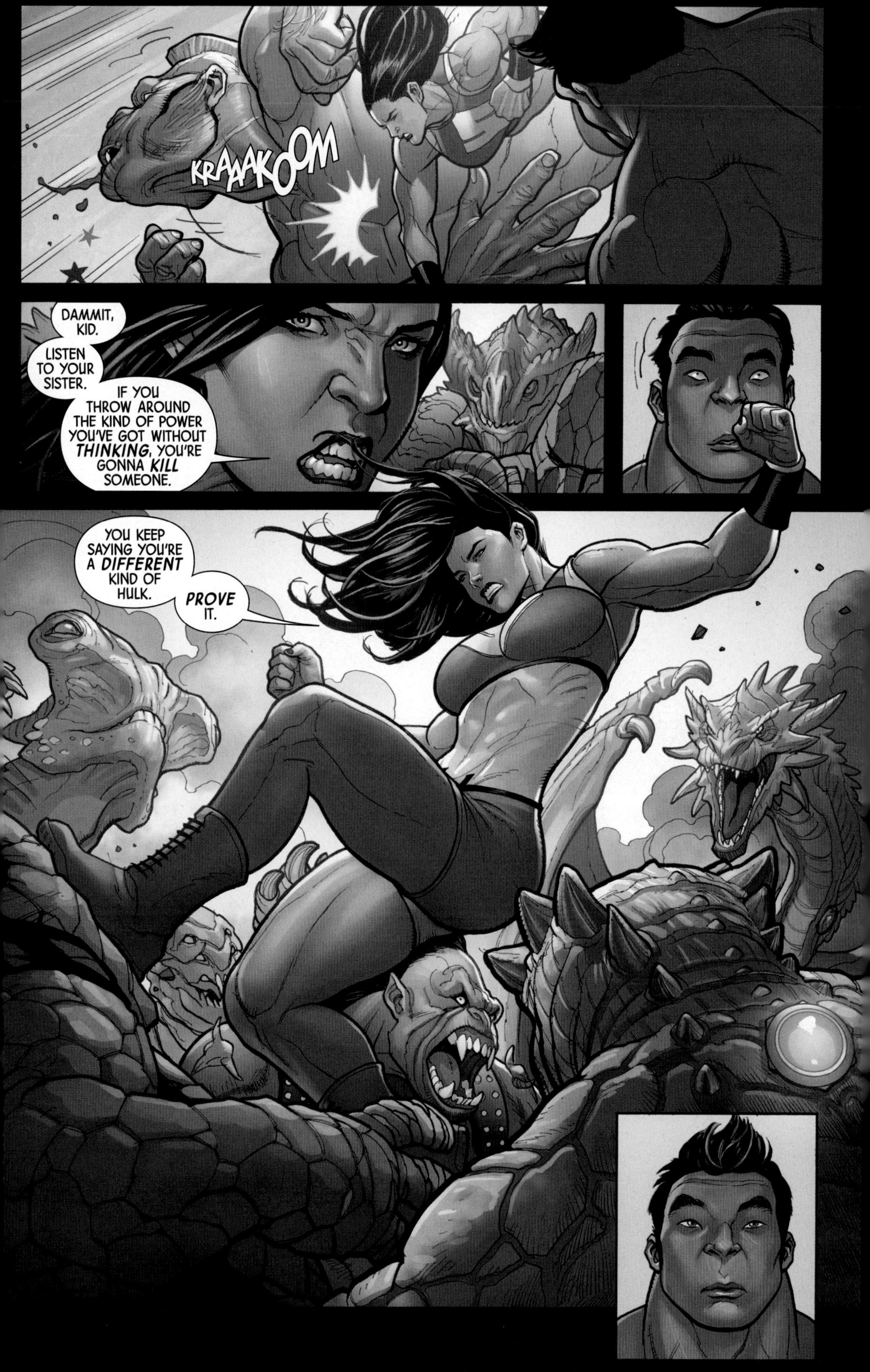
KRAAAKOOM
DAMMIT, KID.
LISTEN TO YOUR SISTER.
IF YOU THROW AROUND THE KIND OF POWER YOU'VE GOT WITHOUT THINKING, YOU'RE GONNA KILL SOMEONE.
YOU KEEP SAYING YOU'RE A DIFFERENT KIND OF HULK.
PROVE IT.

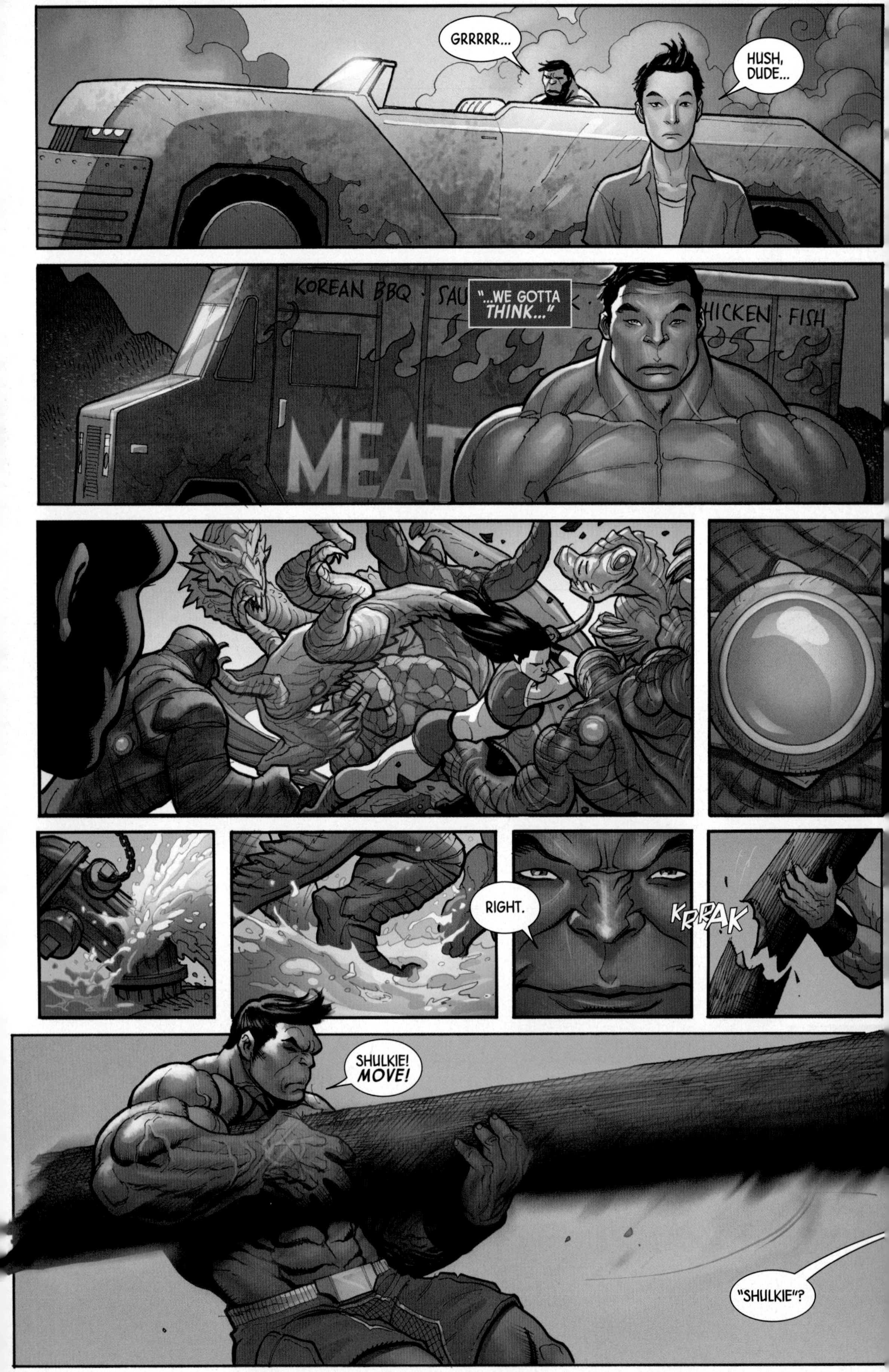
GRRRRR...
HUSH, DUDE...
KOREAN BBQ · SAU
HICKEN · FISH
MEAT
"...WE GOTTA THINK..."
RIGHT.
KRRAK
SHULKIE! MOVE!
"SHULKIE"?

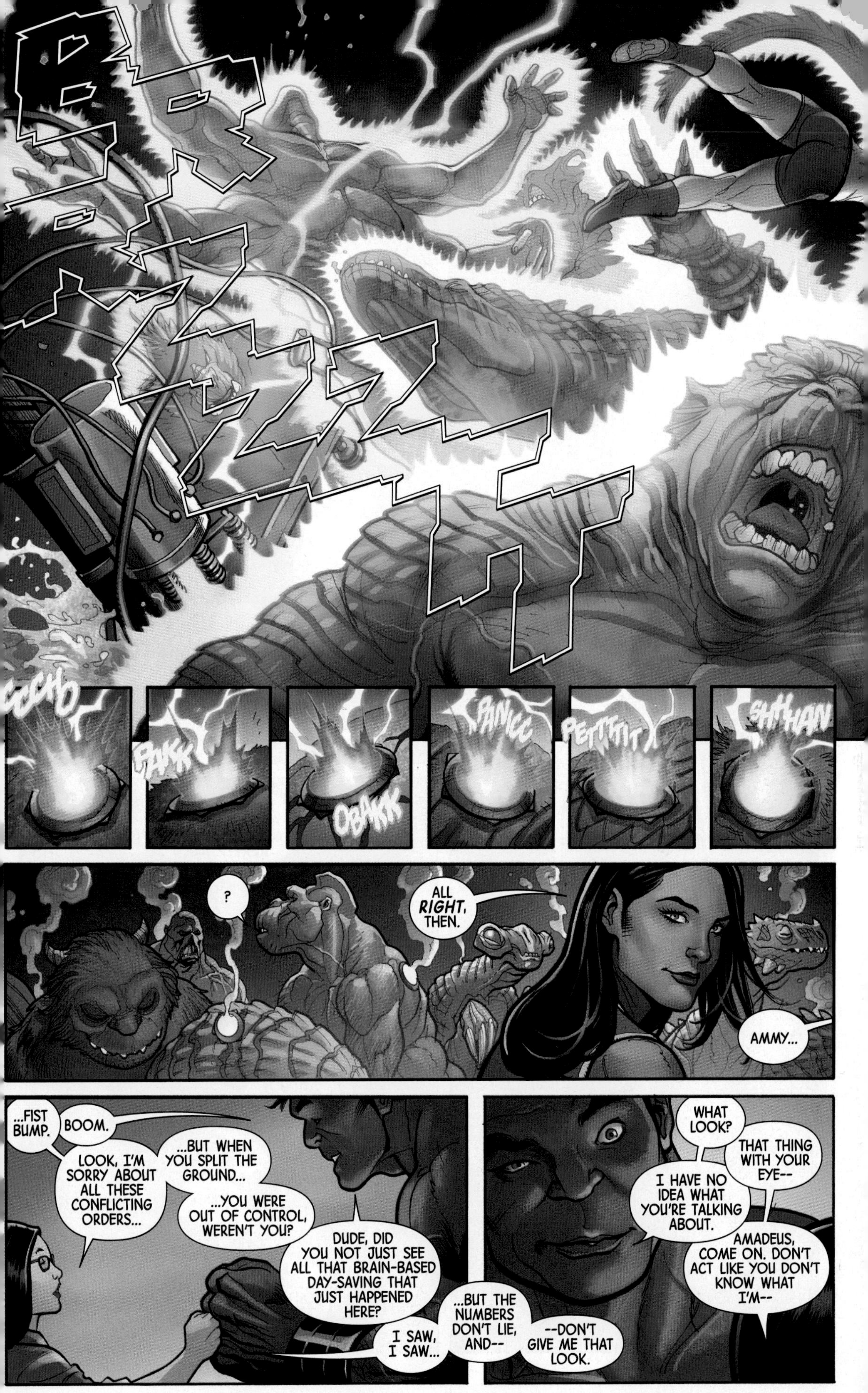
PAKK
OBAKK
PANICC
?
ALL *RIGHT*, THEN.
AMMY...
...FIST BUMP.
BOOM.
LOOK, I'M SORRY ABOUT ALL THESE CONFLICTING ORDERS...
...BUT WHEN YOU SPLIT THE GROUND...
...YOU WERE OUT OF CONTROL, WEREN'T YOU?
DUDE, DID YOU NOT JUST SEE ALL THAT BRAIN-BASED DAY-SAVING THAT JUST HAPPENED HERE?
I SAW, I SAW...
...BUT THE NUMBERS DON'T LIE, AND--
--DON'T GIVE ME THAT LOOK.
WHAT LOOK?
THAT THING WITH YOUR EYE--
I HAVE NO IDEA WHAT YOU'RE TALKING ABOUT.
AMADEUS, COME ON. DON'T ACT LIKE YOU DON'T KNOW WHAT I'M--

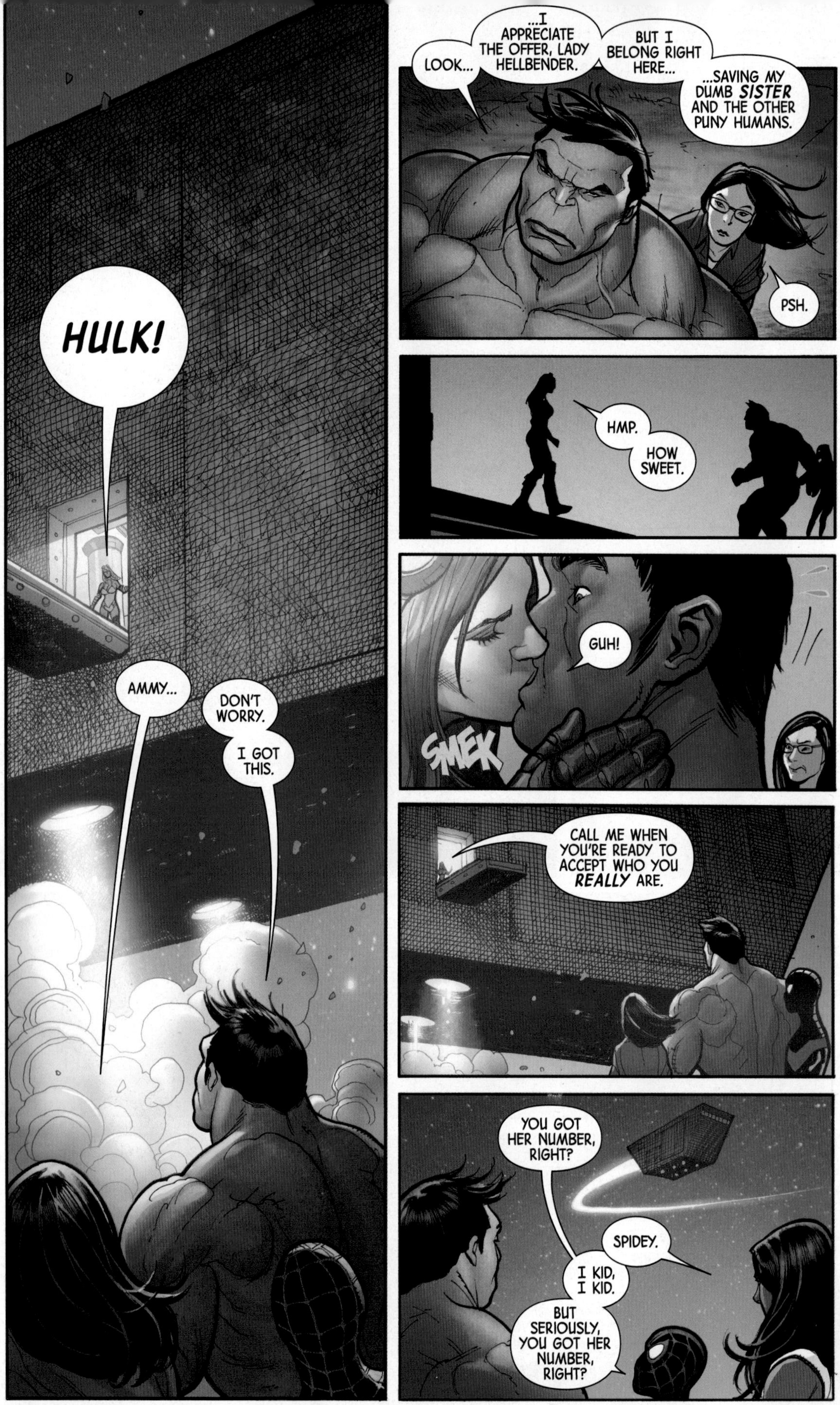
HULK!
AMMY...
DON'T WORRY.
I GOT THIS.
LOOK...
...I APPRECIATE THE OFFER, LADY HELLBENDER.
BUT I BELONG RIGHT HERE...
...SAVING MY DUMB SISTER AND THE OTHER PUNY HUMANS.
PSH.
HMP.
HOW SWEET.
GUH!
SMEK
CALL ME WHEN YOU'RE READY TO ACCEPT WHO YOU REALLY ARE.
YOU GOT HER NUMBER, RIGHT?
SPIDEY.
I KID, I KID.
BUT SERIOUSLY, YOU GOT HER NUMBER, RIGHT?

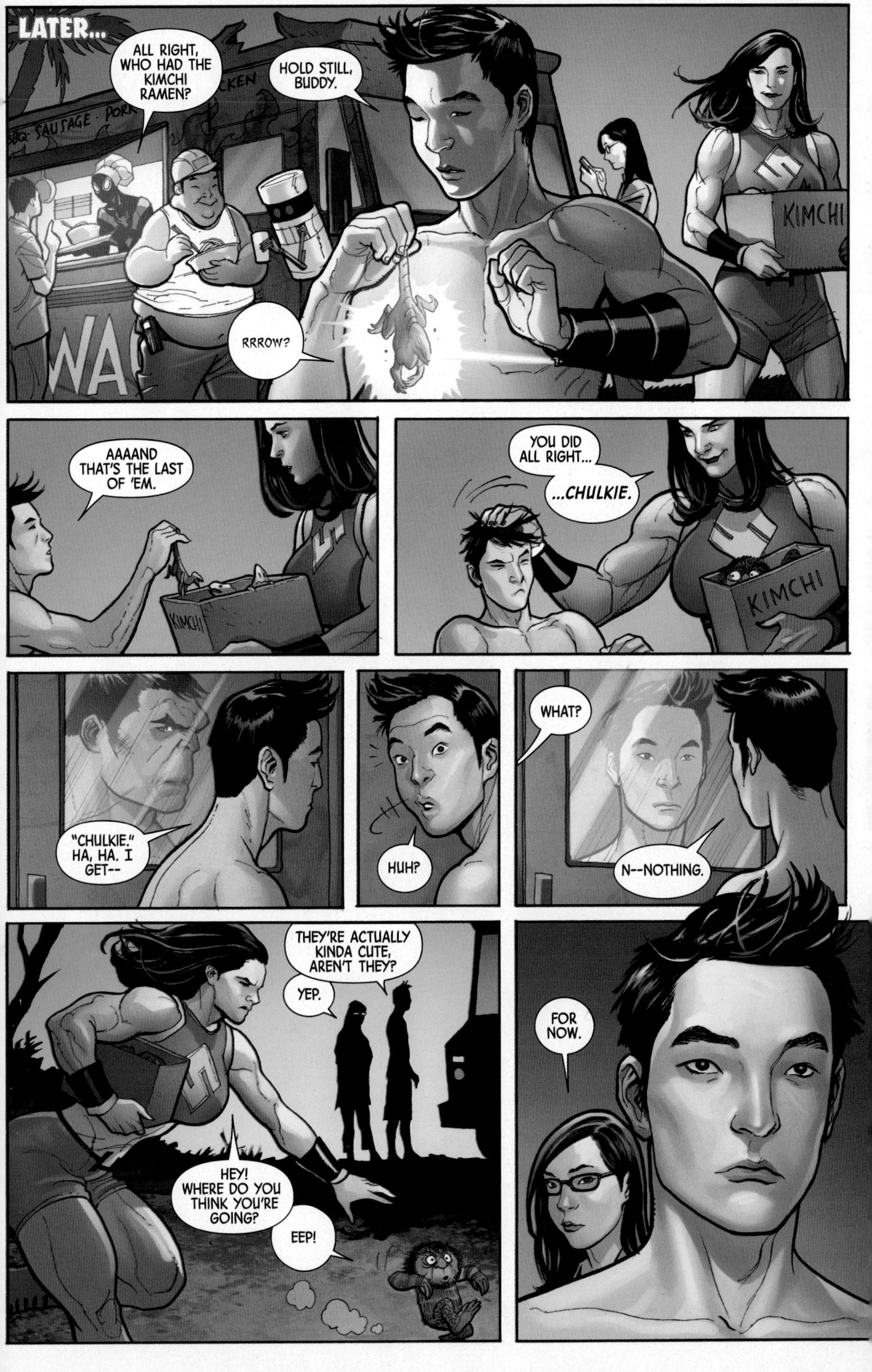
LATER...
ALL RIGHT, WHO HAD THE KIMCHI RAMEN?
HOLD STILL, BUDDY.
RRROW?
KIMCHI
AAAAND THAT'S THE LAST OF 'EM.
KIMCHI
YOU DID ALL RIGHT...
...CHULKIE.
KIMCHI
"CHULKIE." HA, HA. I GET--
HUH?
WHAT?
N--NOTHING.
THEY'RE ACTUALLY KINDA CUTE, AREN'T THEY?
YEP.
HEY! WHERE DO YOU THINK YOU'RE GOING?
EEP!
FOR NOW.

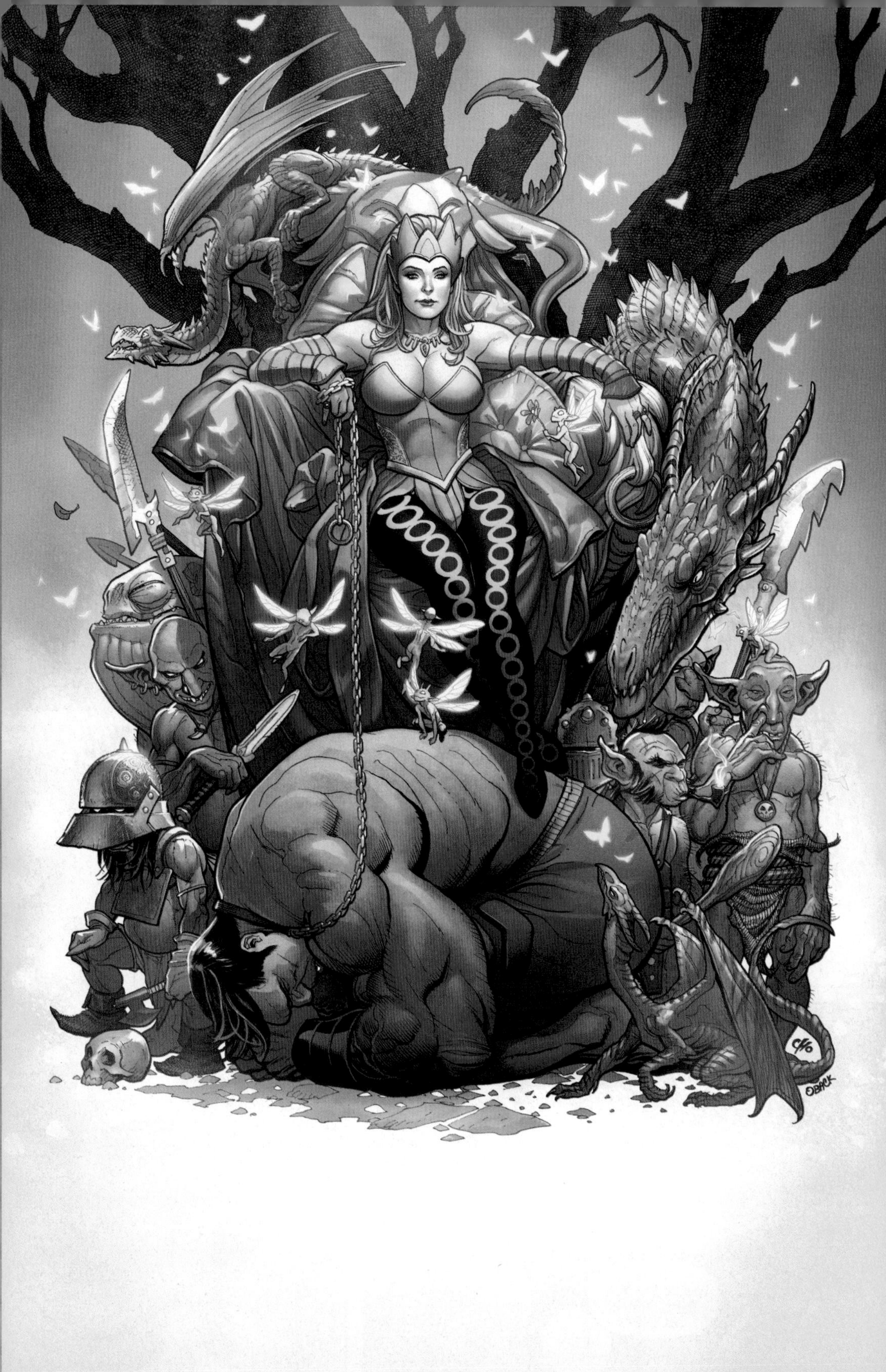

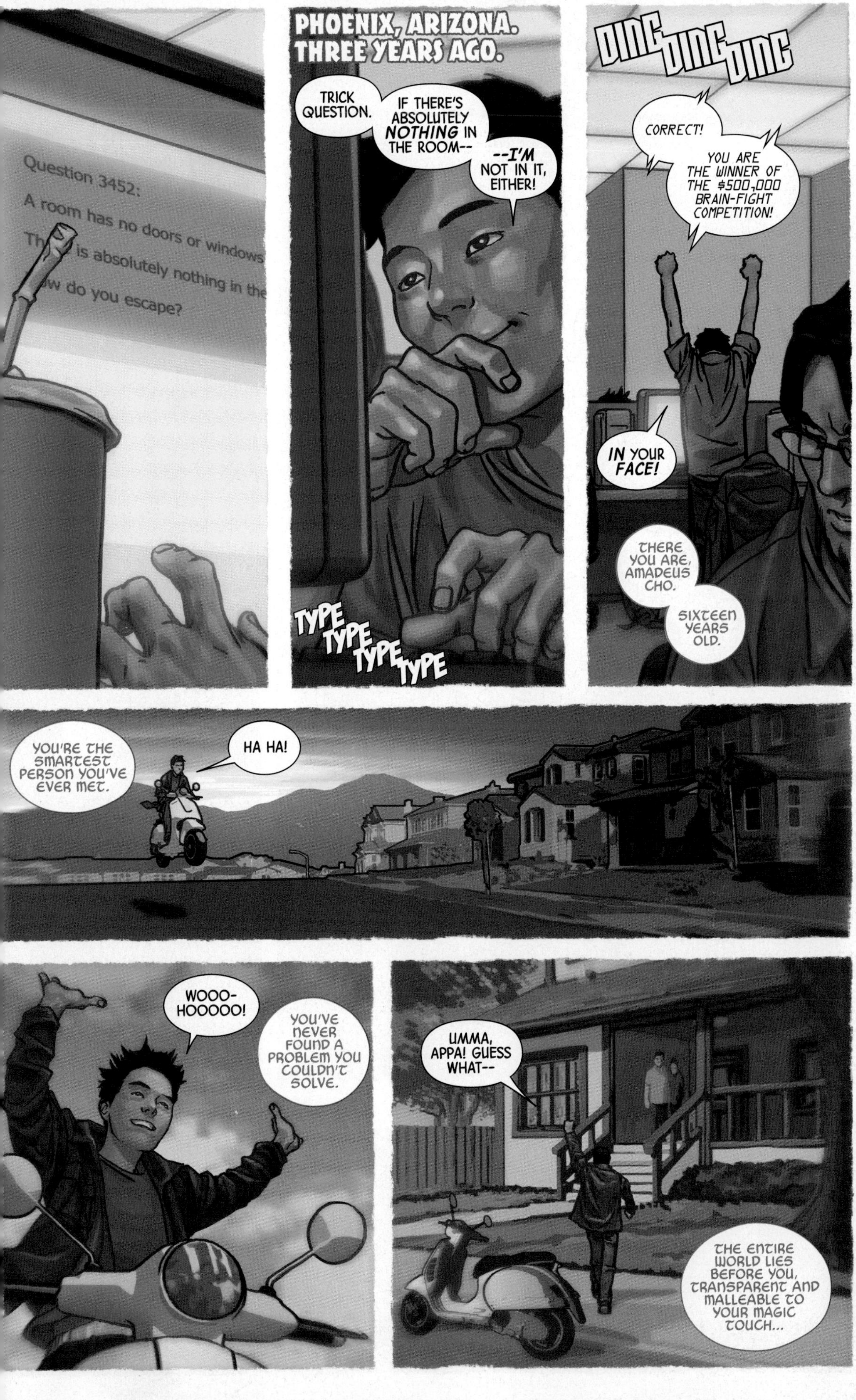
Question 3452:
A room has no doors or windows
is absolutely nothing in the
do you escape?
PHOENIX, ARIZONA.
THREE YEARS AGO.
TRICK QUESTION.
IF THERE'S ABSOLUTELY NOTHING IN THE ROOM--
--I'M NOT IN IT, EITHER!
TYPE TYPE TYPE TYPE
DING DING DING
CORRECT!
YOU ARE THE WINNER OF THE $500,000 BRAIN-FIGHT COMPETITION!
IN YOUR FACE!
THERE YOU ARE, AMADEUS CHO.
SIXTEEN YEARS OLD.
YOU'RE THE SMARTEST PERSON YOU'VE EVER MET.
HA HA!
WOOO-HOOOOO!
YOU'VE NEVER FOUND A PROBLEM YOU COULDN'T SOLVE.
UMMA, APPA! GUESS WHAT--
THE ENTIRE WORLD LIES BEFORE YOU, TRANSPARENT AND MALLEABLE TO YOUR MAGIC TOUCH...

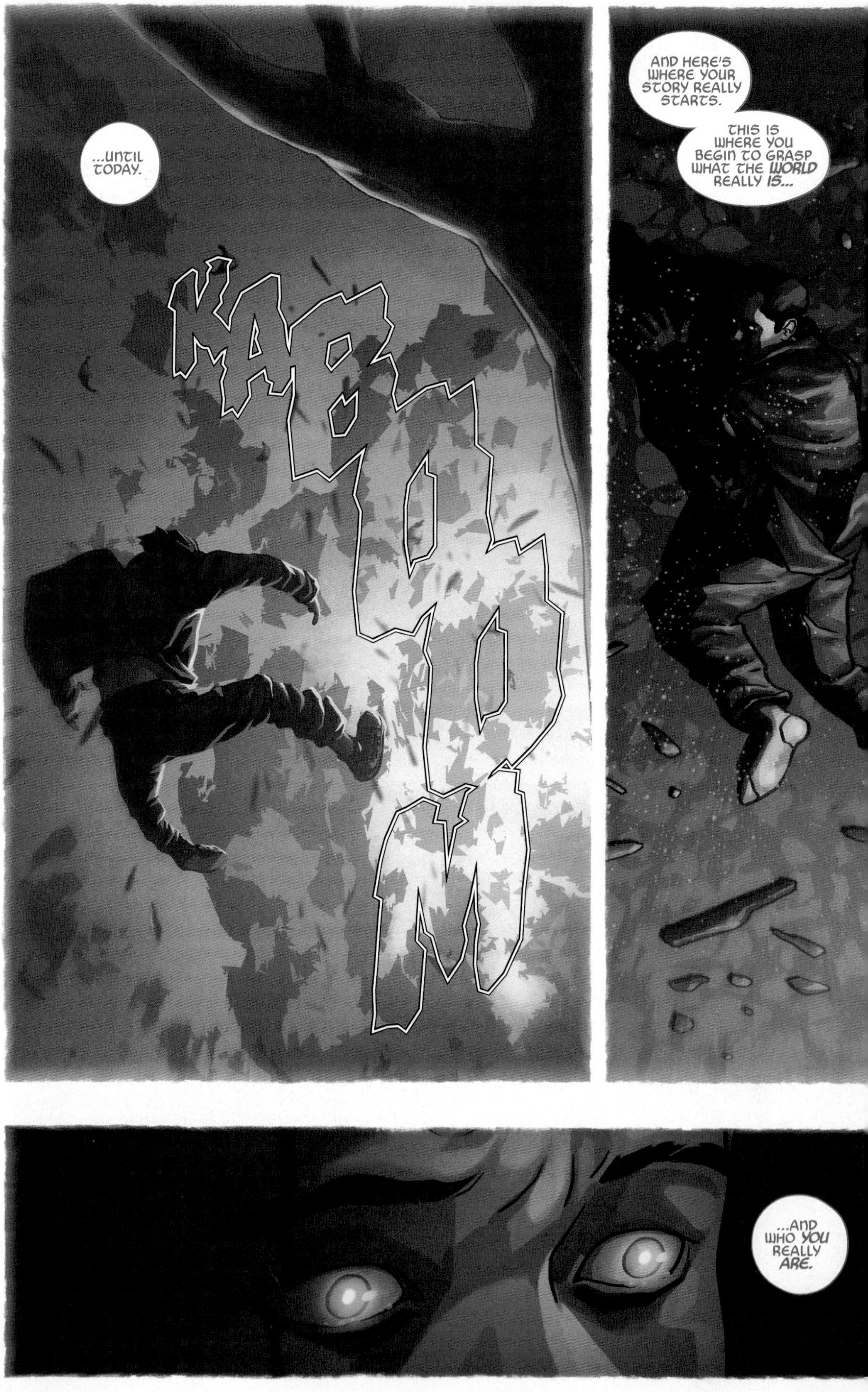
...UNTIL TODAY.
KABOOM
AND HERE'S WHERE YOUR STORY REALLY STARTS.
THIS IS WHERE YOU BEGIN TO GRASP WHAT THE WORLD REALLY IS...
...AND WHO YOU REALLY ARE.

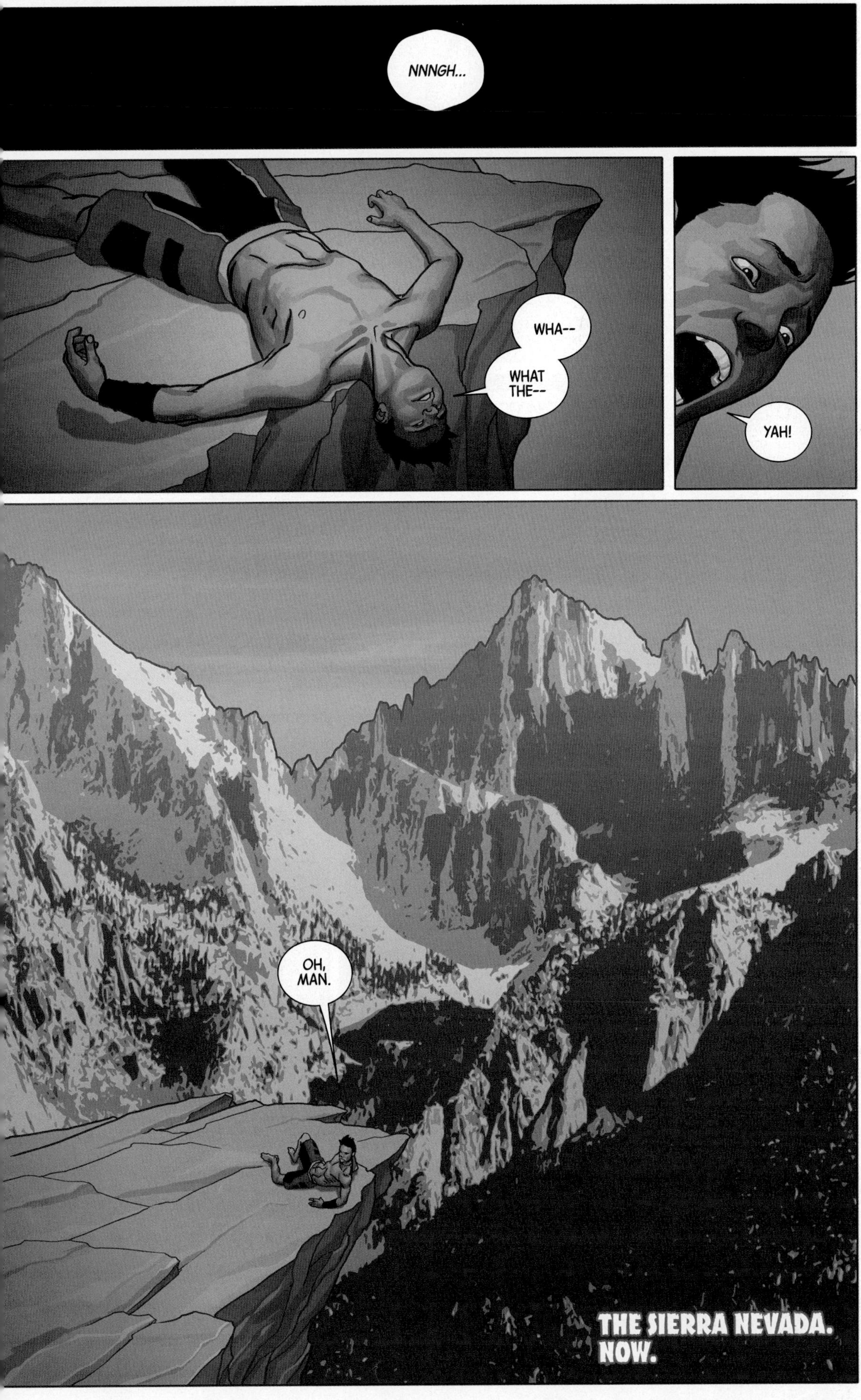
NNNGH...
WHA--
WHAT THE--
YAH!
OH, MAN.
THE SIERRA NEVADA. NOW.

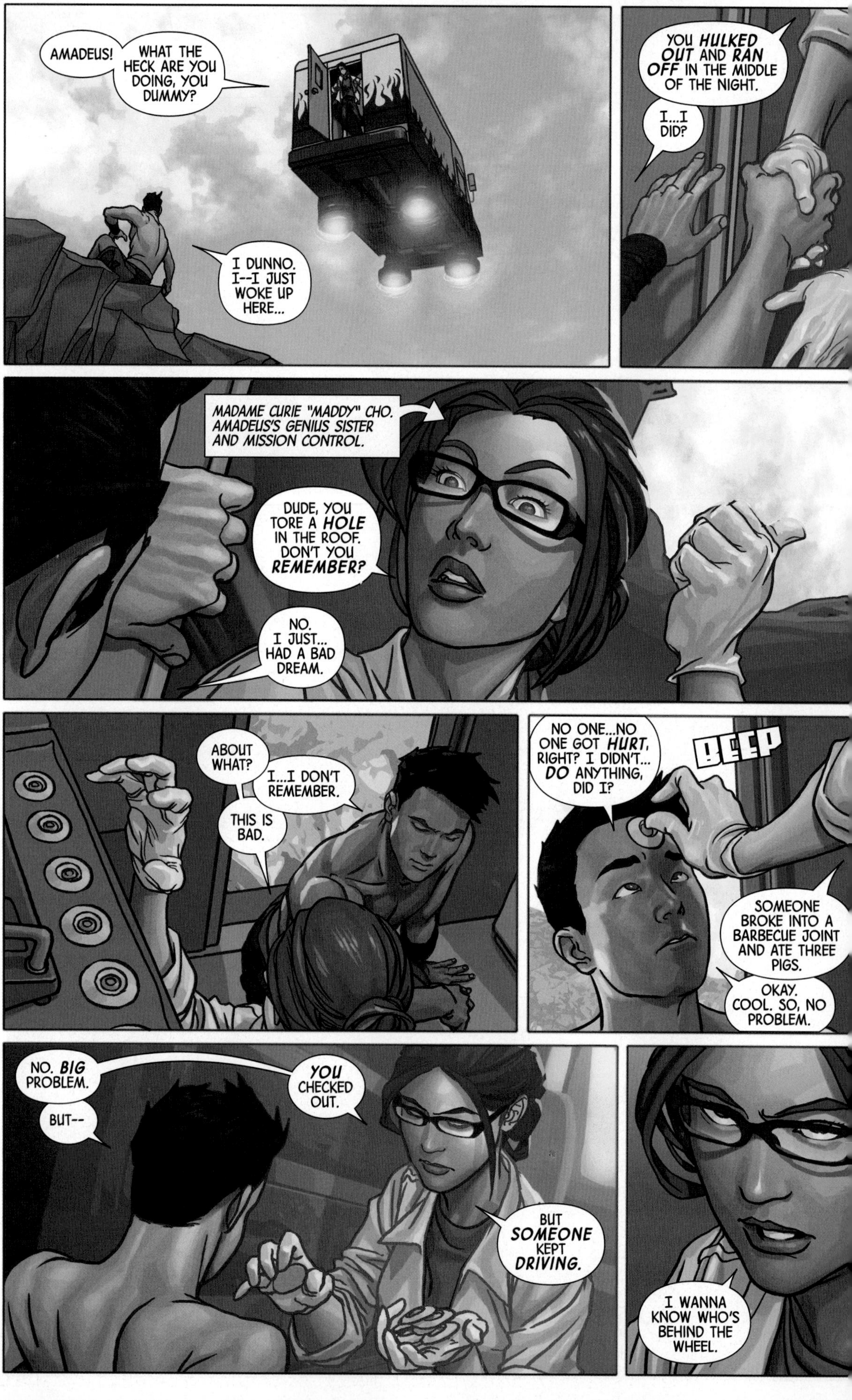
AMADEUS!
WHAT THE HECK ARE YOU DOING, YOU DUMMY?
I DUNNO. I--I JUST WOKE UP HERE...
YOU HULKED OUT AND RAN OFF IN THE MIDDLE OF THE NIGHT.
I...I DID?
MADAME CURIE "MADDY" CHO. AMADEUS'S GENIUS SISTER AND MISSION CONTROL.
DUDE, YOU TORE A HOLE IN THE ROOF. DON'T YOU REMEMBER?
NO. I JUST... HAD A BAD DREAM.
ABOUT WHAT?
I...I DON'T REMEMBER.
THIS IS BAD.
NO ONE...NO ONE GOT HURT, RIGHT? I DIDN'T... DO ANYTHING, DID I?
BEEP
SOMEONE BROKE INTO A BARBECUE JOINT AND ATE THREE PIGS.
OKAY. COOL. SO, NO PROBLEM.
NO. BIG PROBLEM.
YOU CHECKED OUT.
BUT--
BUT SOMEONE KEPT DRIVING.
I WANNA KNOW WHO'S BEHIND THE WHEEL.

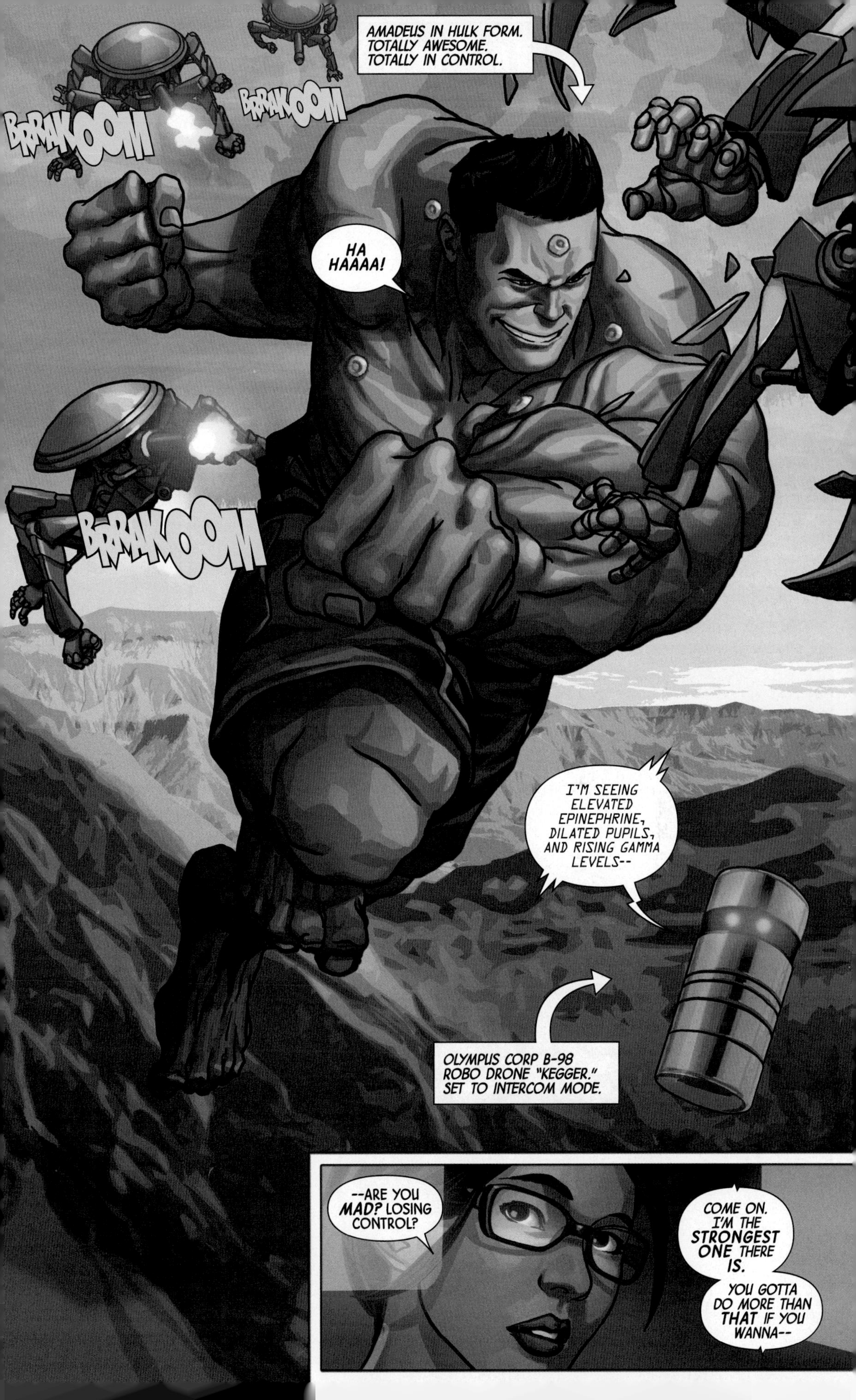
AMADEUS IN HULK FORM. TOTALLY AWESOME. TOTALLY IN CONTROL.
BRRAKOOM
BRRAKOOM
HA HAAAA!
BRRAKOOM
I'M SEEING ELEVATED EPINEPHRINE, DILATED PUPILS, AND RISING GAMMA LEVELS--
OLYMPUS CORP B-98 ROBO DRONE "KEGGER." SET TO INTERCOM MODE.
--ARE YOU MAD? LOSING CONTROL?
COME ON. I'M THE STRONGEST ONE THERE IS.
YOU GOTTA DO MORE THAN THAT IF YOU WANNA--

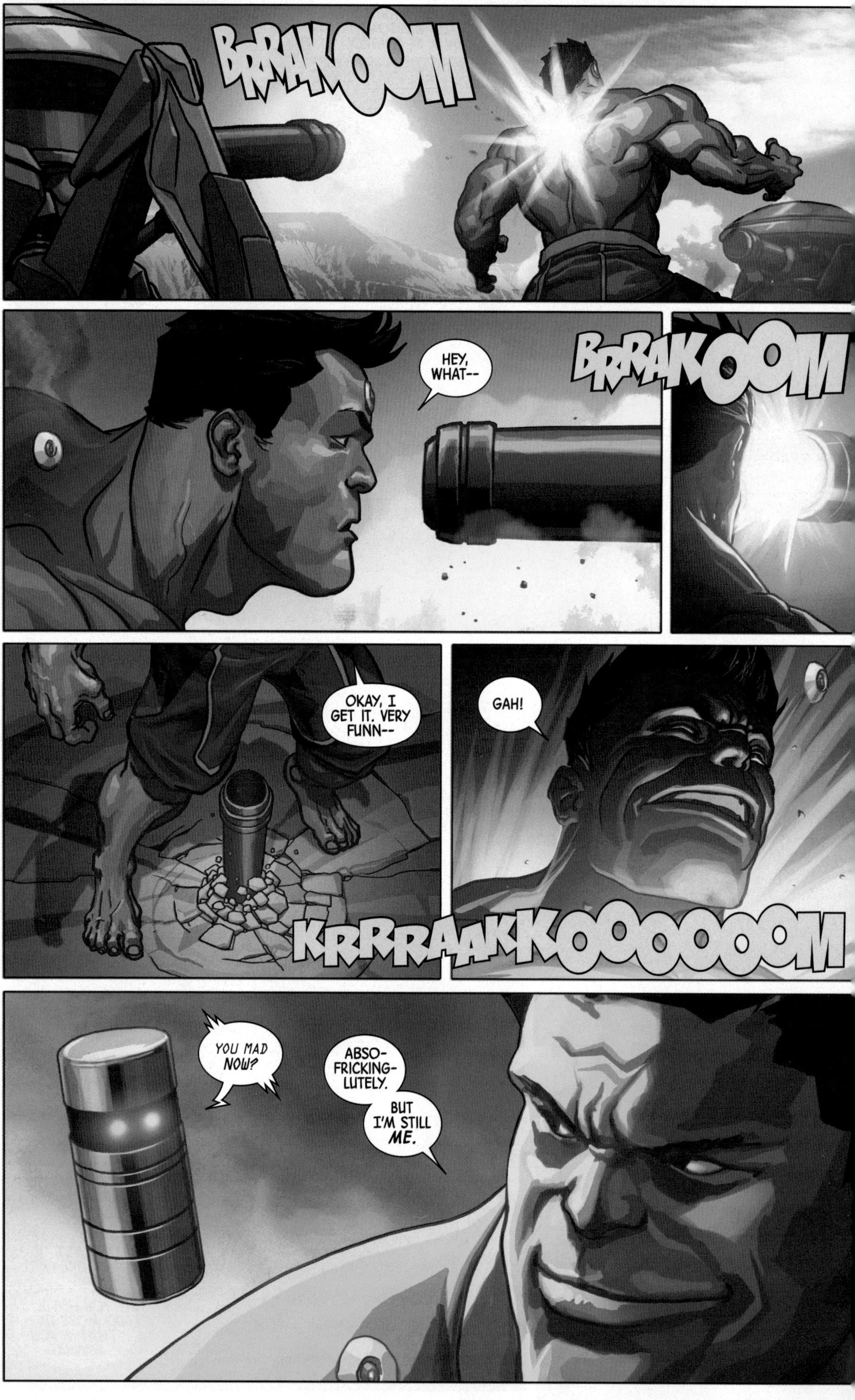
BRRAKOOOM
HEY, WHAT--
BRRAKOOOM
OKAY, I GET IT. VERY FUNN--
GAH!
KRRRAAKKOOOOOOOM
YOU MAD NOW?
ABSO-FRICKING-LUTELY.
BUT I'M STILL ME.

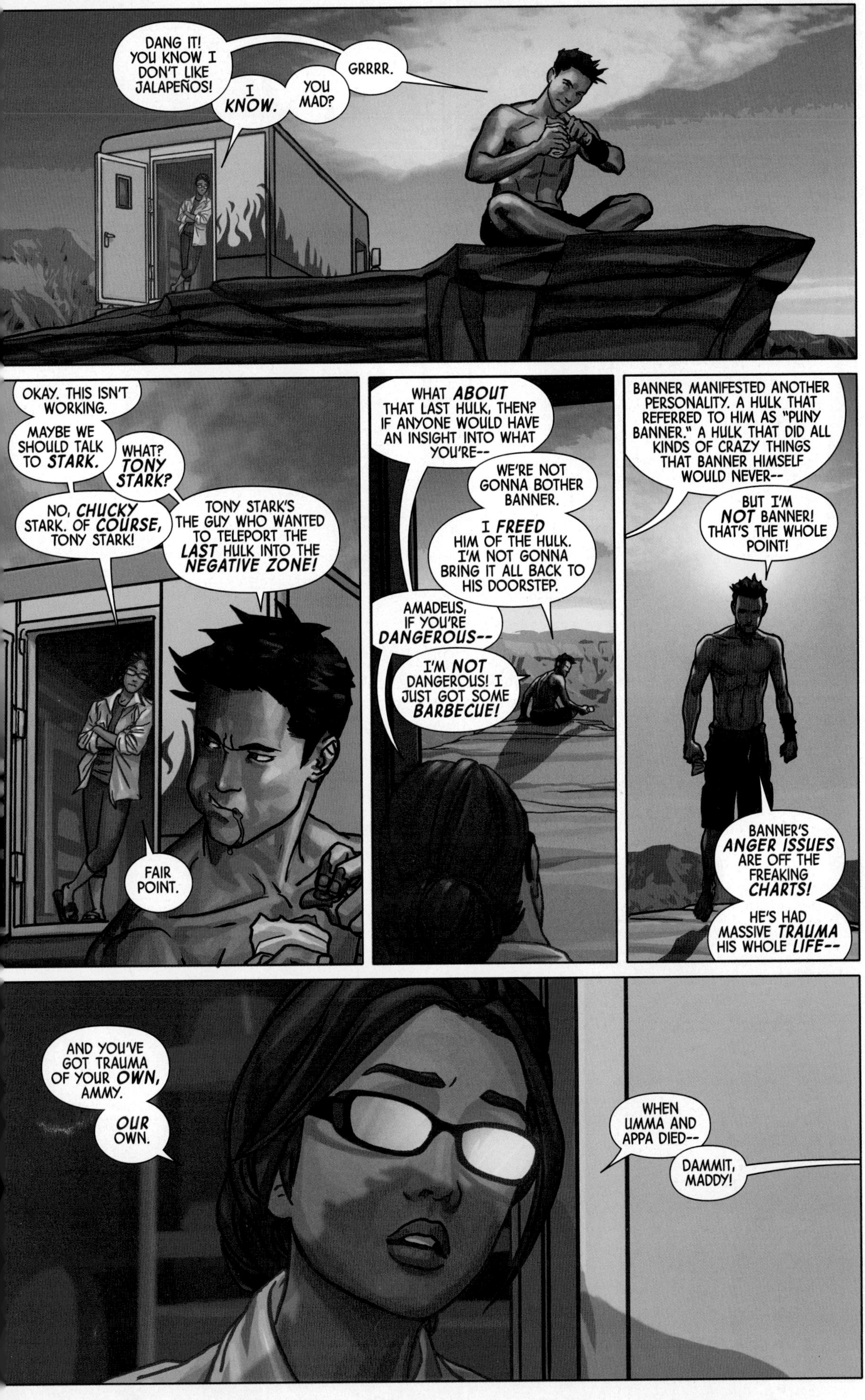
DANG IT! YOU KNOW I DON'T LIKE JALAPEÑOS!
GRRRR.
I KNOW.
YOU MAD?
OKAY. THIS ISN'T WORKING.
MAYBE WE SHOULD TALK TO STARK.
WHAT? TONY STARK?
NO, CHUCKY STARK. OF COURSE, TONY STARK!
TONY STARK'S THE GUY WHO WANTED TO TELEPORT THE LAST HULK INTO THE NEGATIVE ZONE!
FAIR POINT.
WHAT ABOUT THAT LAST HULK, THEN? IF ANYONE WOULD HAVE AN INSIGHT INTO WHAT YOU'RE--
WE'RE NOT GONNA BOTHER BANNER.
I FREED HIM OF THE HULK. I'M NOT GONNA BRING IT ALL BACK TO HIS DOORSTEP.
AMADEUS, IF YOU'RE DANGEROUS--
I'M NOT DANGEROUS! I JUST GOT SOME BARBECUE!
BANNER MANIFESTED ANOTHER PERSONALITY. A HULK THAT REFERRED TO HIM AS "PUNY BANNER." A HULK THAT DID ALL KINDS OF CRAZY THINGS THAT BANNER HIMSELF WOULD NEVER--
BUT I'M NOT BANNER! THAT'S THE WHOLE POINT!
BANNER'S ANGER ISSUES ARE OFF THE FREAKING CHARTS!
HE'S HAD MASSIVE TRAUMA HIS WHOLE LIFE--
AND YOU'VE GOT TRAUMA OF YOUR OWN, AMMY.
OUR OWN.
WHEN UMMA AND APPA DIED--
DAMMIT, MADDY!

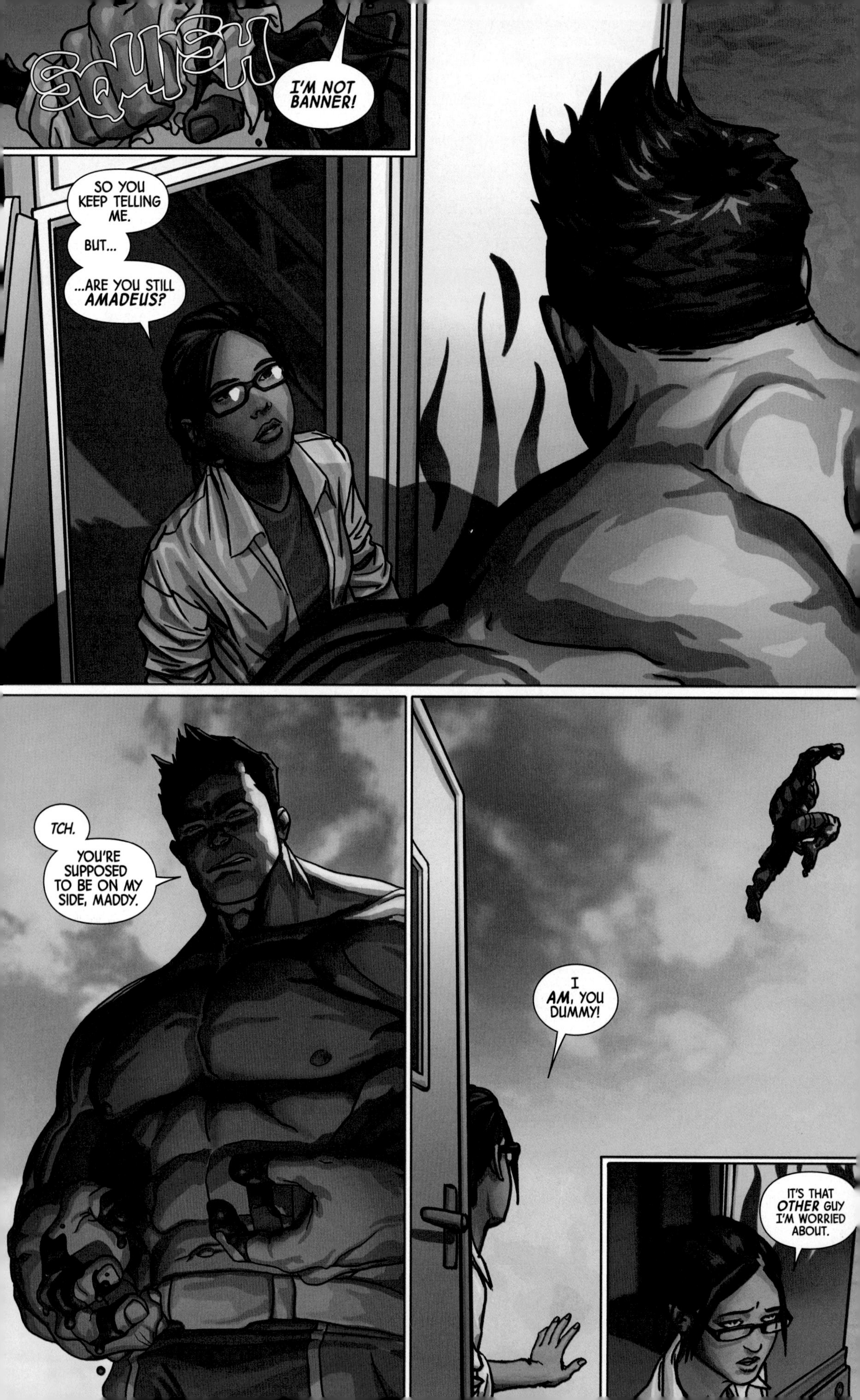
SQUISH
I'M NOT BANNER!
SO YOU KEEP TELLING ME.
BUT...
...ARE YOU STILL AMADEUS?
TCH.
YOU'RE SUPPOSED TO BE ON MY SIDE, MADDY.
I AM, YOU DUMMY!
IT'S THAT OTHER GUY I'M WORRIED ABOUT.

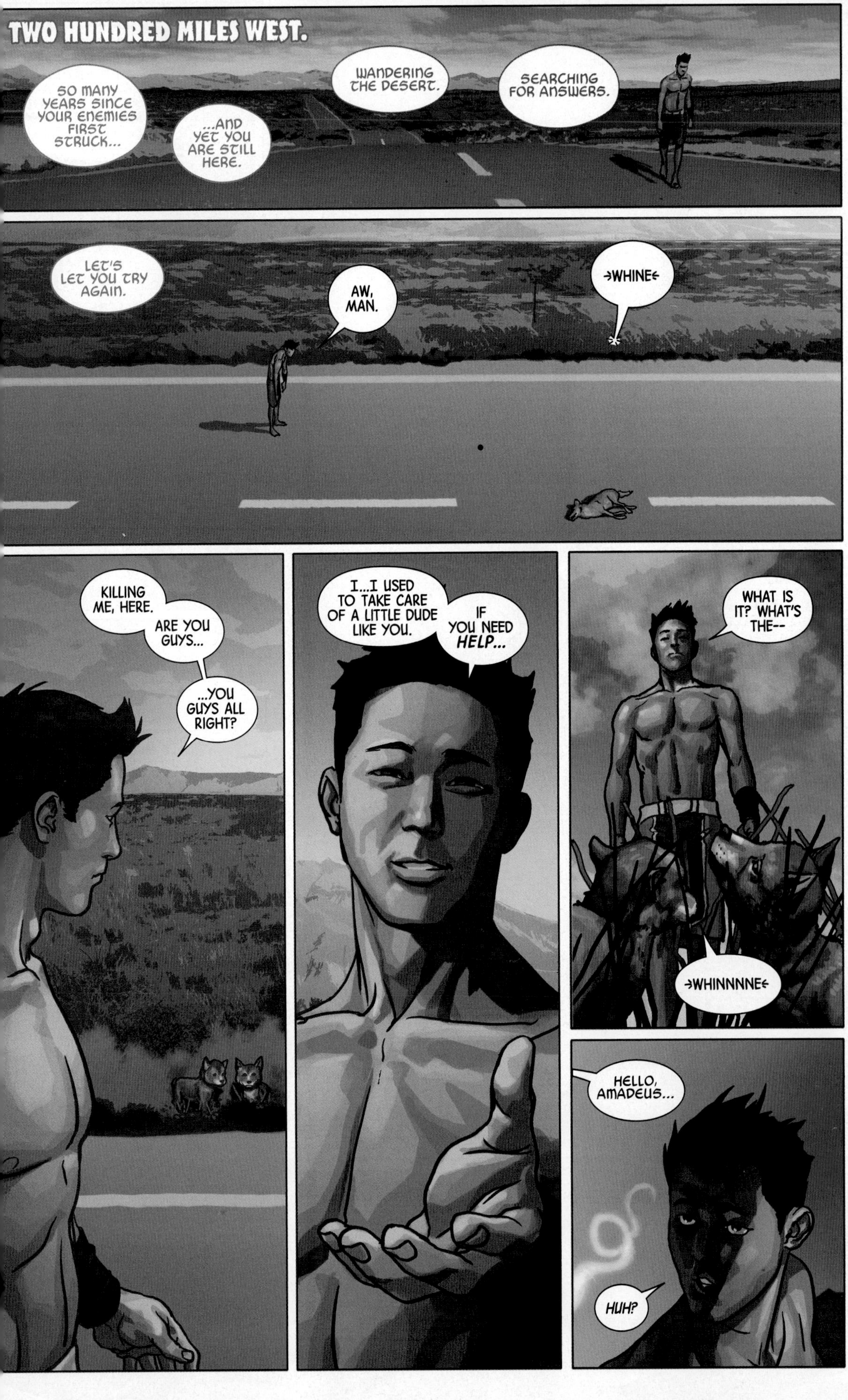
TWO HUNDRED MILES WEST.
SO MANY YEARS SINCE YOUR ENEMIES FIRST STRUCK...
...AND YET YOU ARE STILL HERE.
WANDERING THE DESERT.
SEARCHING FOR ANSWERS.
LET'S LET YOU TRY AGAIN.
AW, MAN.
WHINE
KILLING ME, HERE.
ARE YOU GUYS...
...YOU GUYS ALL RIGHT?
I...I USED TO TAKE CARE OF A LITTLE DUDE LIKE YOU.
IF YOU NEED HELP...
WHAT IS IT? WHAT'S THE--
WHINNNNE
HELLO, AMADEUS...
HUH?

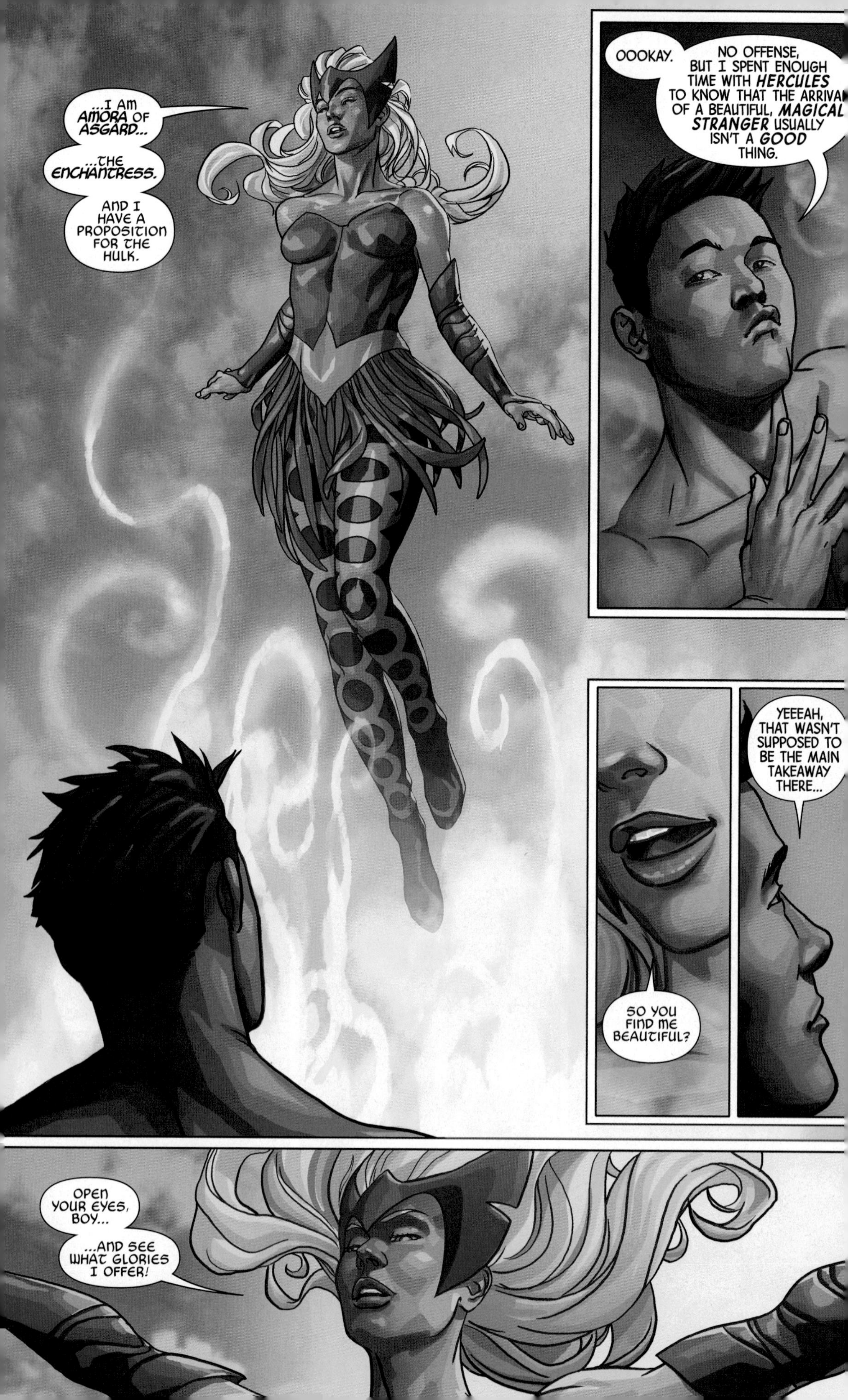

...I AM AMORA OF ASGARD...
...THE ENCHANTRESS.
AND I HAVE A PROPOSITION FOR THE HULK.
OOOKAY.
NO OFFENSE, BUT I SPENT ENOUGH TIME WITH HERCULES TO KNOW THAT THE ARRIVAL OF A BEAUTIFUL, MAGICAL STRANGER USUALLY ISN'T A GOOD THING.
SO YOU FIND ME BEAUTIFUL?
YEEEAH, THAT WASN'T SUPPOSED TO BE THE MAIN TAKEAWAY THERE...
OPEN YOUR EYES, BOY...
...AND SEE WHAT GLORIES I OFFER!

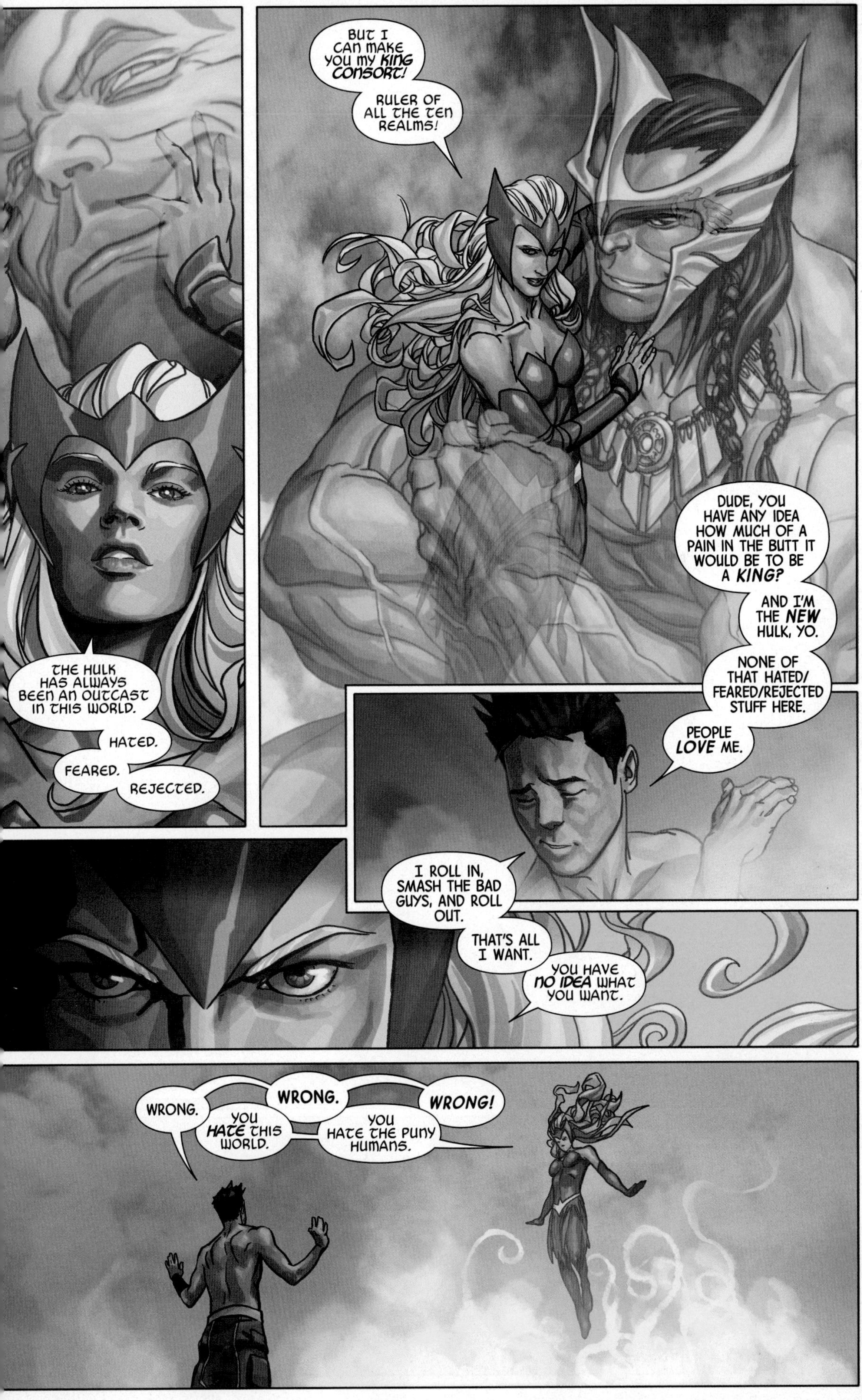

THE HULK HAS ALWAYS BEEN AN OUTCAST IN THIS WORLD.
HATED.
FEARED.
REJECTED.
BUT I CAN MAKE YOU MY KING CONSORT!
RULER OF ALL THE TEN REALMS!
DUDE, YOU HAVE ANY IDEA HOW MUCH OF A PAIN IN THE BUTT IT WOULD BE TO BE A KING?
AND I'M THE NEW HULK, YO.
NONE OF THAT HATED/ FEARED/REJECTED STUFF HERE.
PEOPLE LOVE ME.
I ROLL IN, SMASH THE BAD GUYS, AND ROLL OUT.
THAT'S ALL I WANT.
YOU HAVE NO IDEA WHAT YOU WANT.
WRONG.
YOU HATE THIS WORLD.
WRONG.
YOU HATE THE PUNY HUMANS.
WRONG!

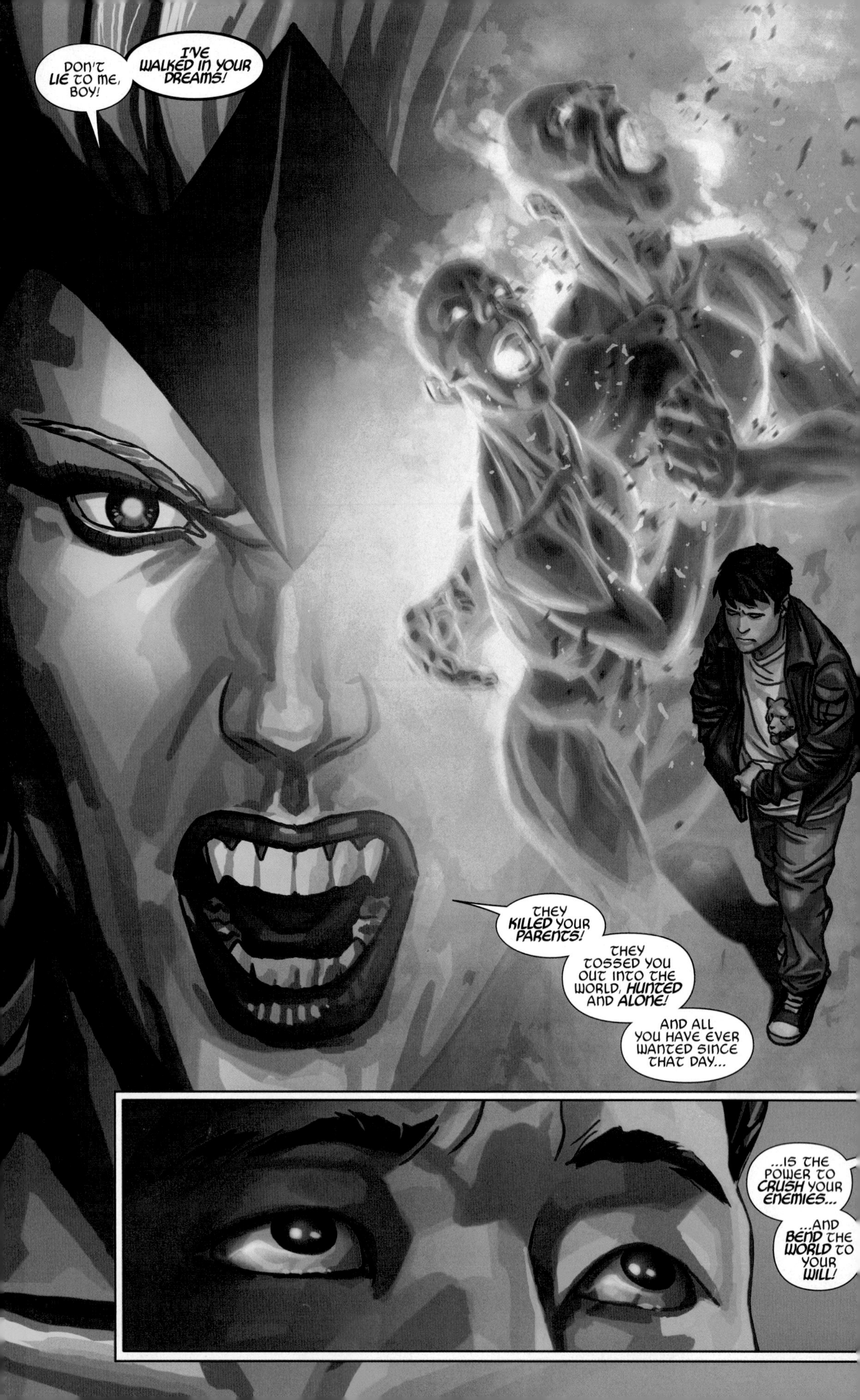
DON'T LIE TO ME, BOY!
I'VE WALKED IN YOUR DREAMS!
THEY KILLED YOUR PARENTS!
THEY TOSSED YOU OUT INTO THE WORLD, HUNTED AND ALONE!
AND ALL YOU HAVE EVER WANTED SINCE THAT DAY...
...IS THE POWER TO CRUSH YOUR ENEMIES...
...AND BEND THE WORLD TO YOUR WILL!

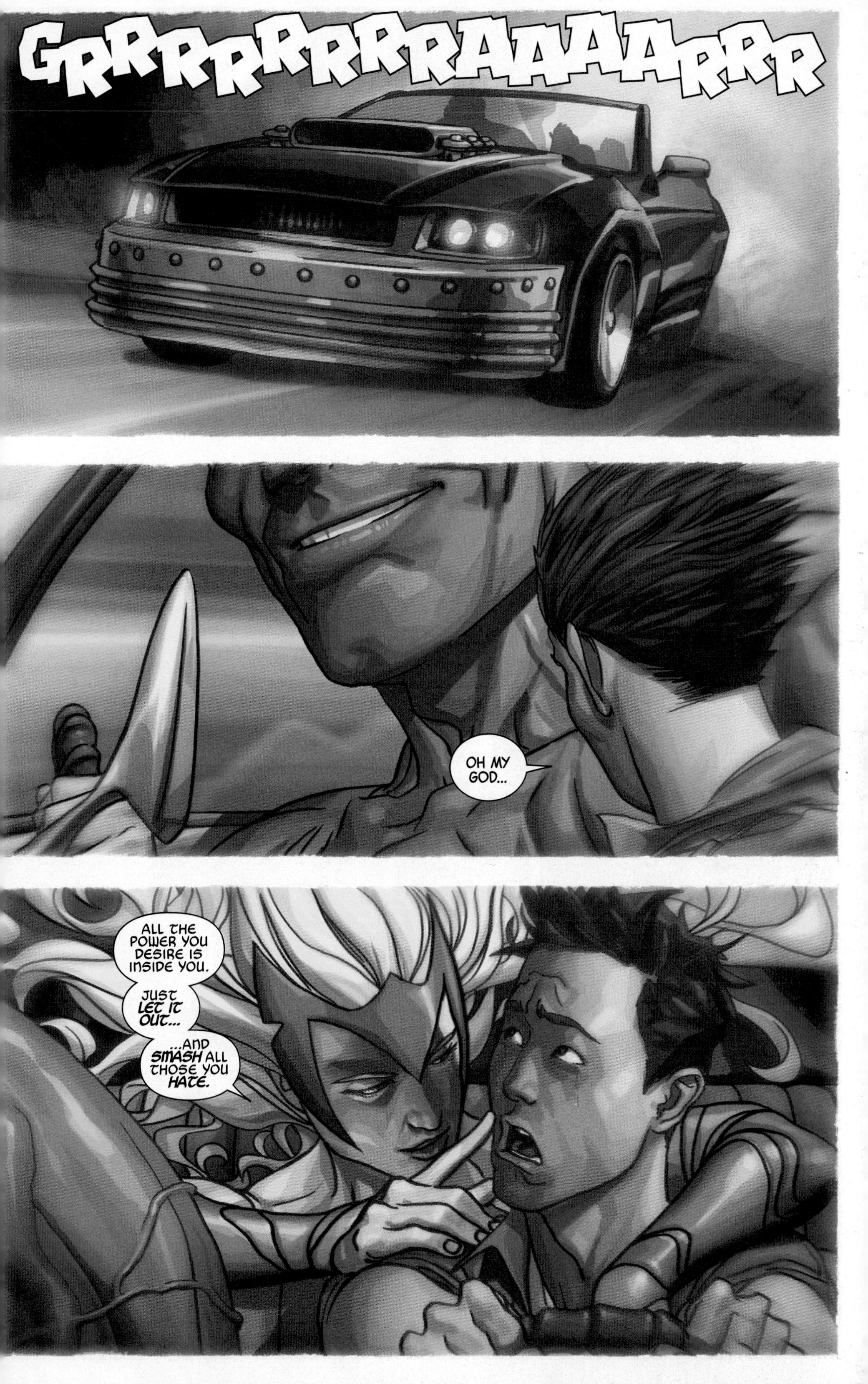
GRRRRRRRAAAAARRR
OH MY GOD...
ALL THE POWER YOU DESIRE IS INSIDE YOU.
JUST LET IT OUT...
...AND SMASH ALL THOSE YOU HATE.

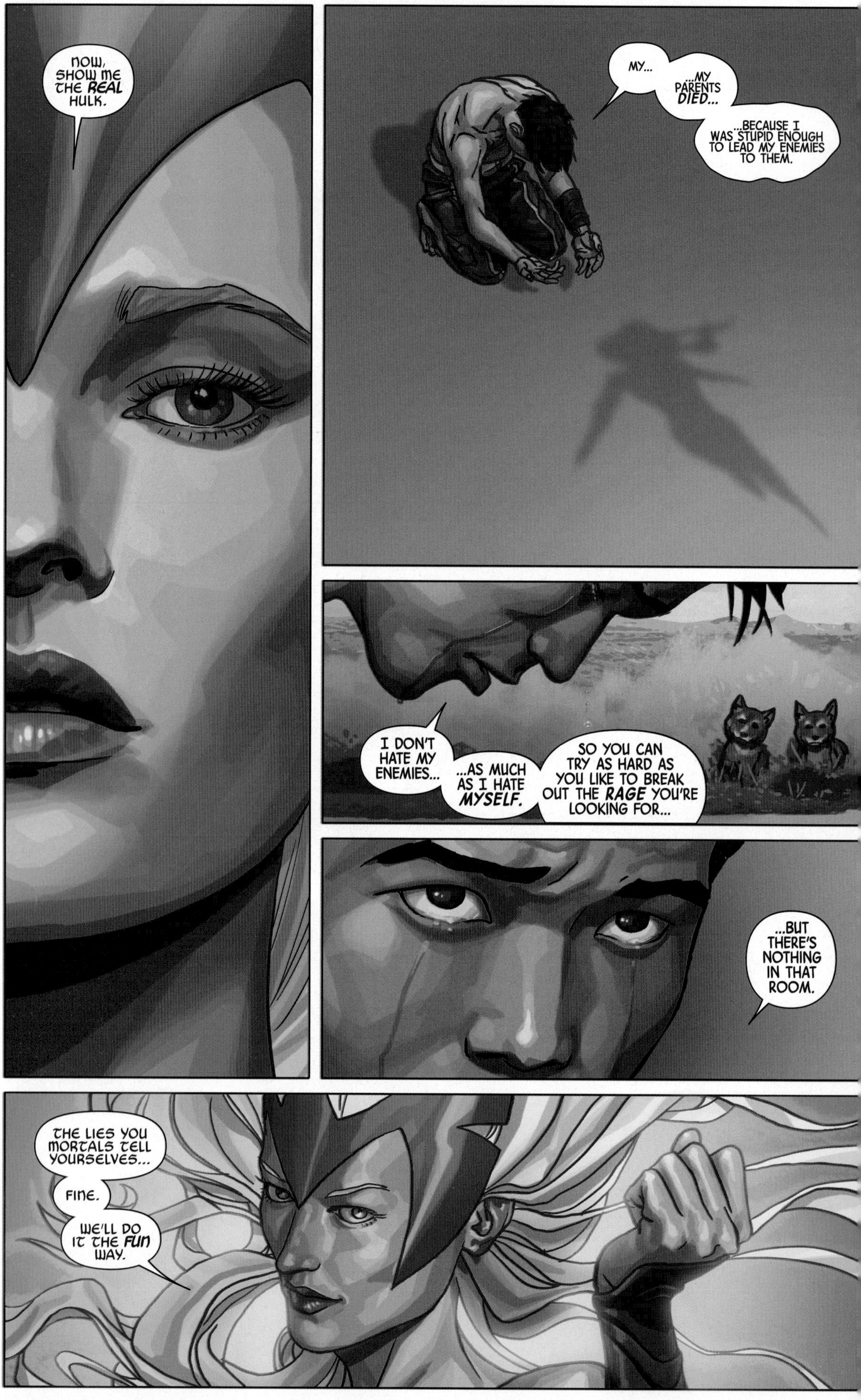
NOW, SHOW ME THE REAL HULK.
MY...
...MY PARENTS DIED...
...BECAUSE I WAS STUPID ENOUGH TO LEAD MY ENEMIES TO THEM.
I DON'T HATE MY ENEMIES...
...AS MUCH AS I HATE MYSELF.
SO YOU CAN TRY AS HARD AS YOU LIKE TO BREAK OUT THE RAGE YOU'RE LOOKING FOR...
...BUT THERE'S NOTHING IN THAT ROOM.
THE LIES YOU MORTALS TELL YOURSELVES...
FINE.
WE'LL DO IT THE FUN WAY.

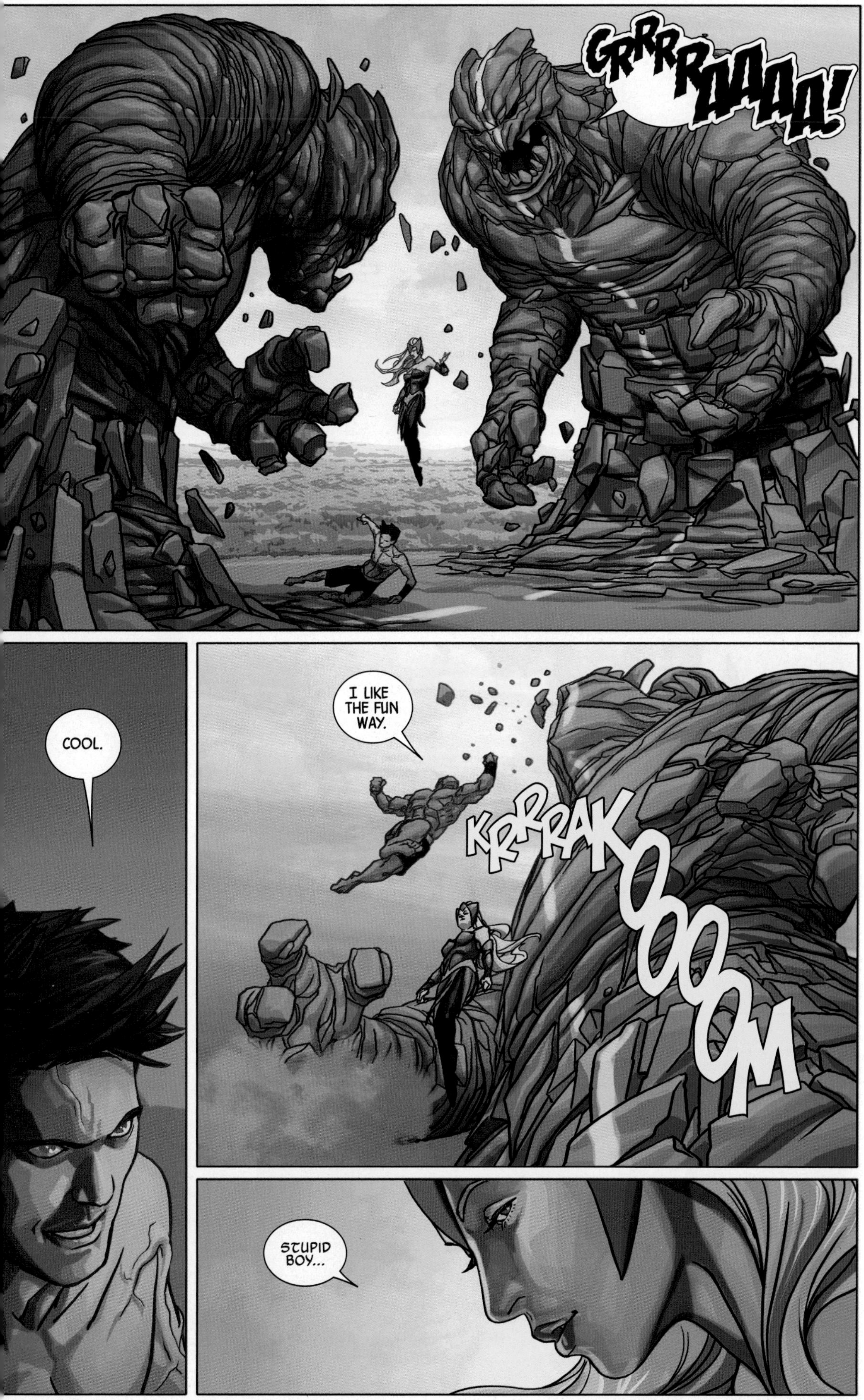
GRRRRAAAAA!
COOL.
I LIKE THE FUN WAY.
KRRRAKOOOOOM
STUPID BOY...

...DID YOU THINK *YOU* WERE THE TARGET?

KUHOOM

YIPE!

GRRAAAA!

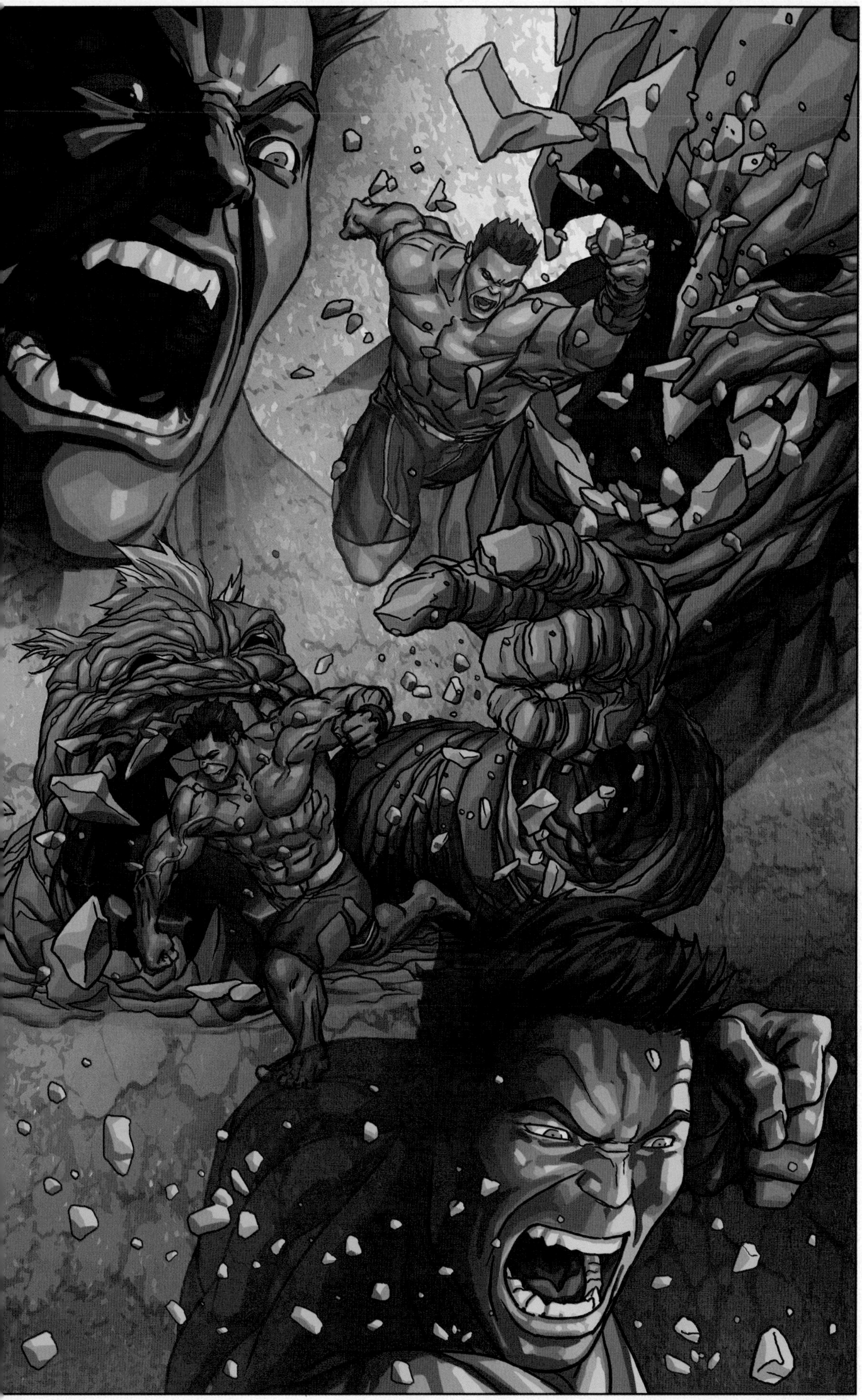

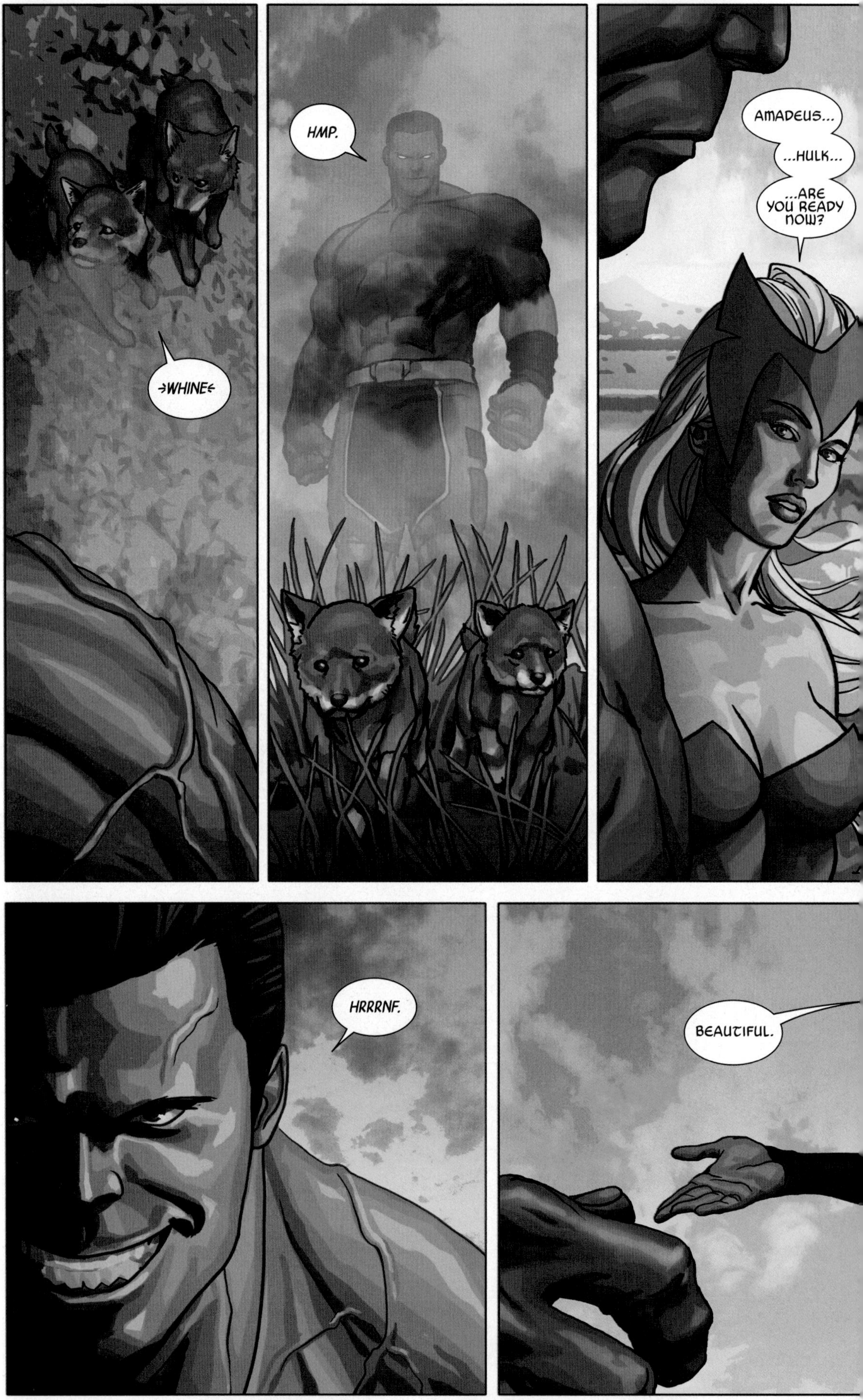

>WHINE<
HMP.
AMADEUS...
...HULK...
...ARE YOU READY NOW?
HRRRNF.
BEAUTIFUL.

[redacted]

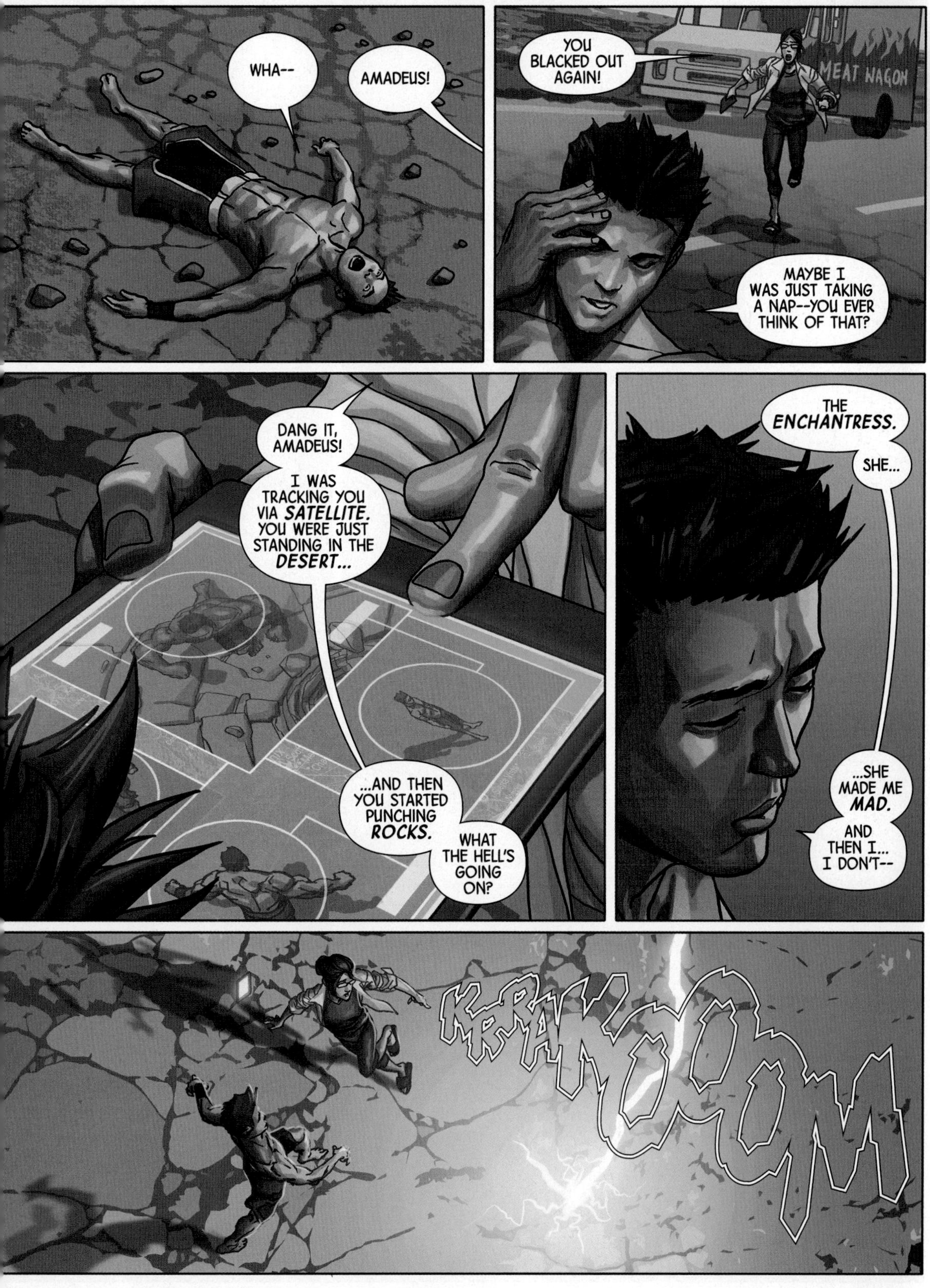
WHA--
AMADEUS!
YOU BLACKED OUT AGAIN!
MAYBE I WAS JUST TAKING A NAP--YOU EVER THINK OF THAT?
DANG IT, AMADEUS!
I WAS TRACKING YOU VIA *SATELLITE.* YOU WERE JUST STANDING IN THE *DESERT...*
...AND THEN YOU STARTED PUNCHING *ROCKS.*
WHAT THE HELL'S GOING ON?
THE *ENCHANTRESS.*
SHE...
...SHE MADE ME *MAD.*
AND THEN I... I DON'T--
MEAT WAGON
KRAKOOOM

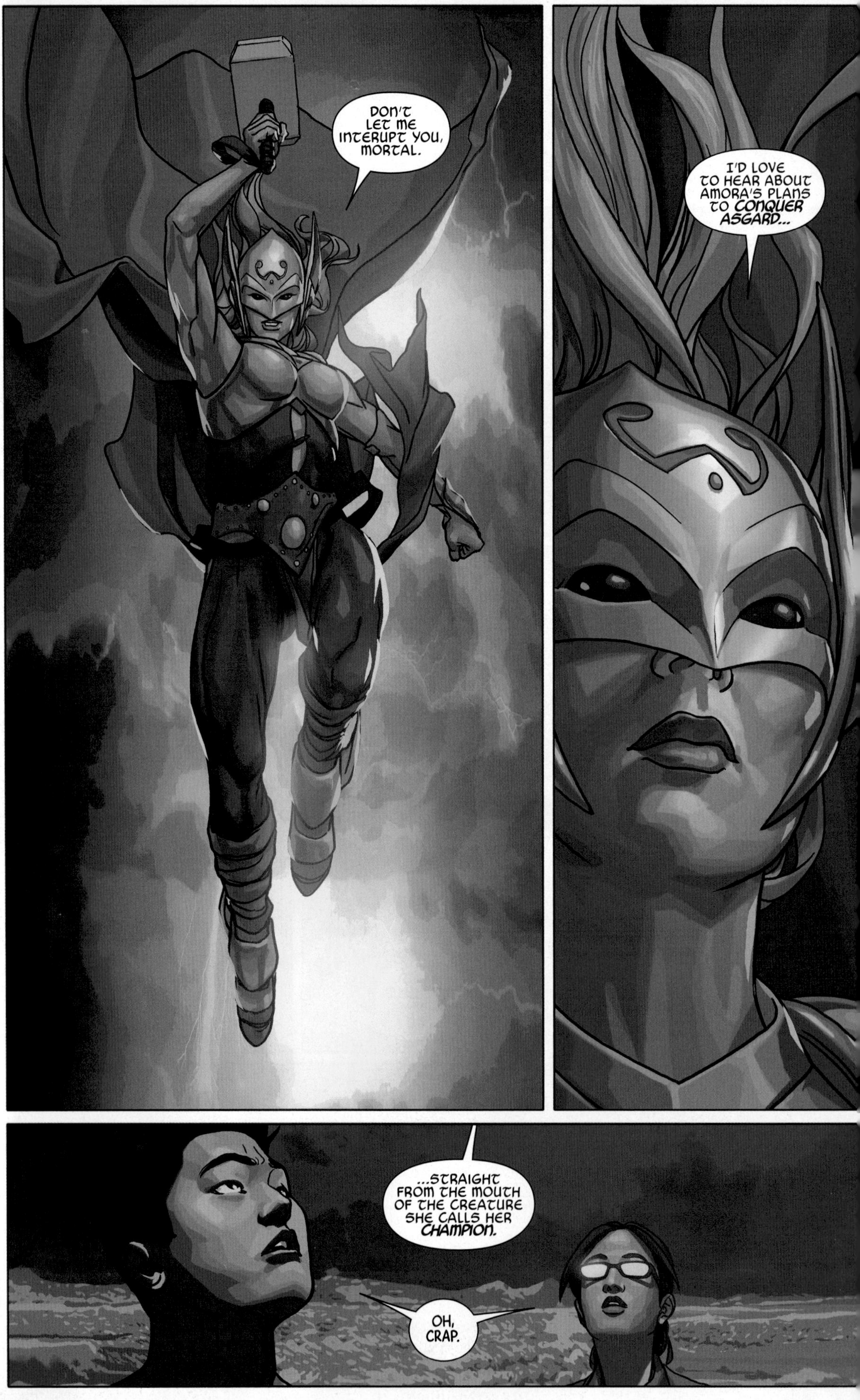
DON'T LET ME INTERUPT YOU, MORTAL.
I'D LOVE TO HEAR ABOUT AMORA'S PLANS TO CONQUER ASGARD...
...STRAIGHT FROM THE MOUTH OF THE CREATURE SHE CALLS HER CHAMPION.
OH, CRAP.

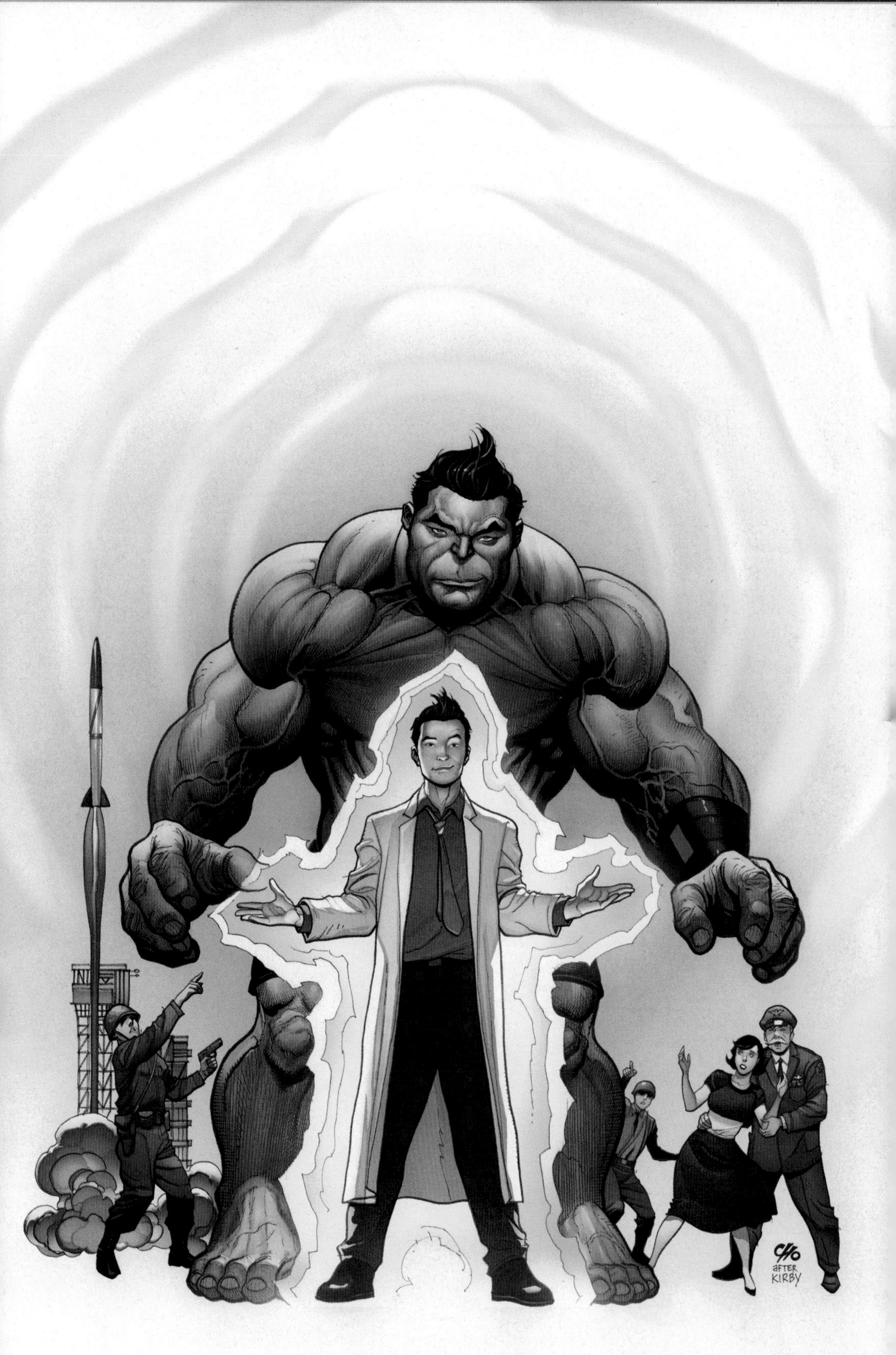
CHO
after
KIRBY

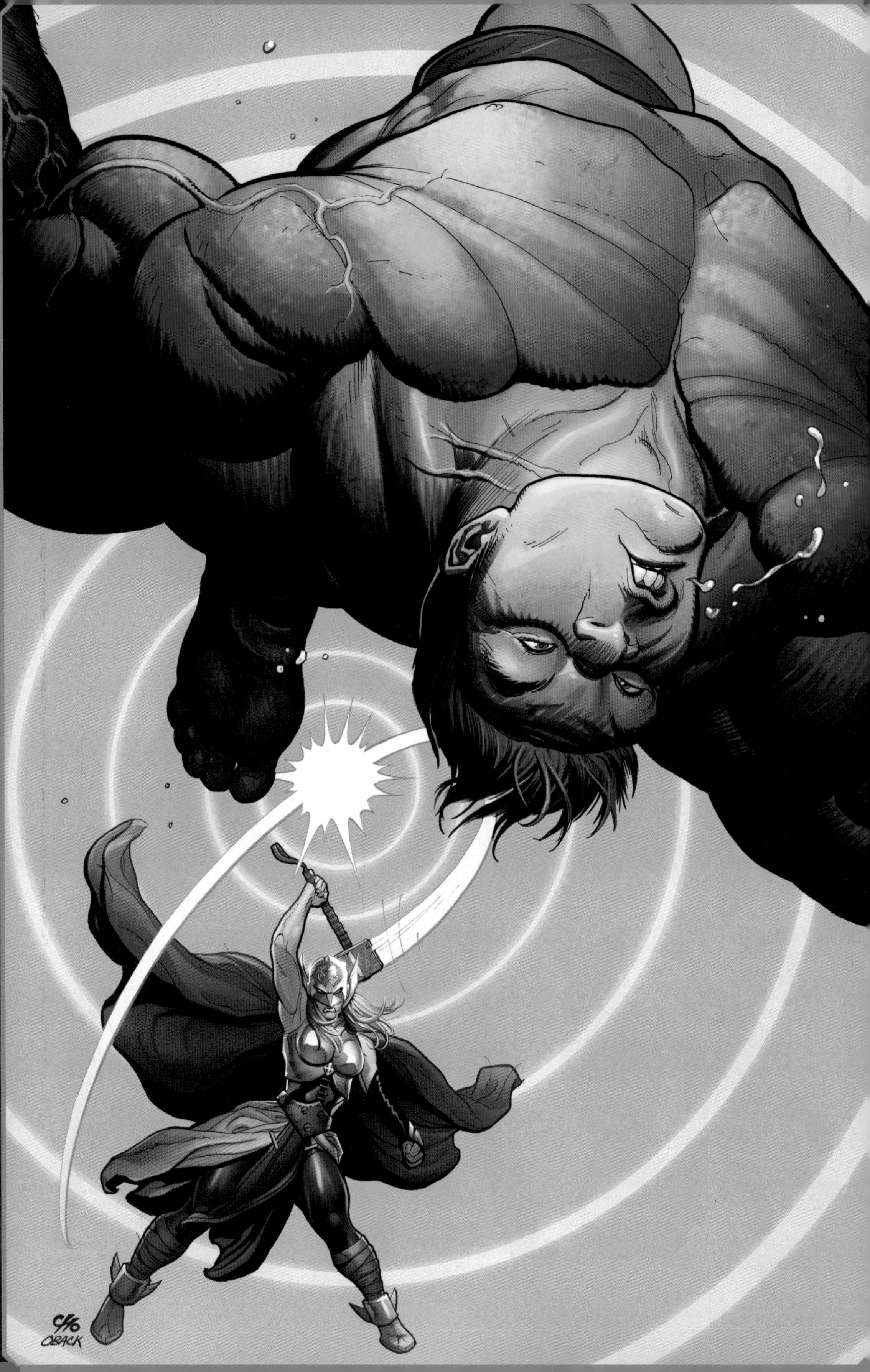

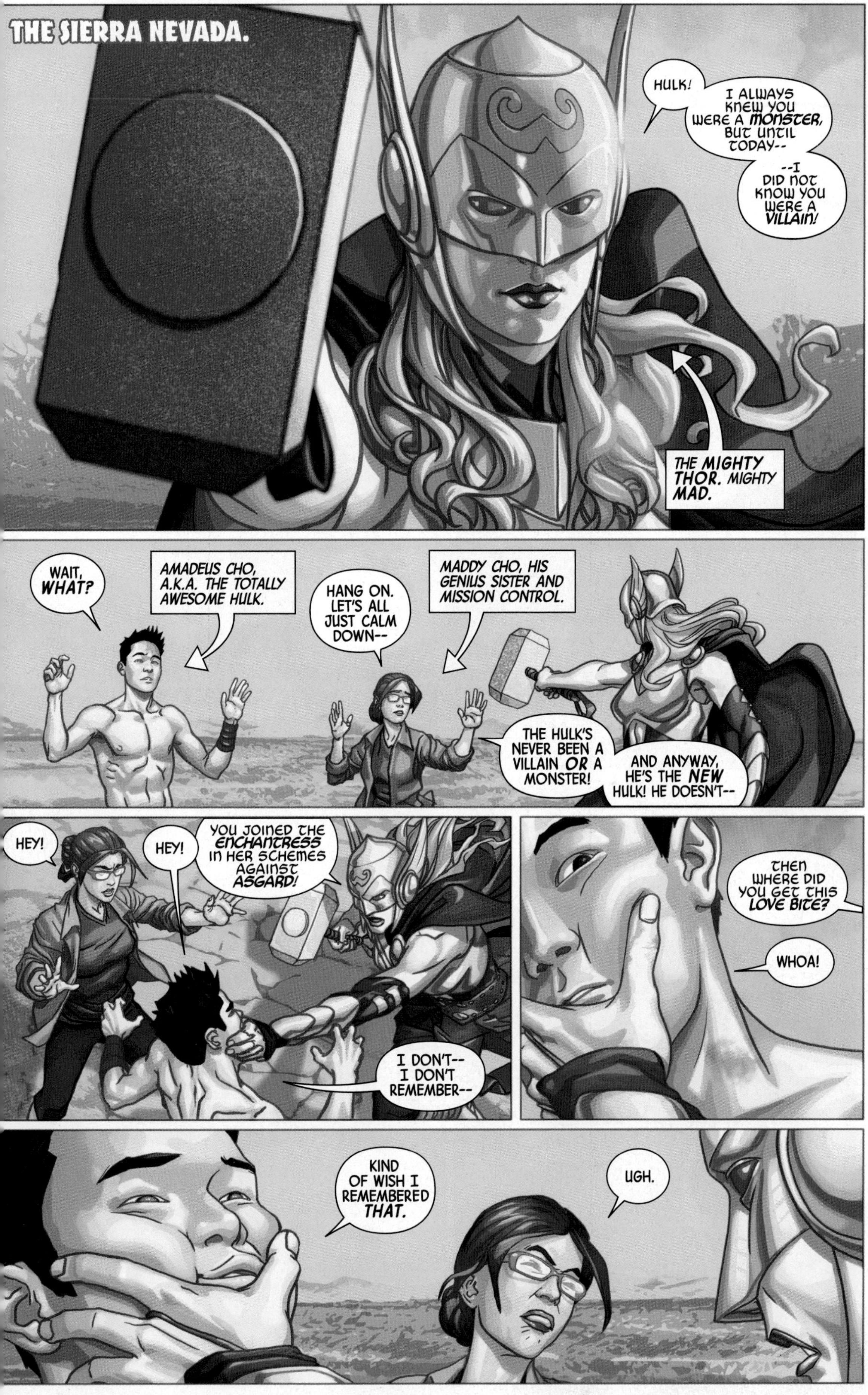
THE SIERRA NEVADA.
HULK!
I ALWAYS KNEW YOU WERE A MONSTER, BUT UNTIL TODAY--
--I DID NOT KNOW YOU WERE A VILLAIN!
THE MIGHTY THOR. MIGHTY MAD.
WAIT, WHAT?
AMADEUS CHO, A.K.A. THE TOTALLY AWESOME HULK.
HANG ON. LET'S ALL JUST CALM DOWN--
MADDY CHO, HIS GENIUS SISTER AND MISSION CONTROL.
THE HULK'S NEVER BEEN A VILLAIN OR A MONSTER!
AND ANYWAY, HE'S THE NEW HULK! HE DOESN'T--
HEY!
HEY!
YOU JOINED THE ENCHANTRESS IN HER SCHEMES AGAINST ASGARD!
I DON'T-- I DON'T REMEMBER--
THEN WHERE DID YOU GET THIS LOVE BITE?
WHOA!
KIND OF WISH I REMEMBERED THAT.
UGH.

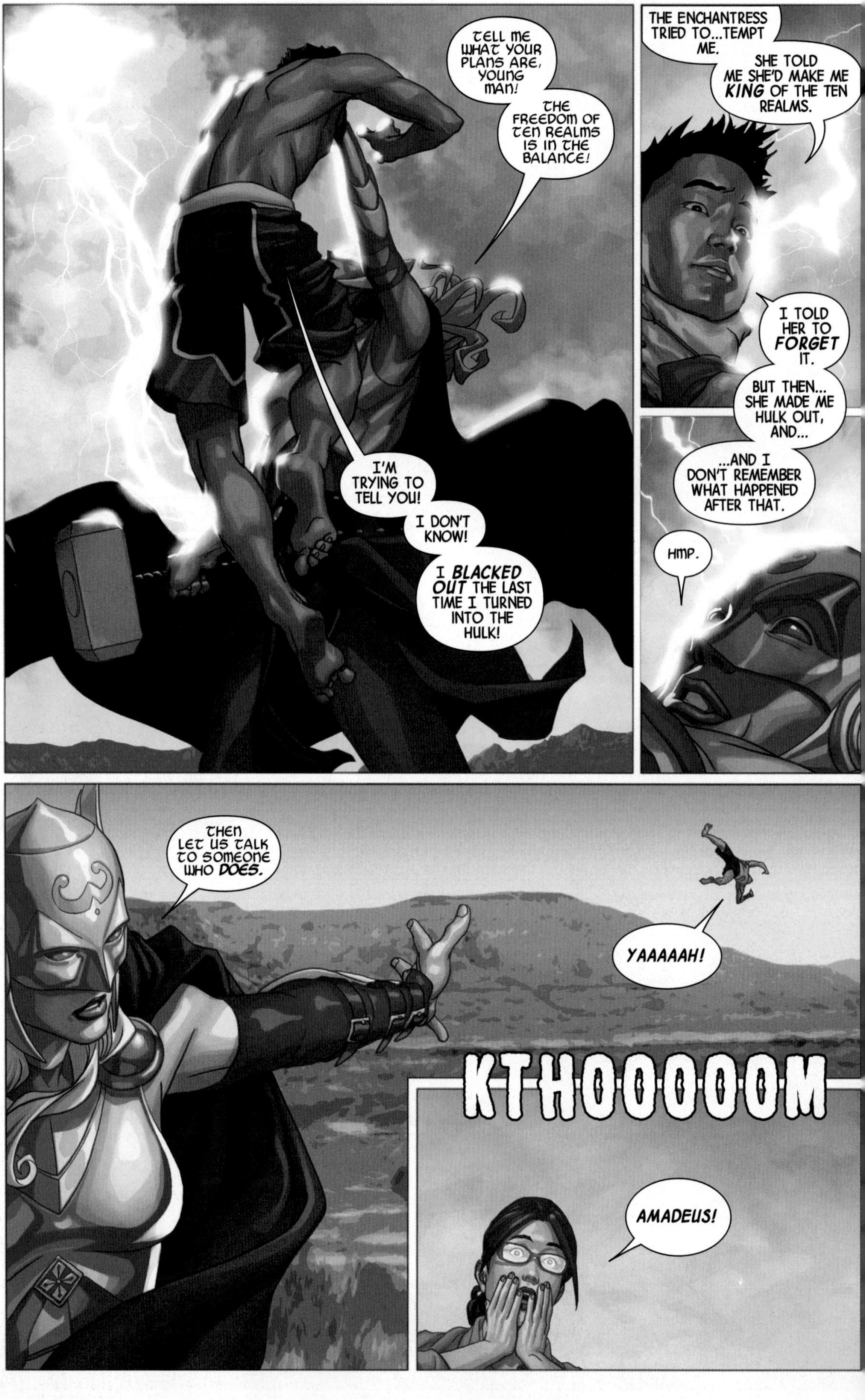
TELL ME WHAT YOUR PLANS ARE, YOUNG MAN!
THE FREEDOM OF TEN REALMS IS IN THE BALANCE!
I'M TRYING TO TELL YOU!
I DON'T KNOW!
I BLACKED OUT THE LAST TIME I TURNED INTO THE HULK!
THE ENCHANTRESS TRIED TO...TEMPT ME.
SHE TOLD ME SHE'D MAKE ME KING OF THE TEN REALMS.
I TOLD HER TO FORGET IT.
BUT THEN... SHE MADE ME HULK OUT, AND...
...AND I DON'T REMEMBER WHAT HAPPENED AFTER THAT.
HMP.
THEN LET US TALK TO SOMEONE WHO DOES.
YAAAAAH!
KTHOOOOOM
AMADEUS!

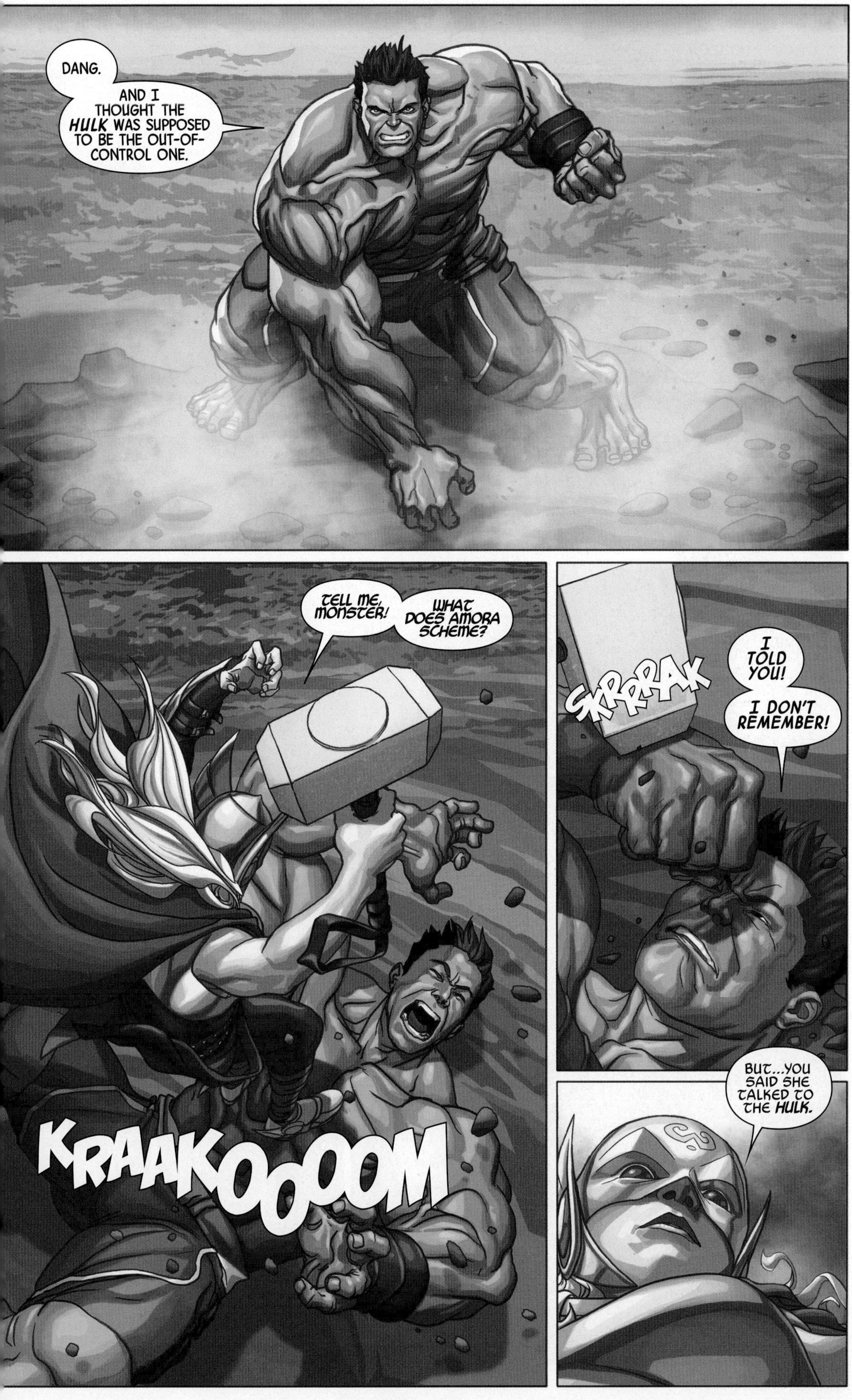

DANG.
AND I THOUGHT THE HULK WAS SUPPOSED TO BE THE OUT-OF-CONTROL ONE.
TELL ME, MONSTER!
WHAT DOES AMORA SCHEME?
KRAAKOOOOM
SKRRRAK
I TOLD YOU!
I DON'T REMEMBER!
BUT...YOU SAID SHE TALKED TO THE HULK.

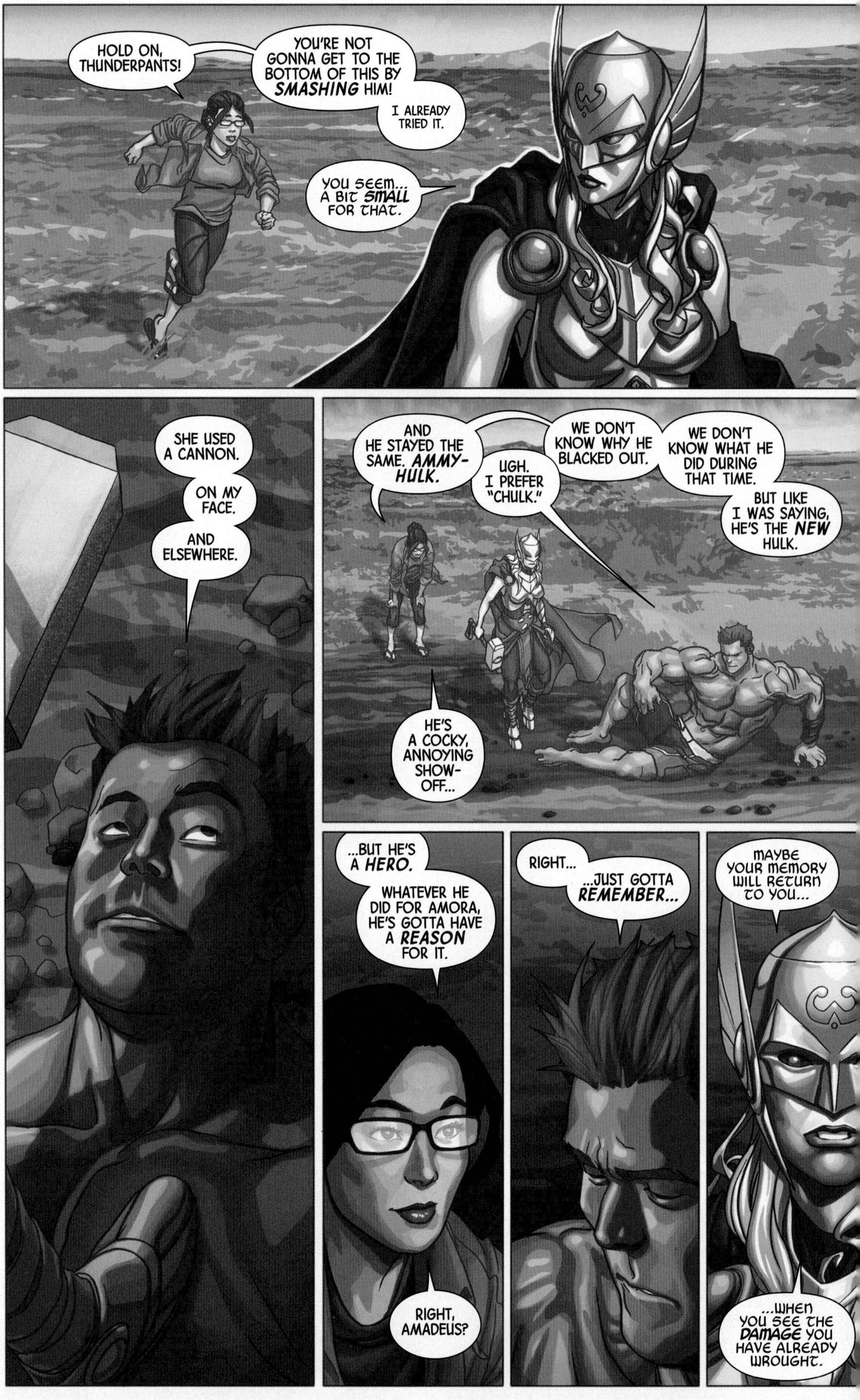
HOLD ON, THUNDERPANTS!
YOU'RE NOT GONNA GET TO THE BOTTOM OF THIS BY SMASHING HIM!
I ALREADY TRIED IT.
YOU SEEM... A BIT SMALL FOR THAT.
SHE USED A CANNON.
ON MY FACE.
AND ELSEWHERE.
AND HE STAYED THE SAME. AMMY-HULK.
UGH. I PREFER "CHULK."
WE DON'T KNOW WHY HE BLACKED OUT.
WE DON'T KNOW WHAT HE DID DURING THAT TIME.
BUT LIKE I WAS SAYING, HE'S THE NEW HULK.
HE'S A COCKY, ANNOYING SHOW-OFF...
...BUT HE'S A HERO.
WHATEVER HE DID FOR AMORA, HE'S GOTTA HAVE A REASON FOR IT.
RIGHT, AMADEUS?
RIGHT...
...JUST GOTTA REMEMBER...
MAYBE YOUR MEMORY WILL RETURN TO YOU...
...WHEN YOU SEE THE DAMAGE YOU HAVE ALREADY WROUGHT.

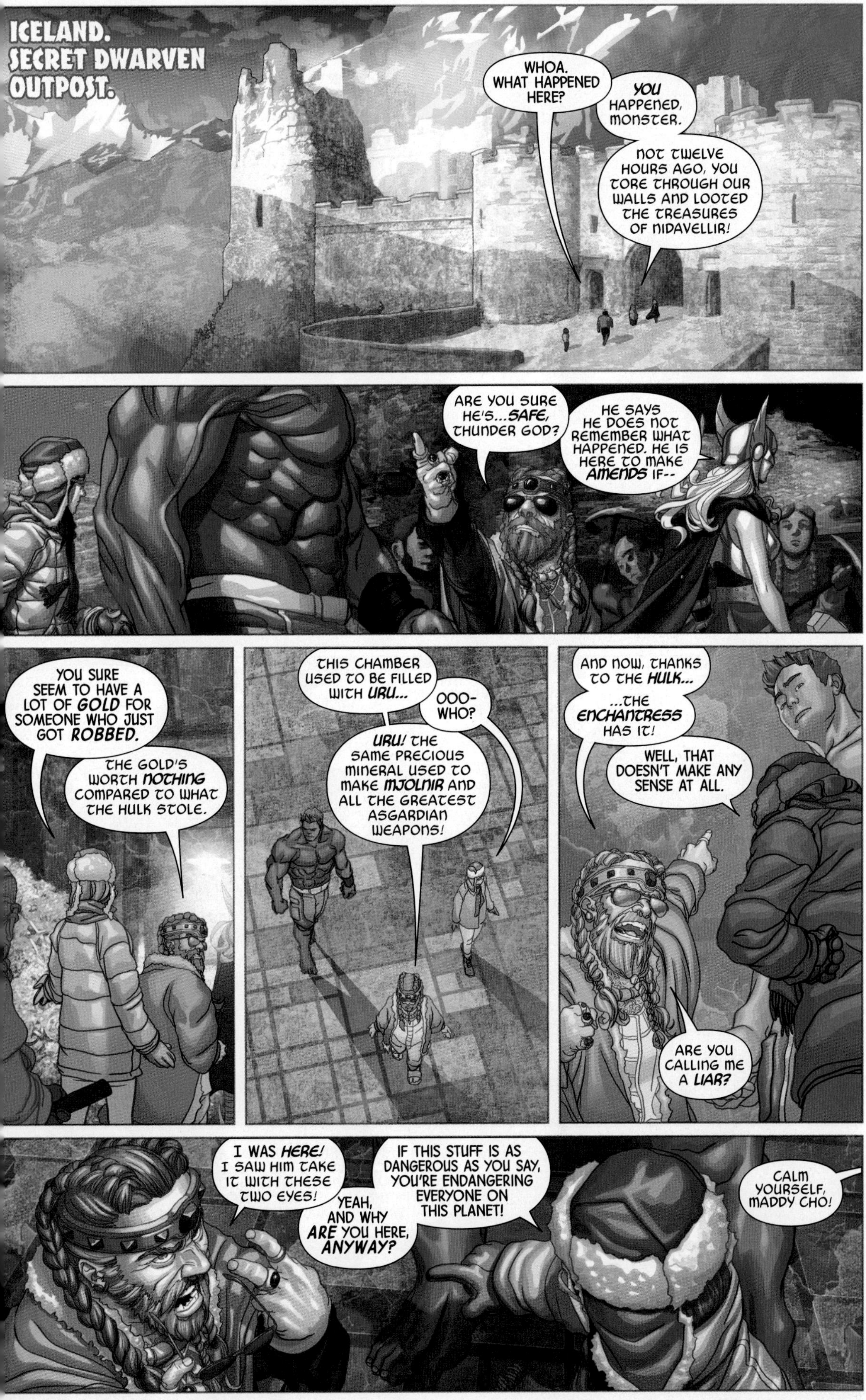

ICELAND. SECRET DWARVEN OUTPOST.
WHOA. WHAT HAPPENED HERE?
YOU HAPPENED, MONSTER.
NOT TWELVE HOURS AGO, YOU TORE THROUGH OUR WALLS AND LOOTED THE TREASURES OF NIDAVELLIR!
ARE YOU SURE HE'S...SAFE, THUNDER GOD?
HE SAYS HE DOES NOT REMEMBER WHAT HAPPENED. HE IS HERE TO MAKE AMENDS IF--
YOU SURE SEEM TO HAVE A LOT OF GOLD FOR SOMEONE WHO JUST GOT ROBBED.
THE GOLD'S WORTH NOTHING COMPARED TO WHAT THE HULK STOLE.
THIS CHAMBER USED TO BE FILLED WITH URU...
OOO-WHO?
URU! THE SAME PRECIOUS MINERAL USED TO MAKE MJOLNIR AND ALL THE GREATEST ASGARDIAN WEAPONS!
AND NOW, THANKS TO THE HULK...
...THE ENCHANTRESS HAS IT!
WELL, THAT DOESN'T MAKE ANY SENSE AT ALL.
ARE YOU CALLING ME A LIAR?
I WAS HERE! I SAW HIM TAKE IT WITH THESE TWO EYES!
YEAH, AND WHY ARE YOU HERE, ANYWAY?
IF THIS STUFF IS AS DANGEROUS AS YOU SAY, YOU'RE ENDANGERING EVERYONE ON THIS PLANET!
CALM YOURSELF, MADDY CHO!

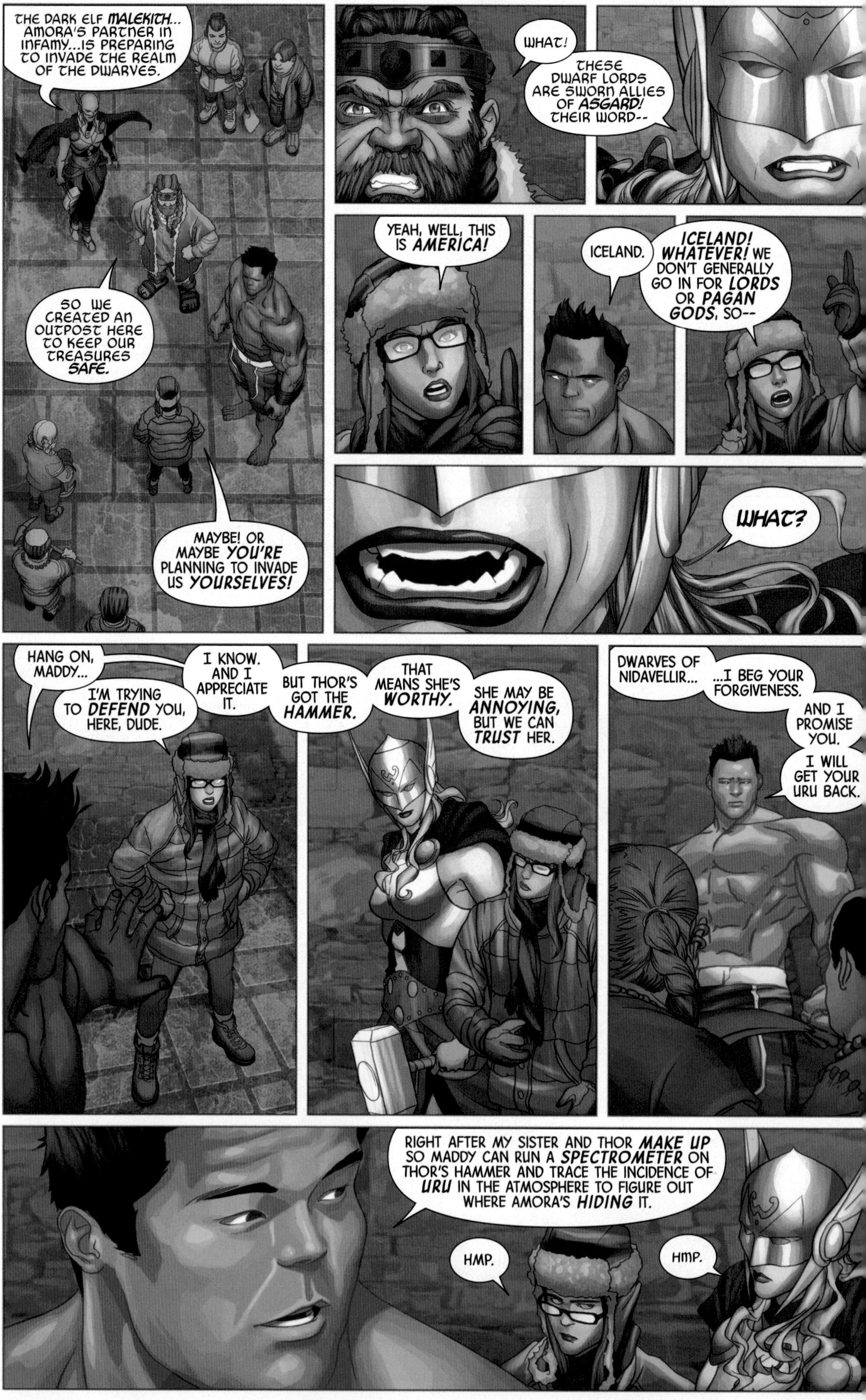
THE DARK ELF MALEKITH... AMORA'S PARTNER IN INFAMY...IS PREPARING TO INVADE THE REALM OF THE DWARVES.
SO WE CREATED AN OUTPOST HERE TO KEEP OUR TREASURES SAFE.
MAYBE! OR MAYBE YOU'RE PLANNING TO INVADE US YOURSELVES!
WHAT!
THESE DWARF LORDS ARE SWORN ALLIES OF ASGARD! THEIR WORD--
YEAH, WELL, THIS IS AMERICA!
ICELAND.
ICELAND! WHATEVER! WE DON'T GENERALLY GO IN FOR LORDS OR PAGAN GODS, SO--
WHAT?
HANG ON, MADDY...
I'M TRYING TO DEFEND YOU, HERE, DUDE.
I KNOW. AND I APPRECIATE IT.
BUT THOR'S GOT THE HAMMER.
THAT MEANS SHE'S WORTHY.
SHE MAY BE ANNOYING, BUT WE CAN TRUST HER.
DWARVES OF NIDAVELLIR...
...I BEG YOUR FORGIVENESS.
AND I PROMISE YOU.
I WILL GET YOUR URU BACK.
RIGHT AFTER MY SISTER AND THOR MAKE UP SO MADDY CAN RUN A SPECTROMETER ON THOR'S HAMMER AND TRACE THE INCIDENCE OF URU IN THE ATMOSPHERE TO FIGURE OUT WHERE AMORA'S HIDING IT.
HMP.
HMP.

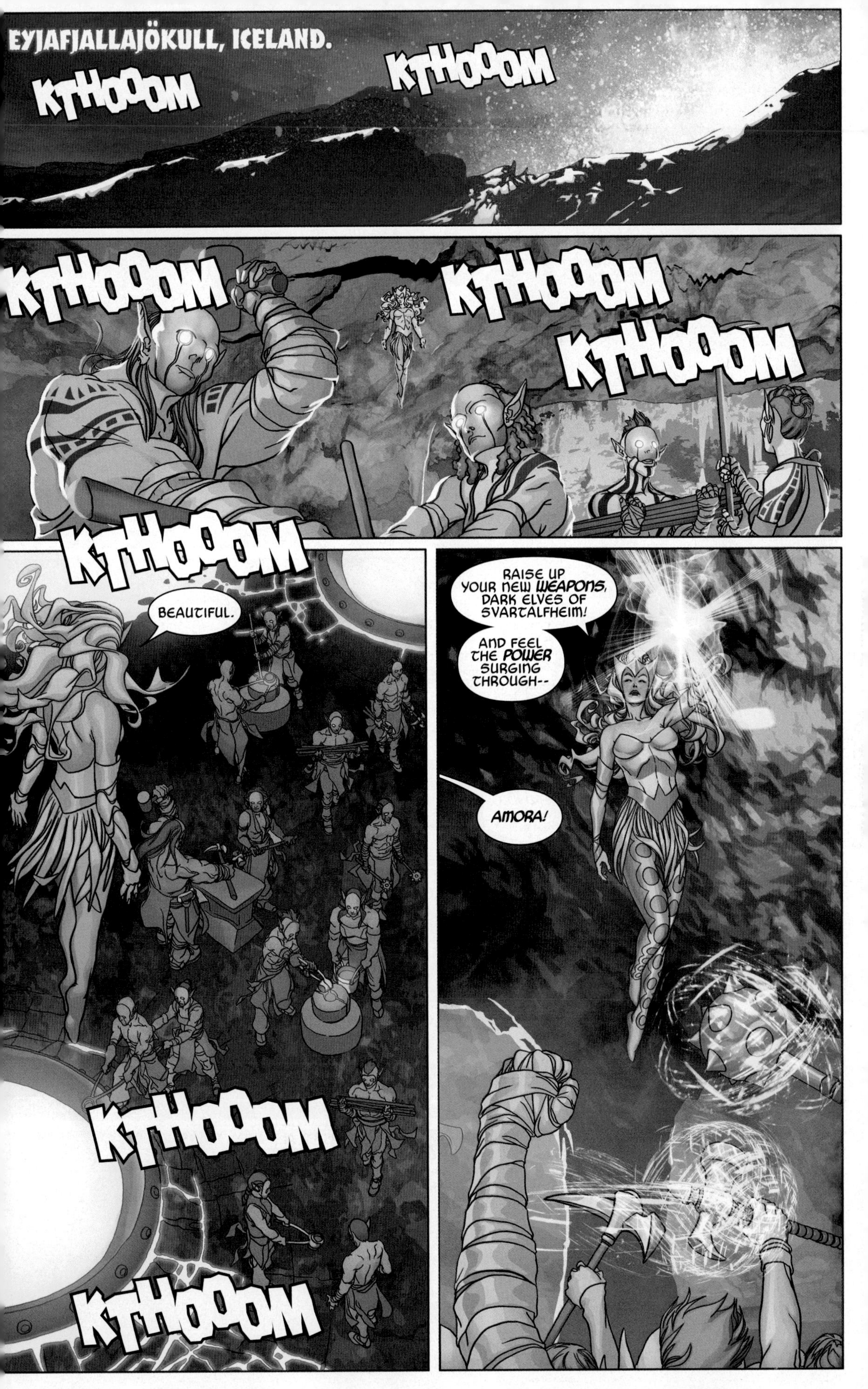
EYJAFJALLAJÖKULL, ICELAND.
KTHOOOM
KTHOOOM
KTHOOOM
KTHOOOM
KTHOOOM
KTHOOOM
BEAUTIFUL.
KTHOOOM
KTHOOOM
RAISE UP YOUR NEW WEAPONS, DARK ELVES OF SVARTALFHEIM!
AND FEEL THE POWER SURGING THROUGH--
AMORA!

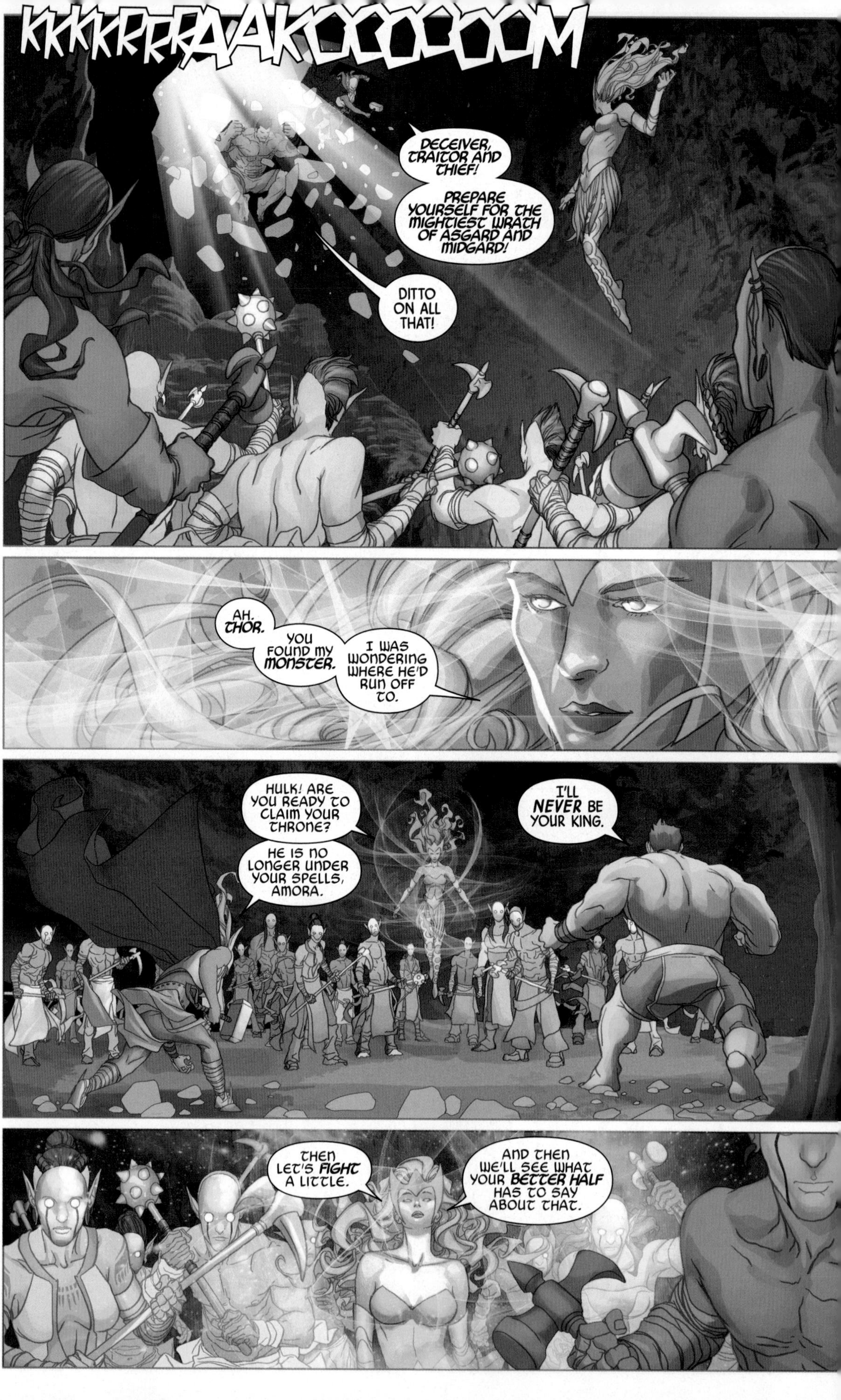
KKKKRRRAAKOOOOOOM
DECEIVER, TRAITOR AND THIEF!
PREPARE YOURSELF FOR THE MIGHTIEST WRATH OF ASGARD AND MIDGARD!
DITTO ON ALL THAT!
AH. THOR.
YOU FOUND MY MONSTER.
I WAS WONDERING WHERE HE'D RUN OFF TO.
HULK! ARE YOU READY TO CLAIM YOUR THRONE?
HE IS NO LONGER UNDER YOUR SPELLS, AMORA.
I'LL NEVER BE YOUR KING.
THEN LET'S FIGHT A LITTLE.
AND THEN WE'LL SEE WHAT YOUR BETTER HALF HAS TO SAY ABOUT THAT.

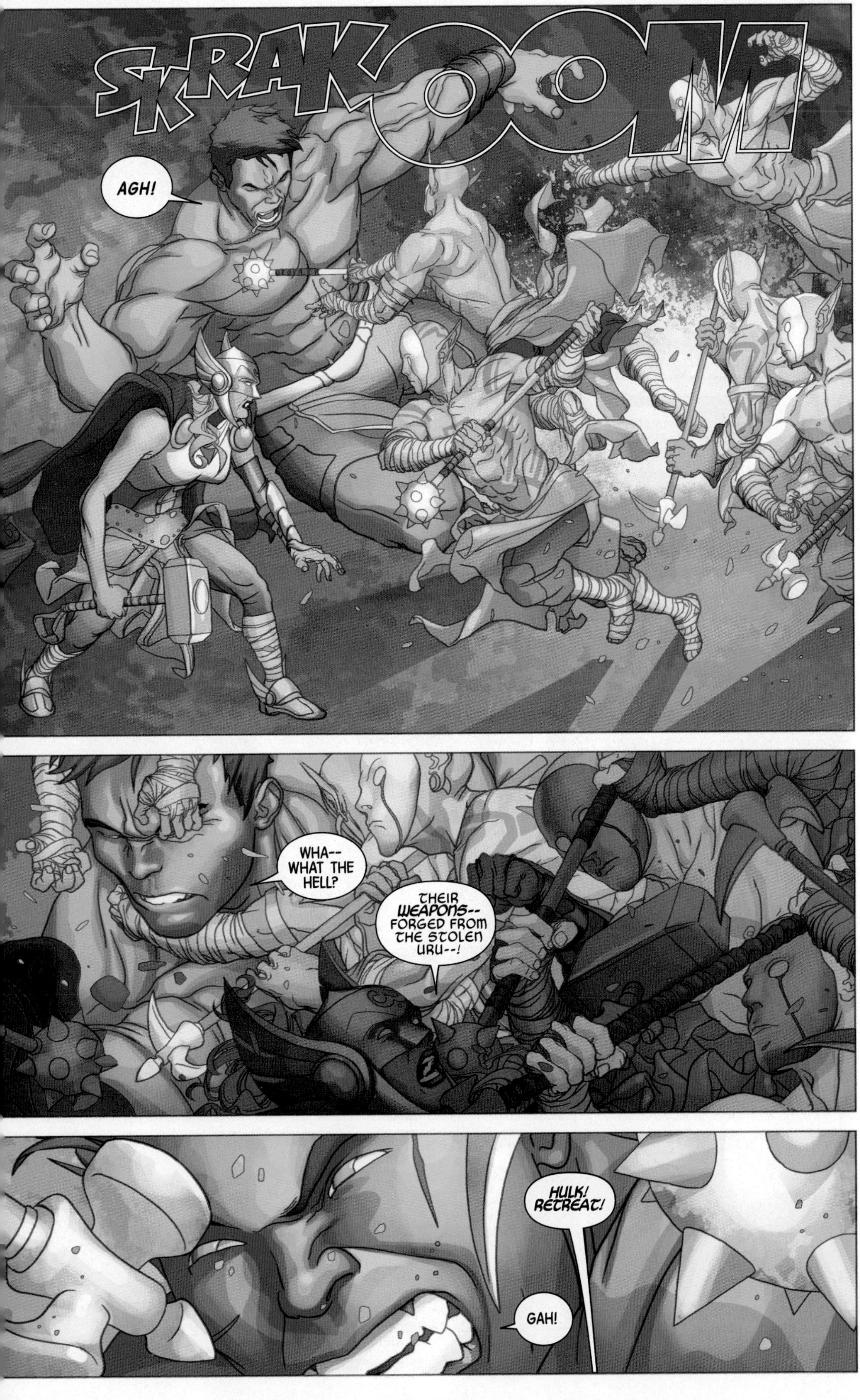
SKRAKOOM
AGH!
WHA-- WHAT THE HELL?
THEIR WEAPONS-- FORGED FROM THE STOLEN URU--!
HULK! RETREAT!
GAH!

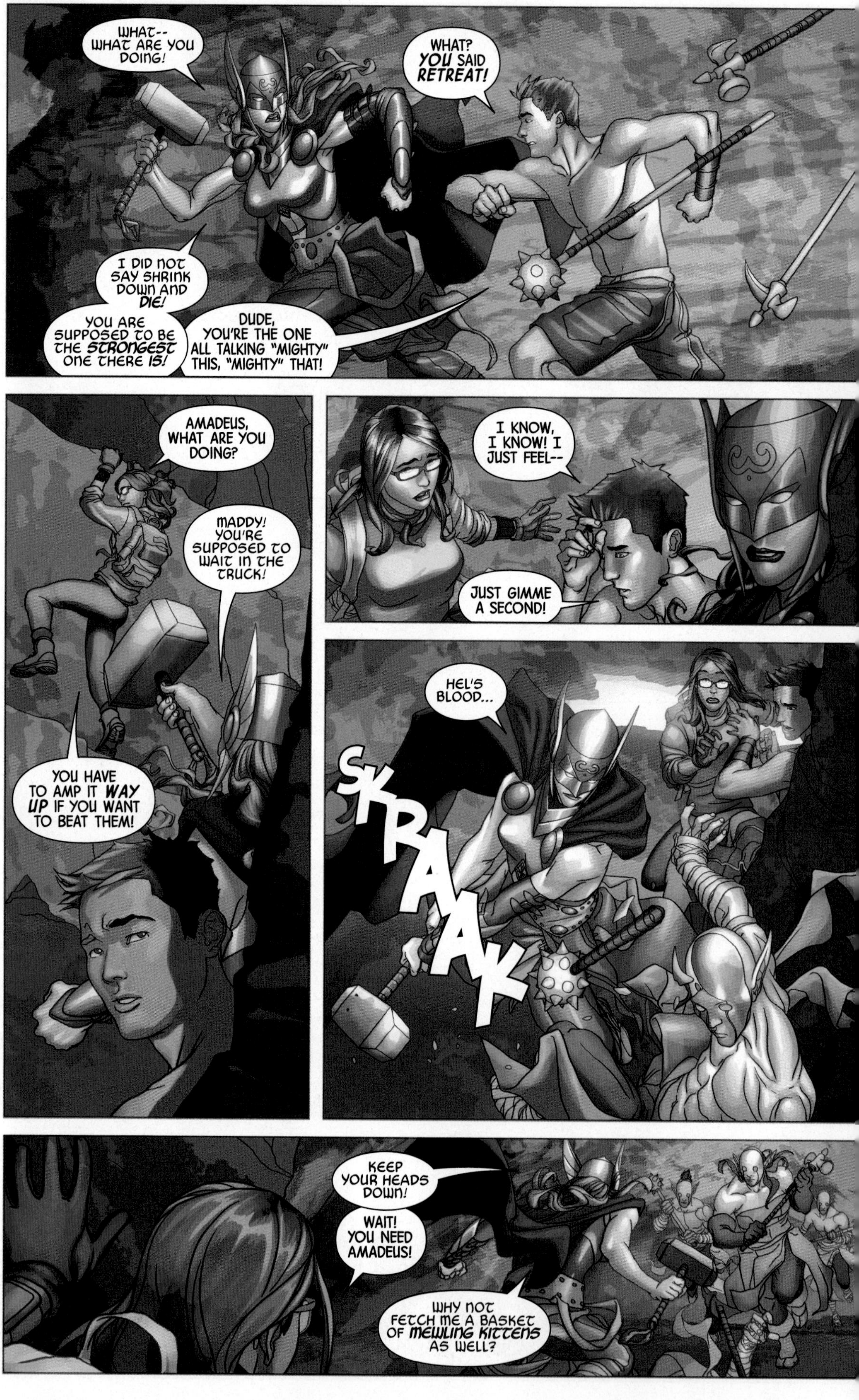

WHAT-- WHAT ARE YOU DOING!
WHAT? YOU SAID RETREAT!
I DID NOT SAY SHRINK DOWN AND DIE!
YOU ARE SUPPOSED TO BE THE STRONGEST ONE THERE IS!
DUDE, YOU'RE THE ONE ALL TALKING "MIGHTY" THIS, "MIGHTY" THAT!
AMADEUS, WHAT ARE YOU DOING?
MADDY! YOU'RE SUPPOSED TO WAIT IN THE TRUCK!
YOU HAVE TO AMP IT WAY UP IF YOU WANT TO BEAT THEM!
I KNOW, I KNOW! I JUST FEEL--
JUST GIMME A SECOND!
HEL'S BLOOD...
SKRAAAK
KEEP YOUR HEADS DOWN!
WAIT! YOU NEED AMADEUS!
WHY NOT FETCH ME A BASKET OF MEWLING KITTENS AS WELL?

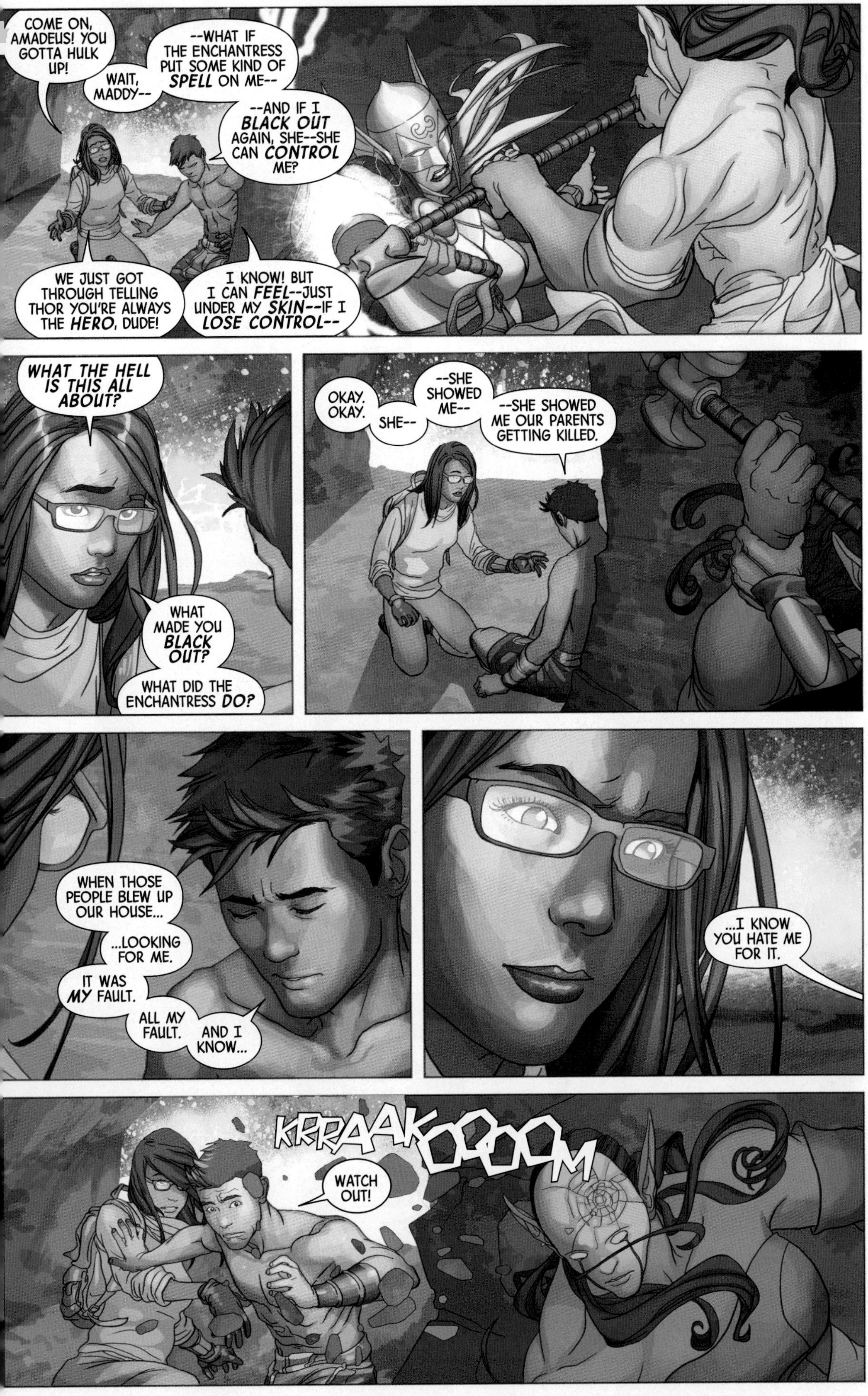
COME ON, AMADEUS! YOU GOTTA HULK UP!
WAIT, MADDY--
--WHAT IF THE ENCHANTRESS PUT SOME KIND OF SPELL ON ME--
--AND IF I BLACK OUT AGAIN, SHE--SHE CAN CONTROL ME?
WE JUST GOT THROUGH TELLING THOR YOU'RE ALWAYS THE HERO, DUDE!
I KNOW! BUT I CAN FEEL--JUST UNDER MY SKIN--IF I LOSE CONTROL--
WHAT THE HELL IS THIS ALL ABOUT?
WHAT MADE YOU BLACK OUT?
WHAT DID THE ENCHANTRESS DO?
OKAY. OKAY.
SHE--
--SHE SHOWED ME--
--SHE SHOWED ME OUR PARENTS GETTING KILLED.
WHEN THOSE PEOPLE BLEW UP OUR HOUSE...
...LOOKING FOR ME.
IT WAS MY FAULT.
ALL MY FAULT.
AND I KNOW...
...I KNOW YOU HATE ME FOR IT.
KRRAAKOOOOM
WATCH OUT!

I'M SO-- I'M SO *SORRY*, MADDY!

I'D JUST WON THAT STUPID BRAIN GAME COMPETITION!

I WASN'T THINKING ABOUT THEM. OR YOU. OR ANYTHING--

--JUST MY OWN STUPID SELF!

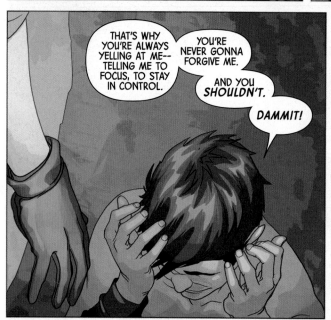

THAT'S WHY YOU'RE ALWAYS YELLING AT ME-- TELLING ME TO FOCUS, TO STAY IN CONTROL.

YOU'RE NEVER GONNA FORGIVE ME.

AND YOU *SHOULDN'T*.

DAMMIT!

AMMY...

...YOU'RE RIGHT.

I *AM* MAD.

I...I MISS THEM SO DAMN MUCH...

...BUT THAT'S OUR BUSINESS.

AND THAT DAMN... *WITCH*...

...HAS NO *RIGHT*...

YOU GO AHEAD AND GET *MAD*, AMADEUS.

BUT GET MAD AT *HER*.

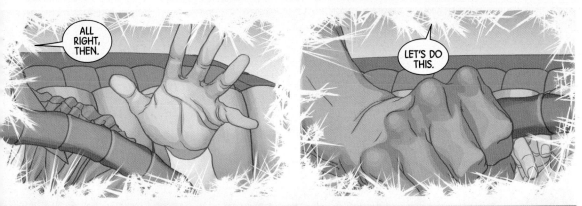

ALL RIGHT, THEN.

LET'S DO THIS.

WHOA!

GGGRAAH!

AH. *THAT* LOOKS LIKE THE MONSTER I KNOW.

NOW COME.

WE MADE A PACT.

I PROMISED YOU A *WEAPON* WORTHY OF YOUR *RAGE*--

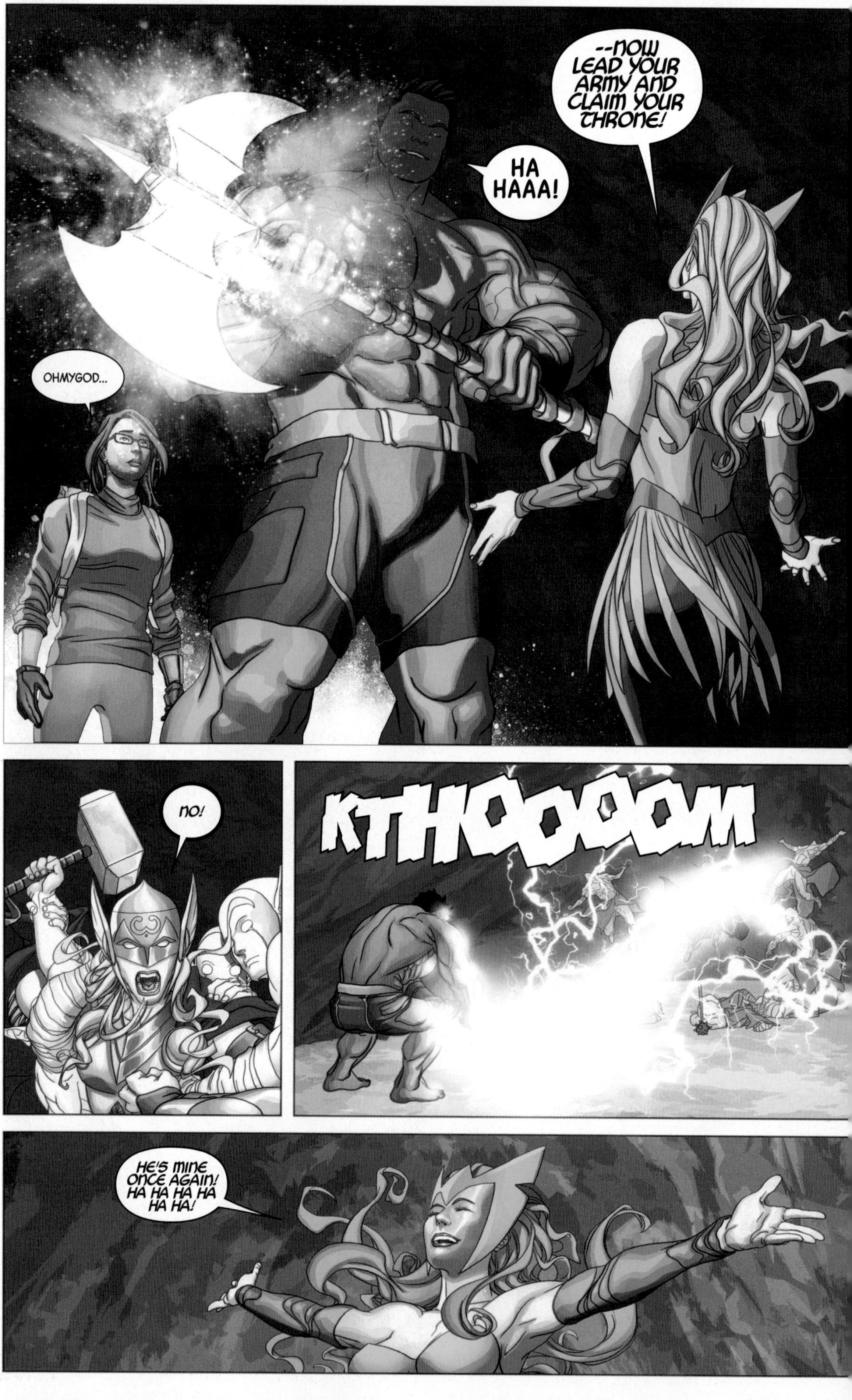
--NOW LEAD YOUR ARMY AND CLAIM YOUR THRONE!
HA HAAA!
OHMYGOD...
NO!
KTHOOOOOM
HE'S MINE ONCE AGAIN! HA HA HA HA HA HA!

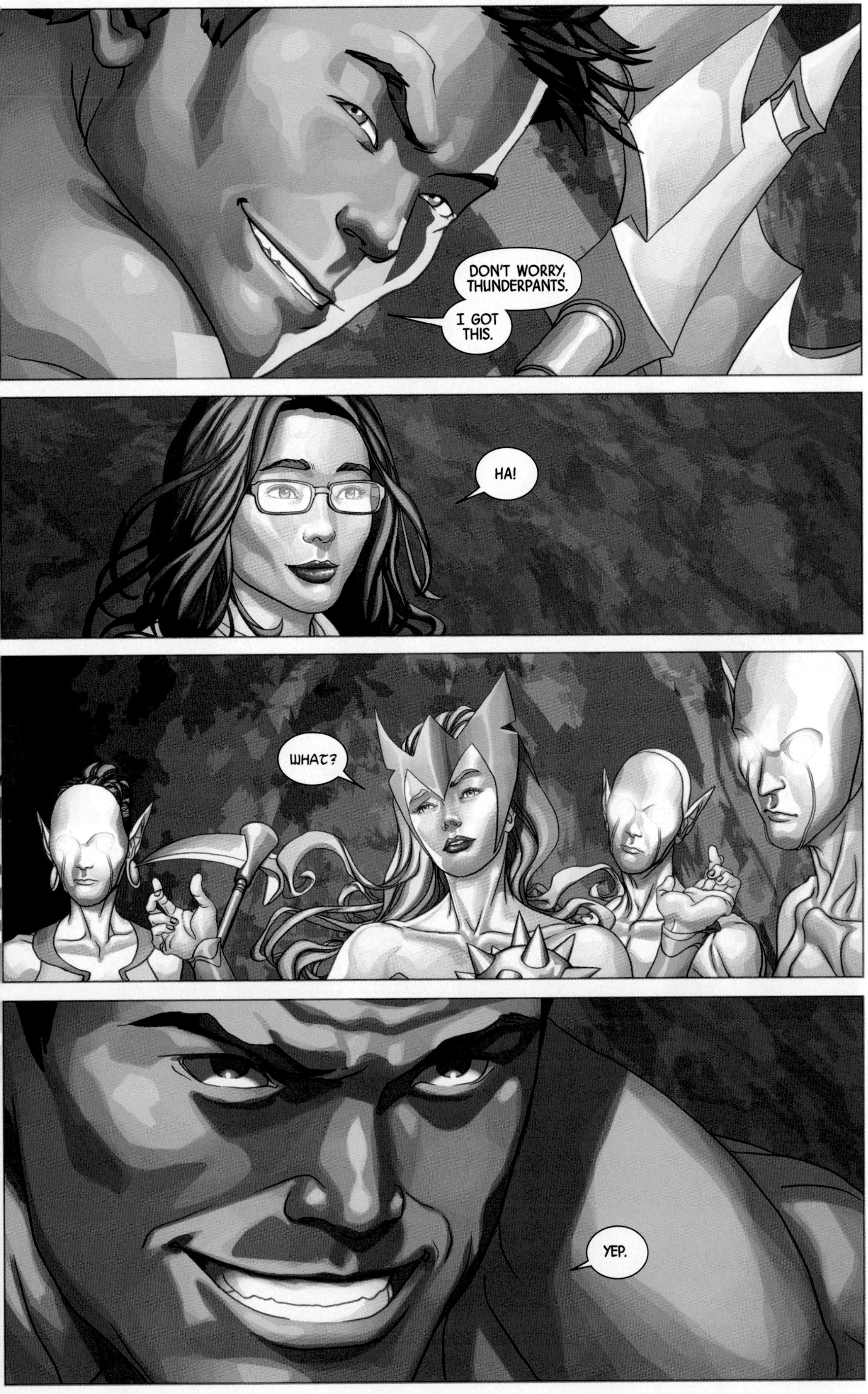
DON'T WORRY, THUNDERPANTS.
I GOT THIS.
HA!
WHAT?
YEP.

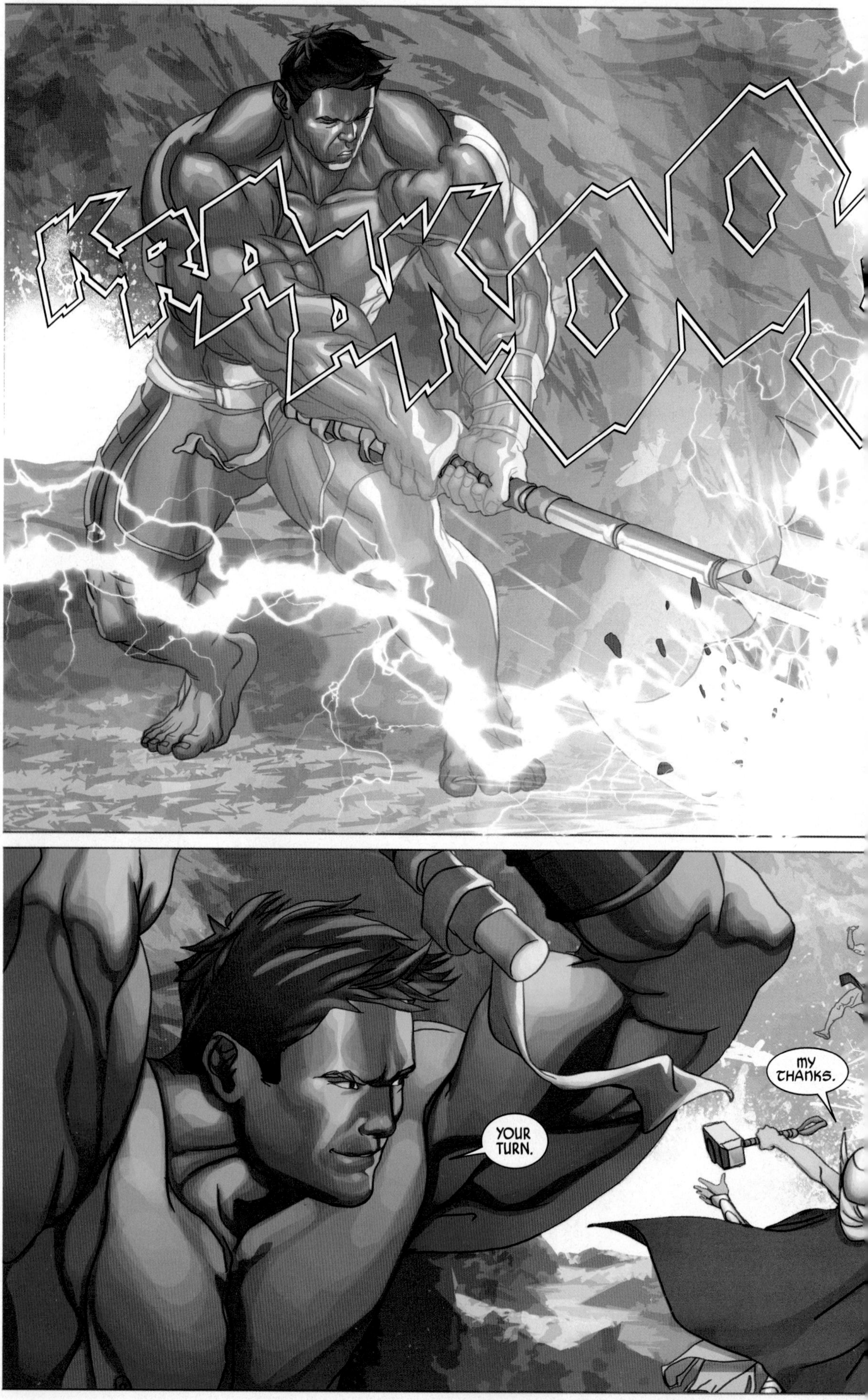
YOUR TURN.
MY THANKS.

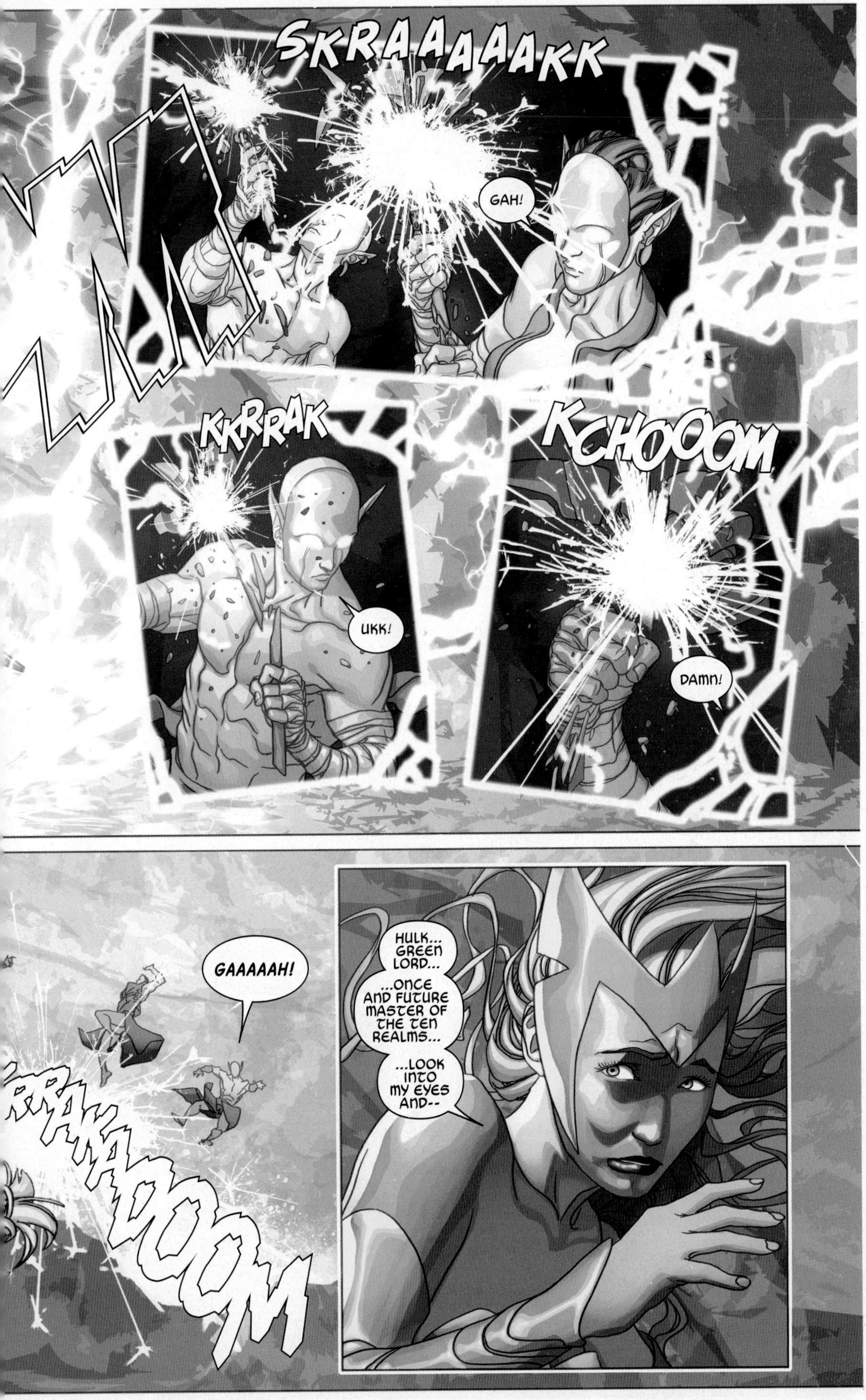
SKRAAAAAAKK
GAH!
KKRRAK
UKK!
KCHOOOM
DAMN!
GAAAAAH!
HULK... GREEN LORD...
...ONCE AND FUTURE MASTER OF THE TEN REALMS...
...LOOK INTO MY EYES AND--

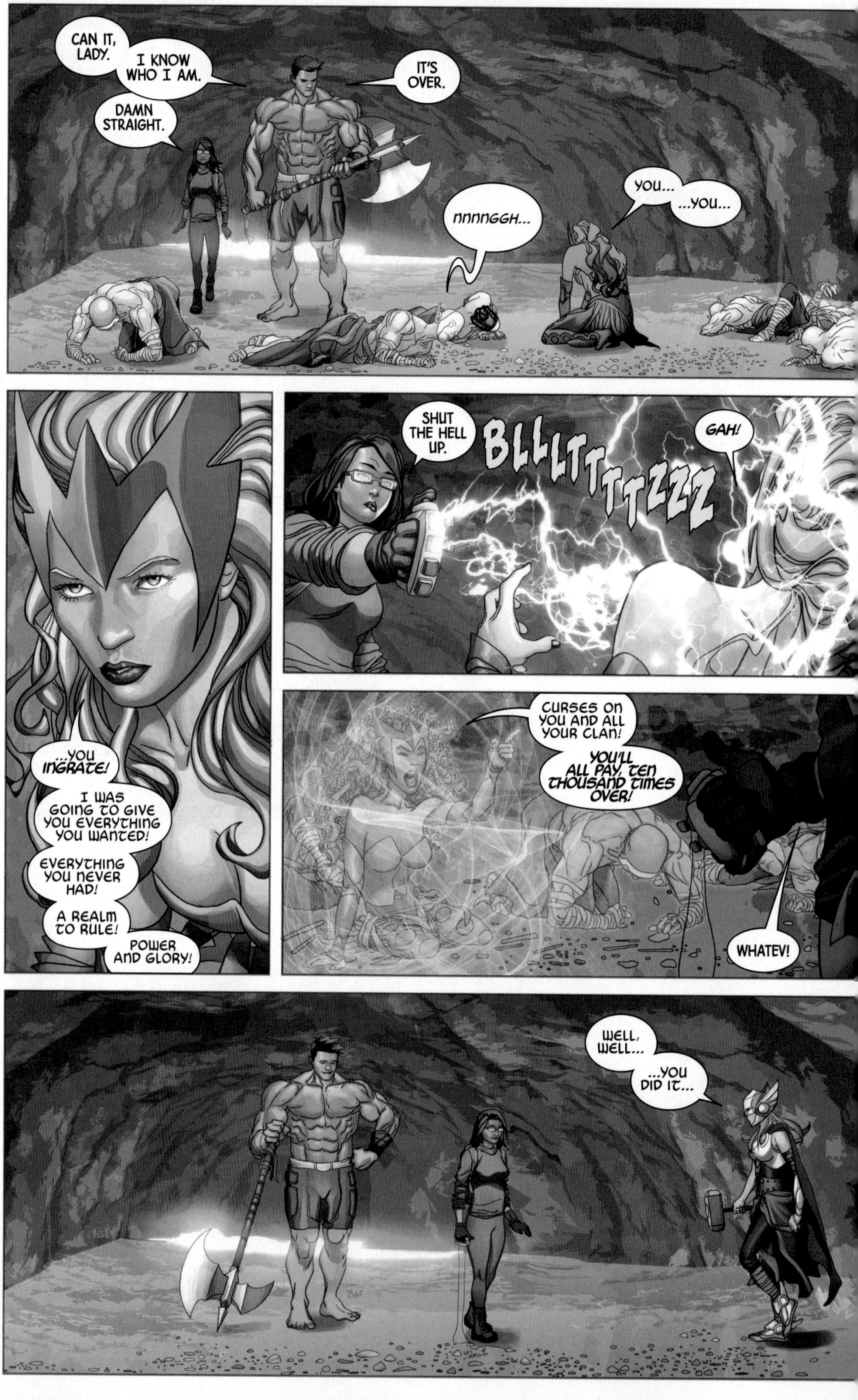
CAN IT, LADY.
I KNOW WHO I AM.
DAMN STRAIGHT.
IT'S OVER.
NNNNGGH...
YOU...
...YOU...
...YOU INGRATE!
I WAS GOING TO GIVE YOU EVERYTHING YOU WANTED!
EVERYTHING YOU NEVER HAD!
A REALM TO RULE!
POWER AND GLORY!
SHUT THE HELL UP.
BLLLTTTTTZZZZ
GAH!
CURSES ON YOU AND ALL YOUR CLAN!
YOU'LL ALL PAY, TEN THOUSAND TIMES OVER!
WHATEV!
WELL, WELL...
...YOU DID IT...

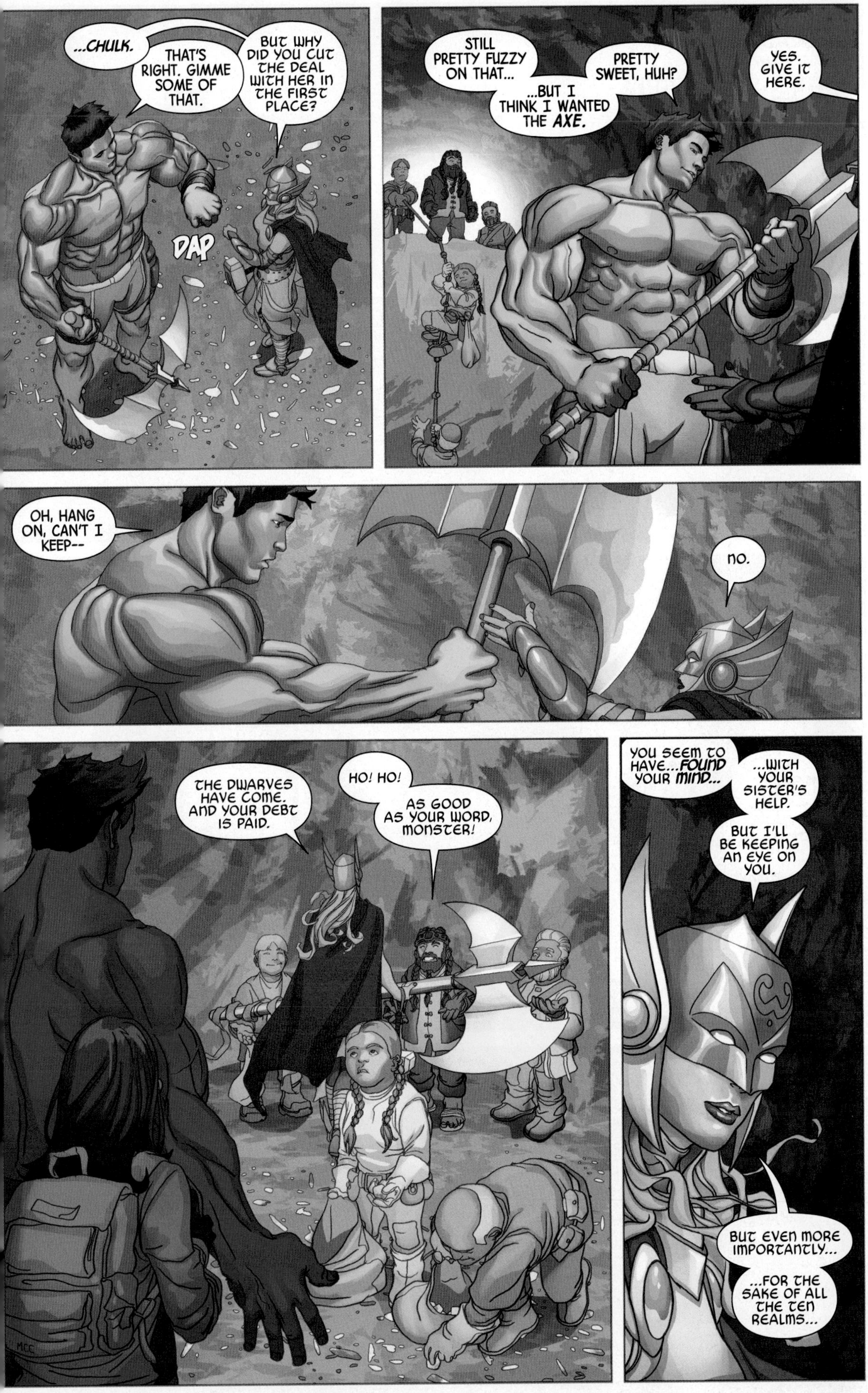
...CHULK.
THAT'S RIGHT. GIMME SOME OF THAT.
BUT WHY DID YOU CUT THE DEAL WITH HER IN THE FIRST PLACE?
DAP
STILL PRETTY FUZZY ON THAT...
...BUT I THINK I WANTED THE AXE.
PRETTY SWEET, HUH?
YES. GIVE IT HERE.
OH, HANG ON, CAN'T I KEEP--
NO.
THE DWARVES HAVE COME. AND YOUR DEBT IS PAID.
HO! HO!
AS GOOD AS YOUR WORD, MONSTER!
YOU SEEM TO HAVE...FOUND YOUR MIND...
...WITH YOUR SISTER'S HELP.
BUT I'LL BE KEEPING AN EYE ON YOU.
BUT EVEN MORE IMPORTANTLY...
...FOR THE SAKE OF ALL THE TEN REALMS...

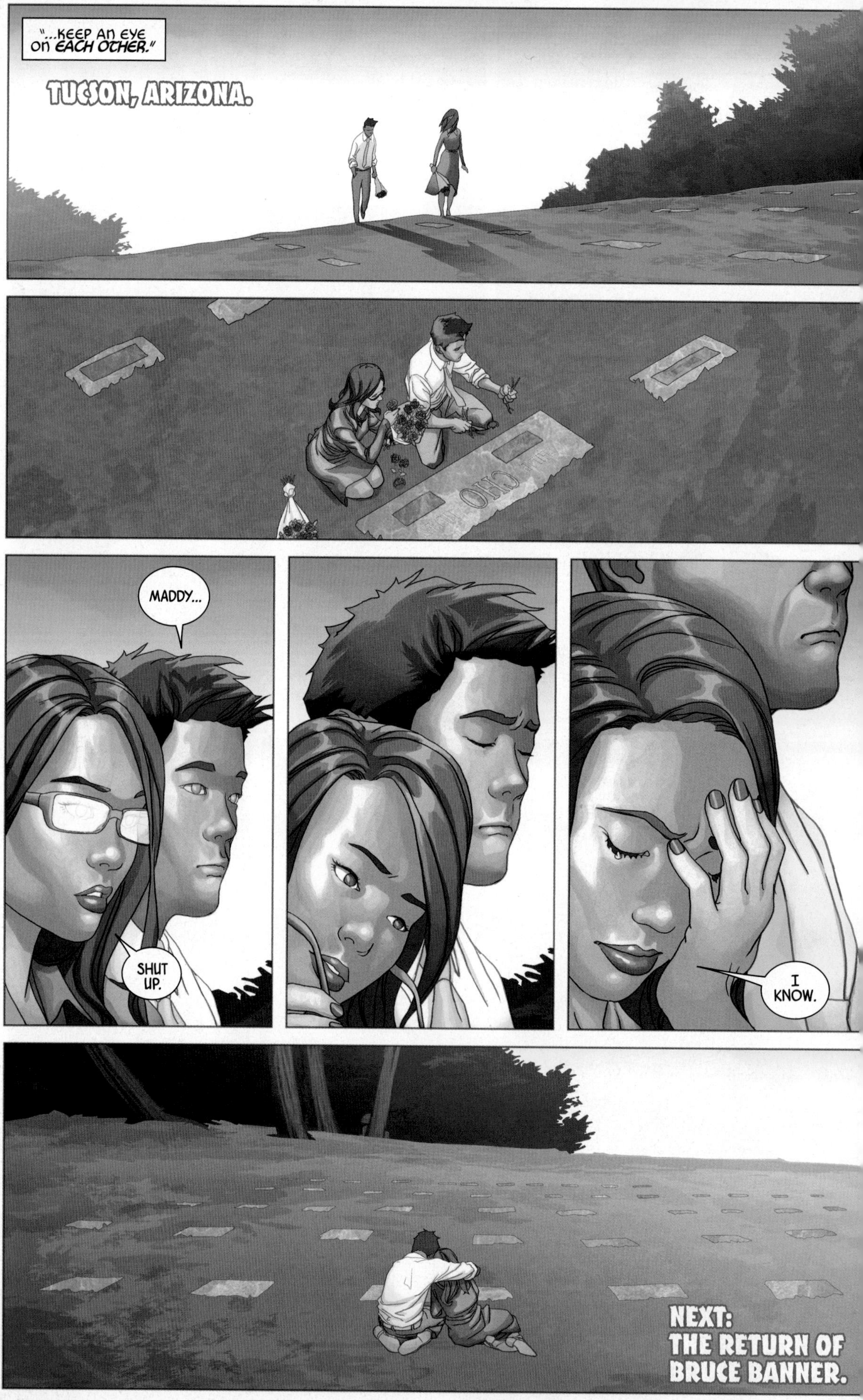
"...KEEP AN EYE ON EACH OTHER."
TUCSON, ARIZONA.
MADDY...
SHUT UP.
I KNOW.
NEXT: THE RETURN OF BRUCE BANNER.

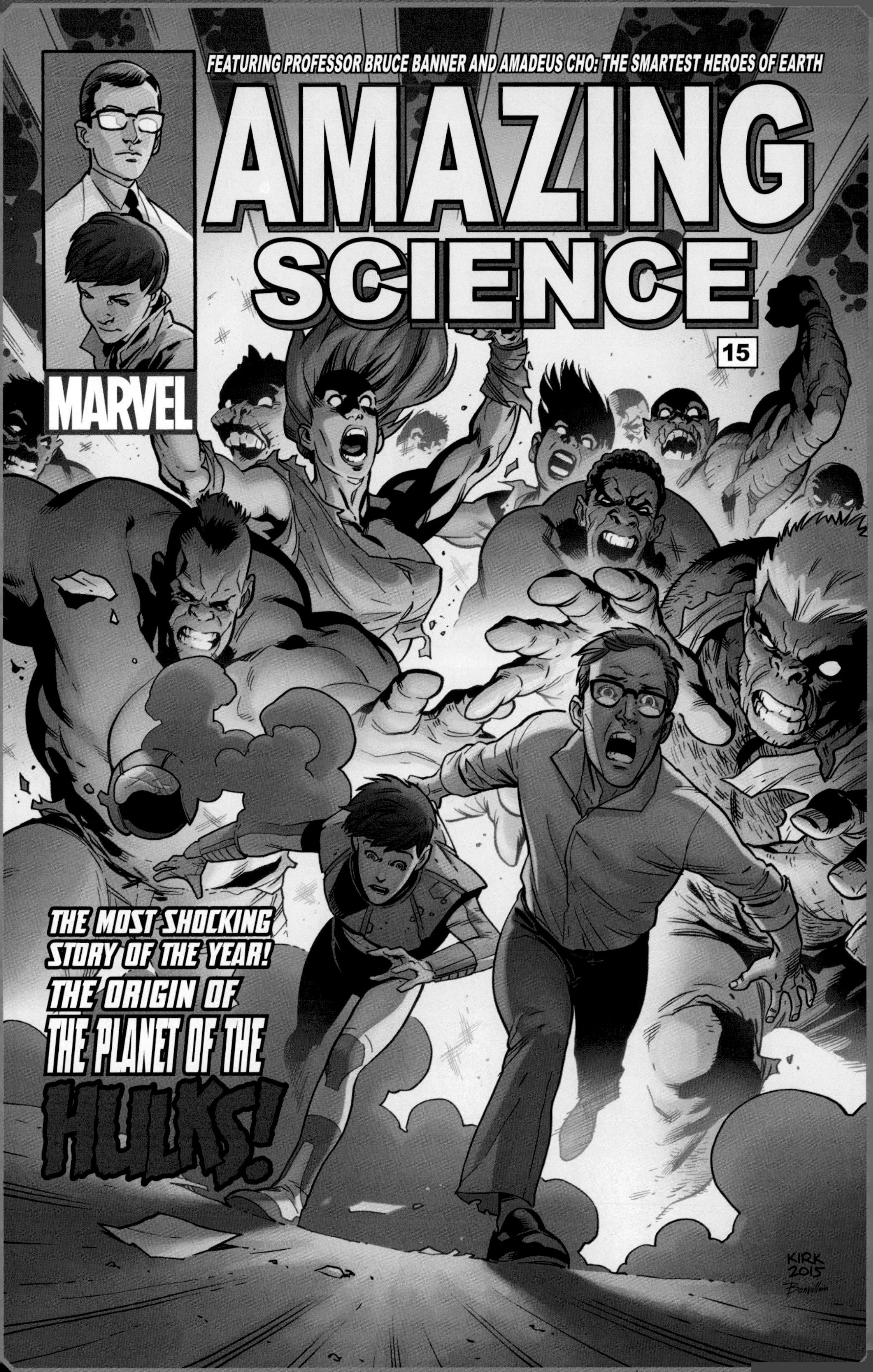
FEATURING PROFESSOR BRUCE BANNER AND AMADEUS CHO: THE SMARTEST HEROES OF EARTH
AMAZING
SCIENCE
15
MARVEL
THE MOST SHOCKING STORY OF THE YEAR!
THE ORIGIN OF
THE PLANET OF THE
HULKS!
KIRK 2015

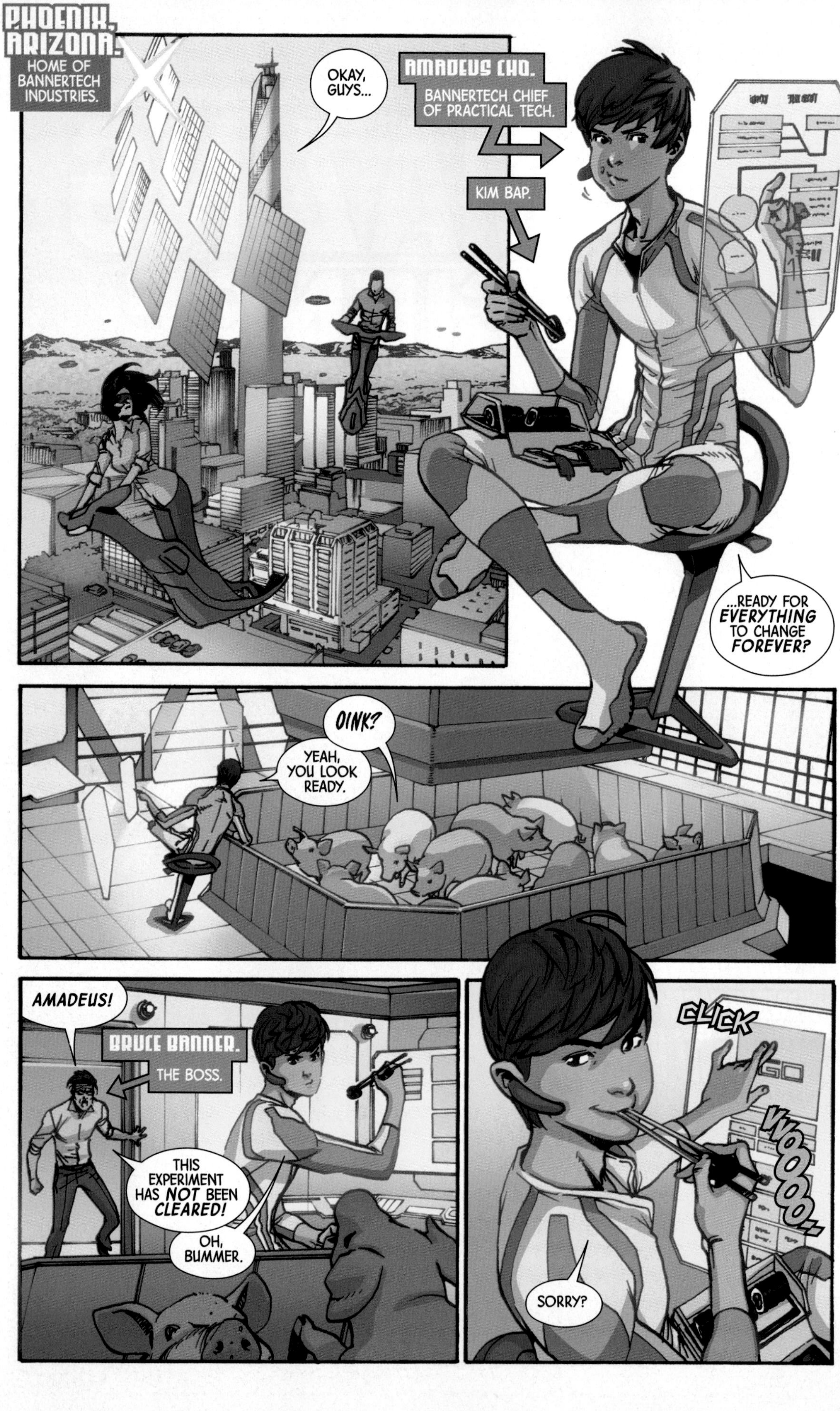
PHOENIX, ARIZONA.
HOME OF BANNERTECH INDUSTRIES.
OKAY, GUYS...
AMADEUS CHO.
BANNERTECH CHIEF OF PRACTICAL TECH.
KIM BAP.
...READY FOR EVERYTHING TO CHANGE FOREVER?
OINK?
YEAH, YOU LOOK READY.
AMADEUS!
BRUCE BANNER.
THE BOSS.
THIS EXPERIMENT HAS NOT BEEN CLEARED!
OH, BUMMER.
CLICK
GO
VWOOOO--
SORRY?

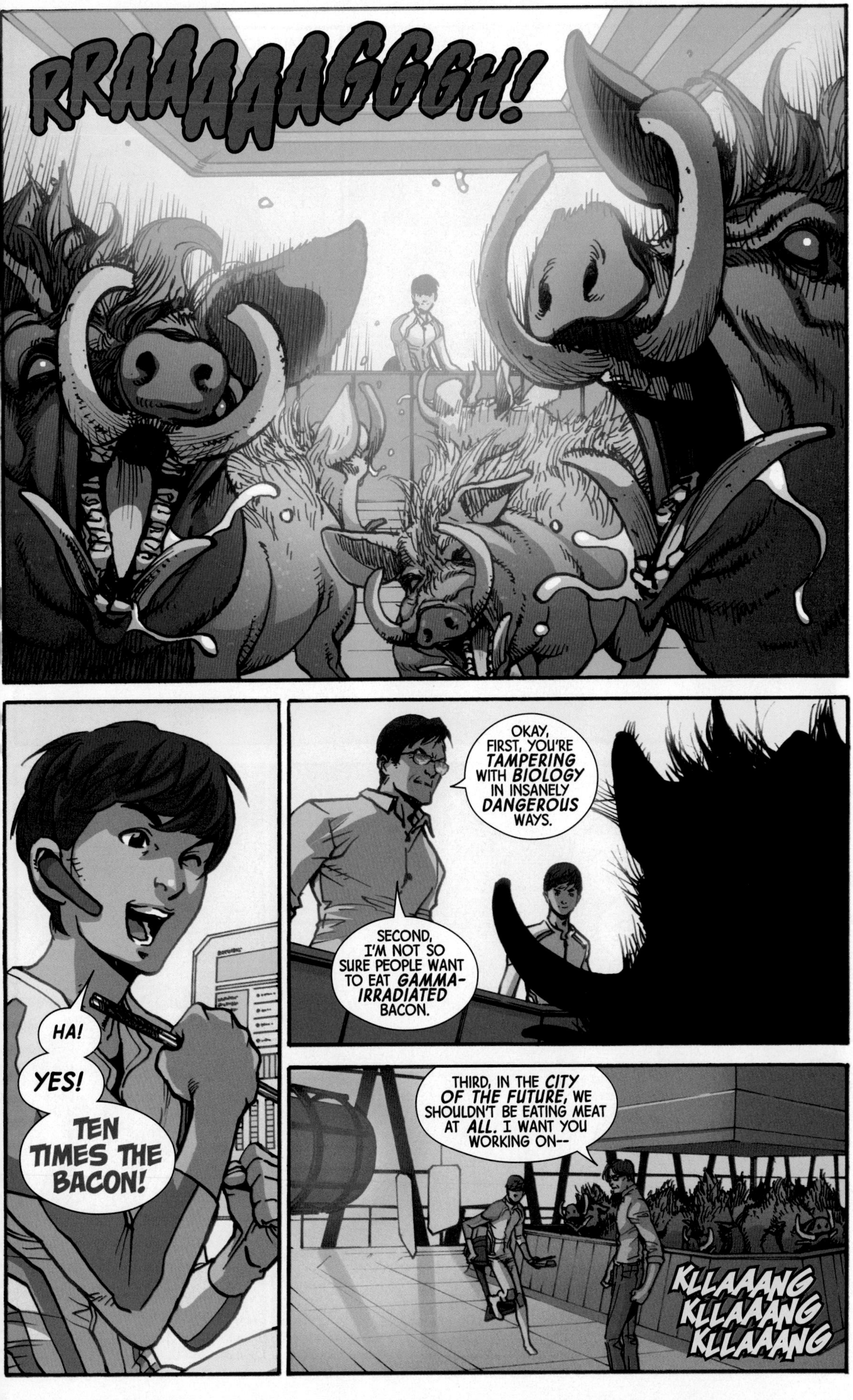
RRAAAAAAGGGGH!
HA!
YES!
TEN TIMES THE BACON!
OKAY, FIRST, YOU'RE TAMPERING WITH BIOLOGY IN INSANELY DANGEROUS WAYS.
SECOND, I'M NOT SO SURE PEOPLE WANT TO EAT GAMMA-IRRADIATED BACON.
THIRD, IN THE CITY OF THE FUTURE, WE SHOULDN'T BE EATING MEAT AT ALL. I WANT YOU WORKING ON--
KLLAAANG KLLAAANG KLLAAANG

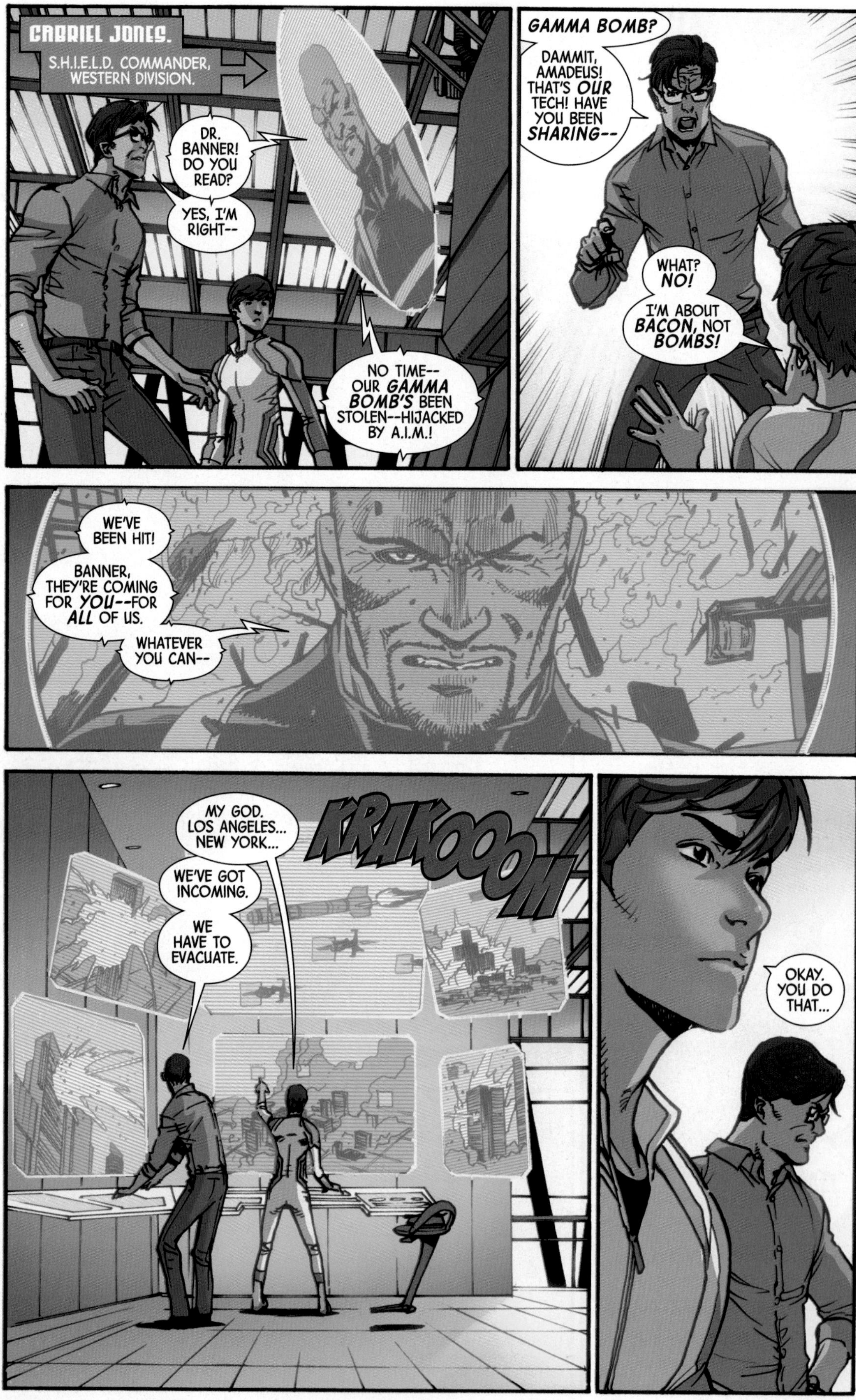
GABRIEL JONES.
S.H.I.E.L.D. COMMANDER, WESTERN DIVISION.
DR. BANNER! DO YOU READ?
YES, I'M RIGHT--
NO TIME--OUR GAMMA BOMB'S BEEN STOLEN--HIJACKED BY A.I.M.!
GAMMA BOMB?
DAMMIT, AMADEUS! THAT'S OUR TECH! HAVE YOU BEEN SHARING--
WHAT? NO!
I'M ABOUT BACON, NOT BOMBS!
WE'VE BEEN HIT!
BANNER, THEY'RE COMING FOR YOU--FOR ALL OF US.
WHATEVER YOU CAN--
MY GOD. LOS ANGELES... NEW YORK...
WE'VE GOT INCOMING.
WE HAVE TO EVACUATE.
KRAKOOOOM
OKAY. YOU DO THAT...

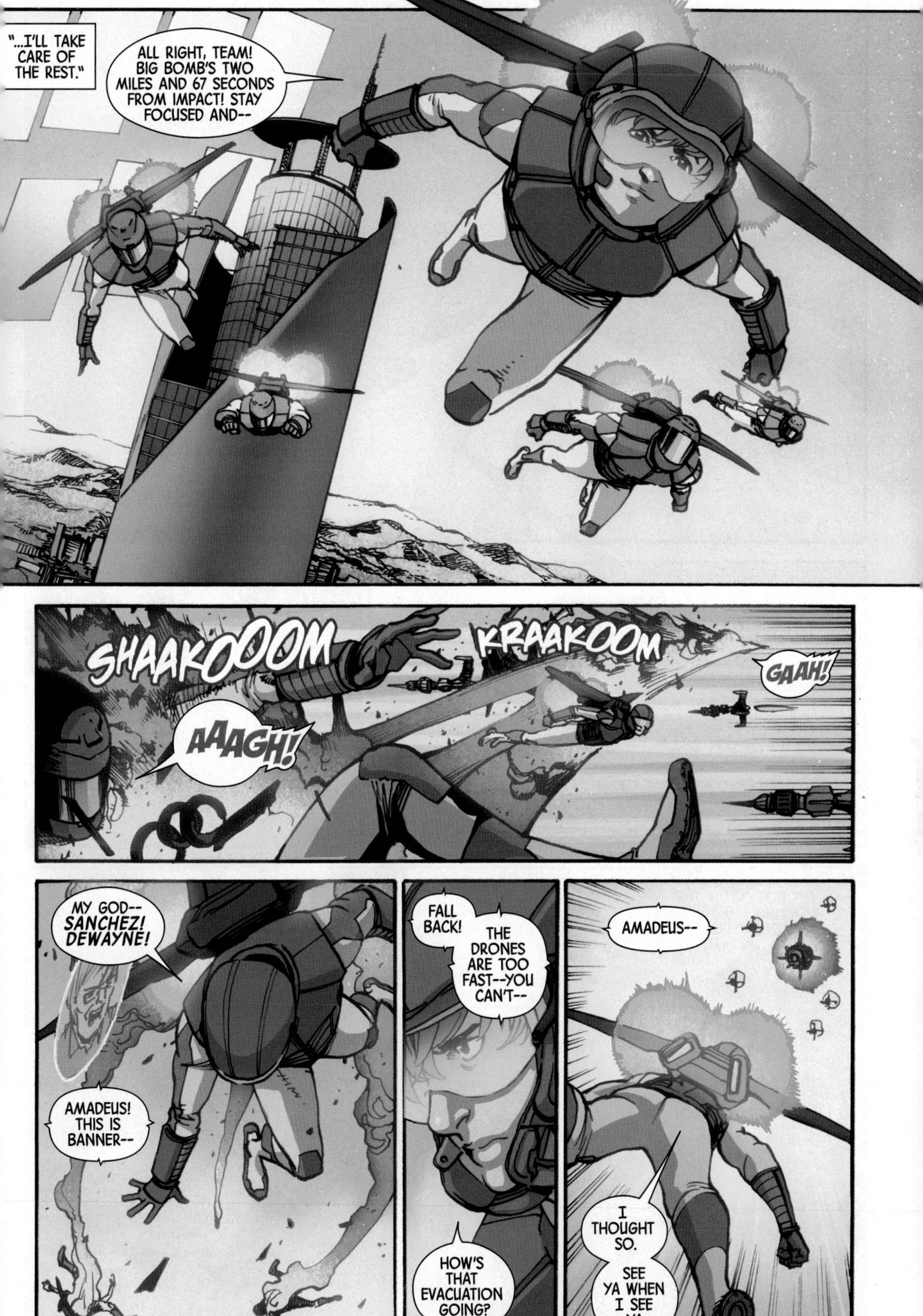
"...I'LL TAKE CARE OF THE REST."
ALL RIGHT, TEAM! BIG BOMB'S TWO MILES AND 67 SECONDS FROM IMPACT! STAY FOCUSED AND--
SHAAKOOOM
KRAAKOOM
GAAH!
AAAGH!
MY GOD-- SANCHEZ! DEWAYNE!
AMADEUS! THIS IS BANNER--
FALL BACK!
THE DRONES ARE TOO FAST--YOU CAN'T--
HOW'S THAT EVACUATION GOING?
AMADEUS--
I THOUGHT SO.
SEE YA WHEN I SEE YA.

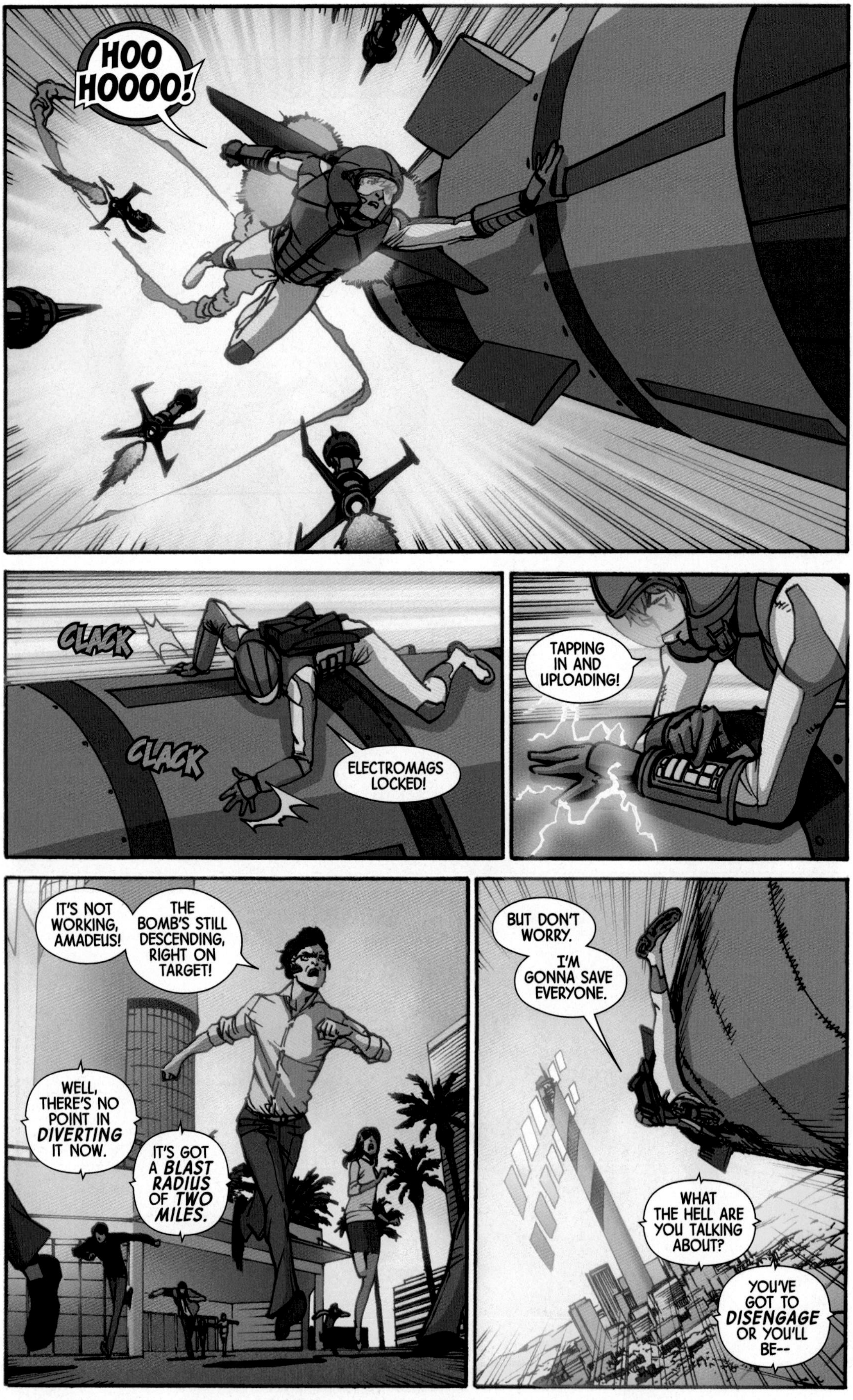
HOO HOOOO!
CLACK
CLACK
ELECTROMAGS LOCKED!
TAPPING IN AND UPLOADING!
IT'S NOT WORKING, AMADEUS!
THE BOMB'S STILL DESCENDING, RIGHT ON TARGET!
WELL, THERE'S NO POINT IN DIVERTING IT NOW.
IT'S GOT A BLAST RADIUS OF TWO MILES.
BUT DON'T WORRY.
I'M GONNA SAVE EVERYONE.
WHAT THE HELL ARE YOU TALKING ABOUT?
YOU'VE GOT TO DISENGAGE OR YOU'LL BE--

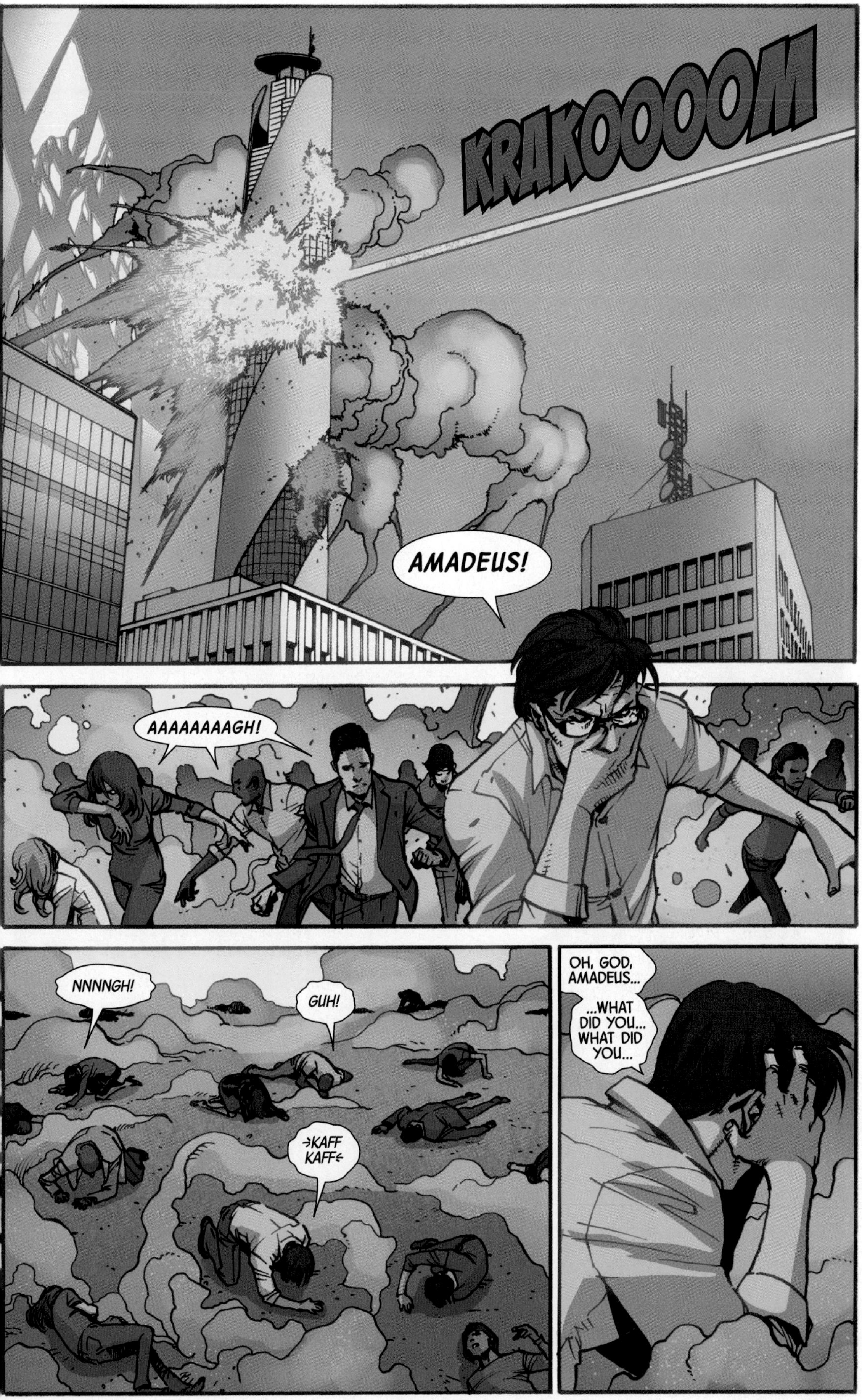
KRAKOOOOM
AMADEUS!
AAAAAAAAGH!
NNNNGH!
GUH!
KAFF KAFF
OH, GOD, AMADEUS...
...WHAT DID YOU... WHAT DID YOU...

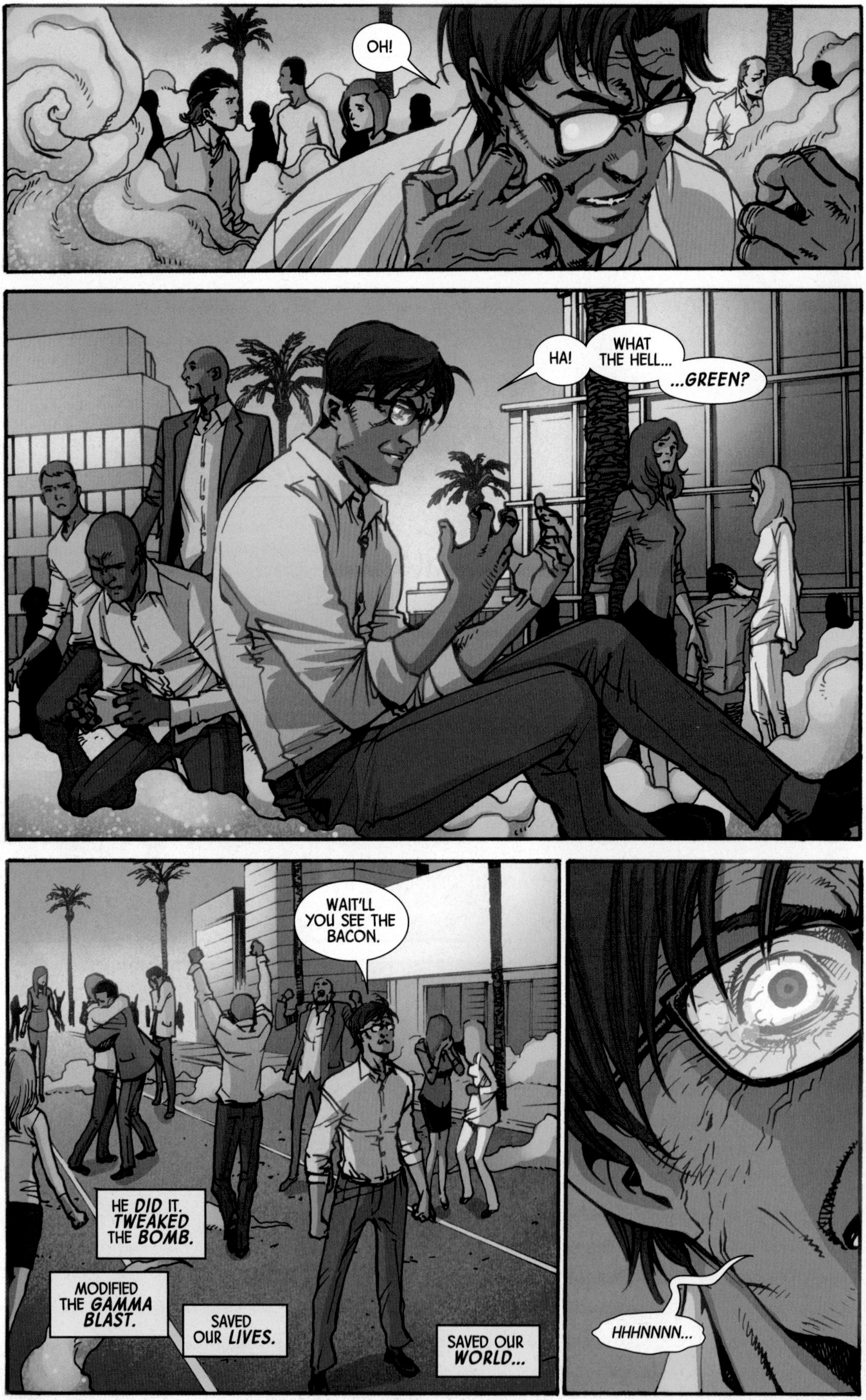
OH!
HA!
WHAT THE HELL...
...GREEN?
WAIT'LL YOU SEE THE BACON.
HE DID IT. TWEAKED THE BOMB.
MODIFIED THE GAMMA BLAST.
SAVED OUR LIVES.
SAVED OUR WORLD...
HHHNNNN...

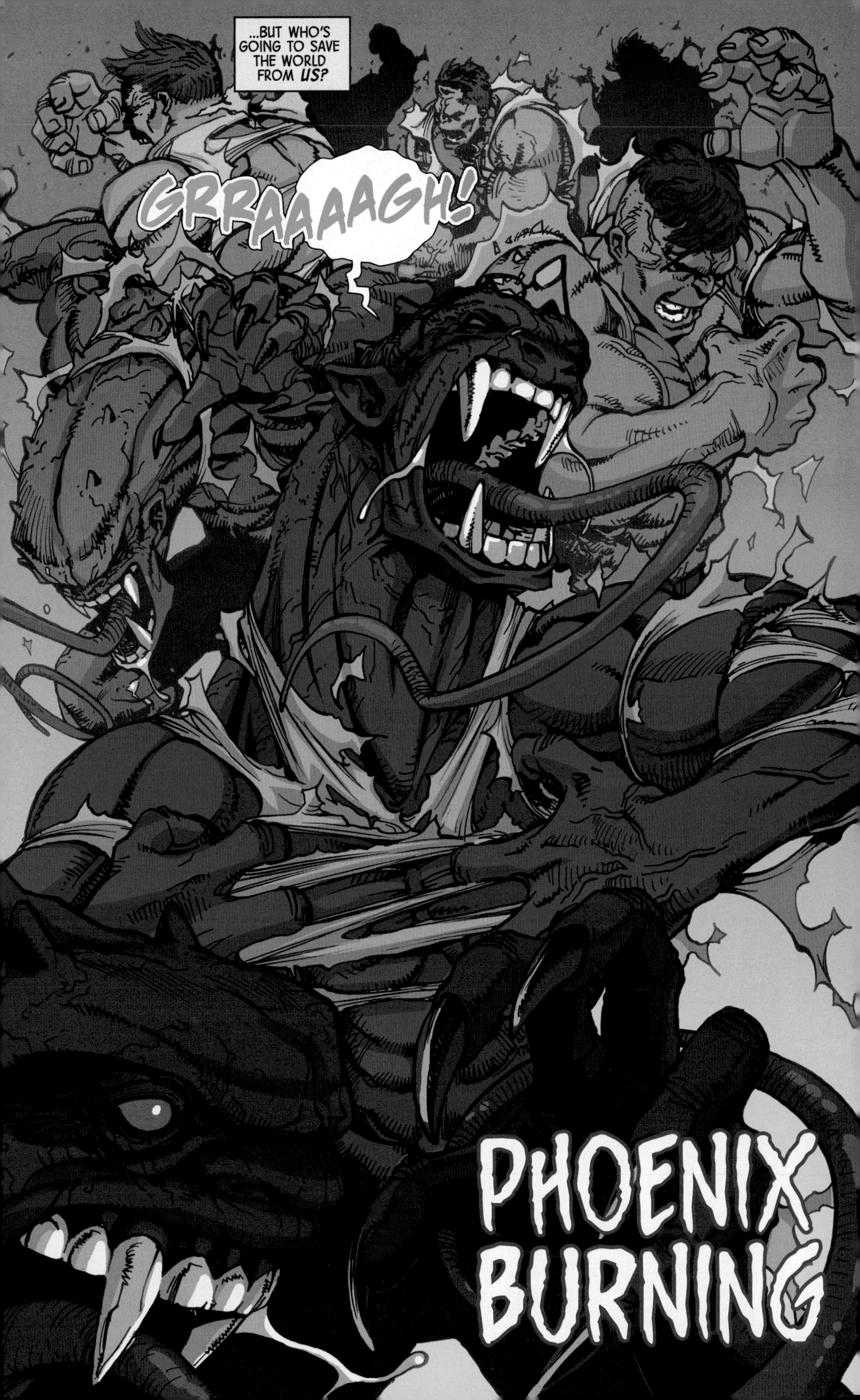
...BUT WHO'S GOING TO SAVE THE WORLD FROM US?
GRRAAAAGH!
PHOENIX BURNING

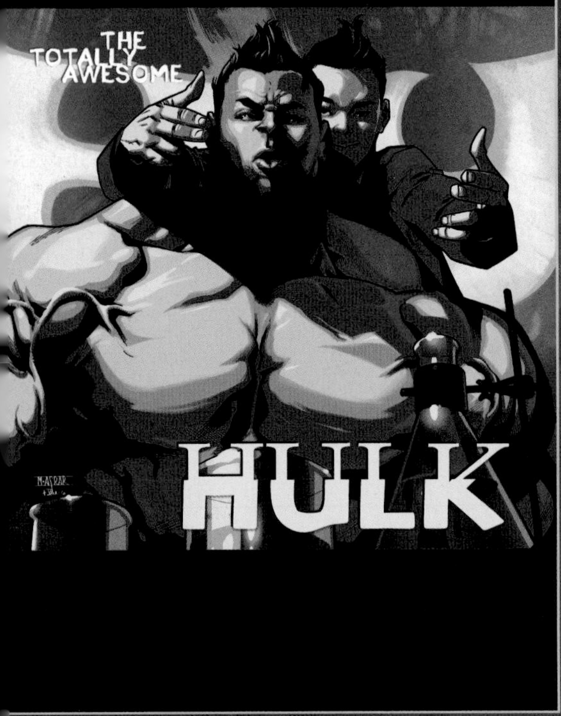
THE TOTALLY AWESOME
HULK

1 HIP-HOP VARIANT BY MAHMUD ASRAR & DAVE McCAIG

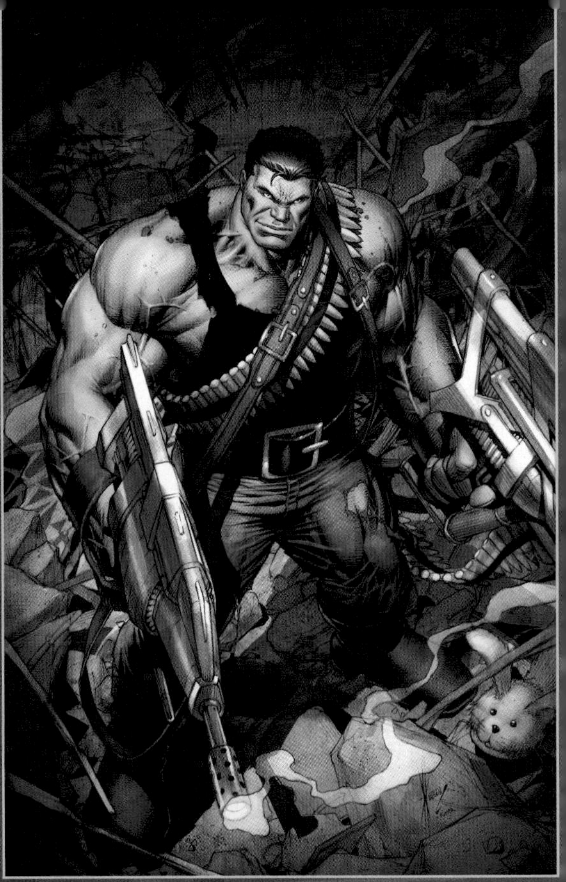

1 MARVEL '92 VARIANT BY DALE KEOWN & JASON KEITH

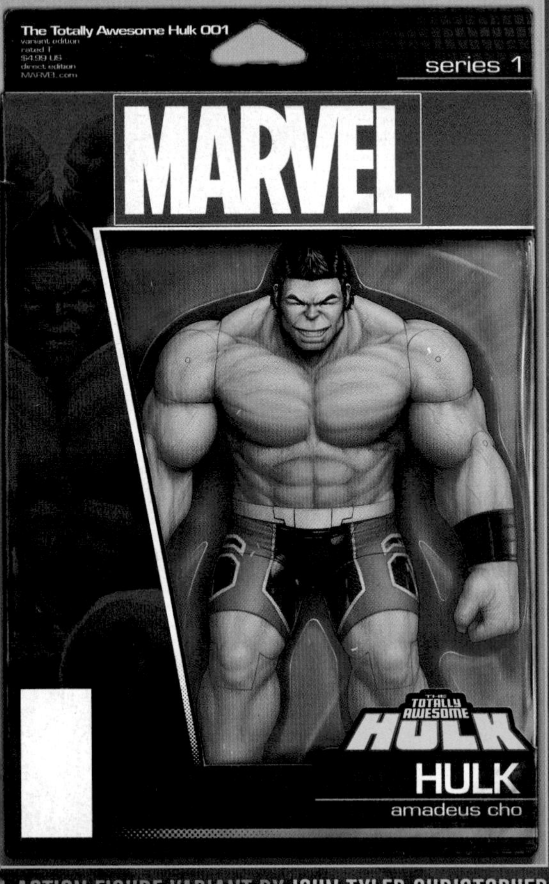
The Totally Awesome Hulk 001
variant edition
rated T
$4.99 US
direct edition
MARVEL.com
series 1
MARVEL
THE TOTALLY AWESOME HULK
HULK
amadeus cho

ACTION FIGURE VARIANT BY JOHN TYLER CHRISTOPHER

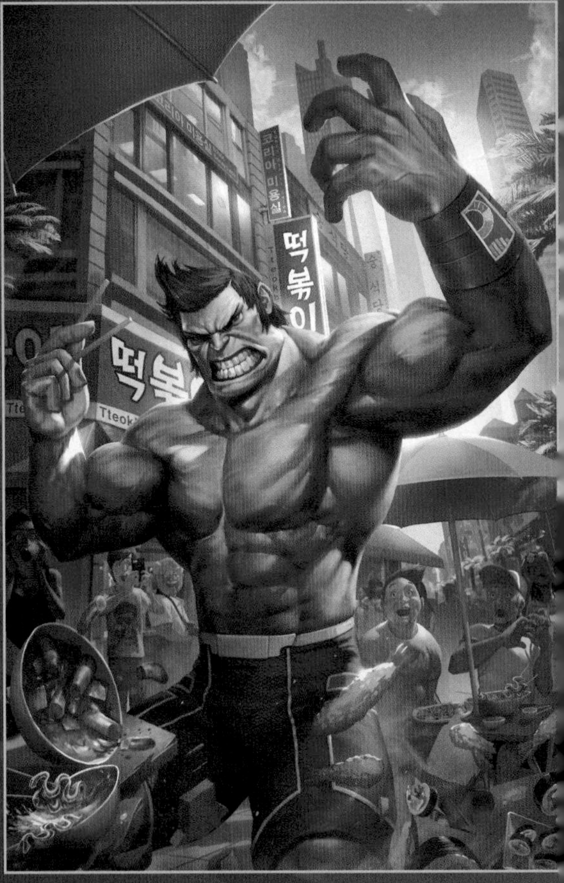
떡볶이

1 VARIANT BY WOO CHUL LEE

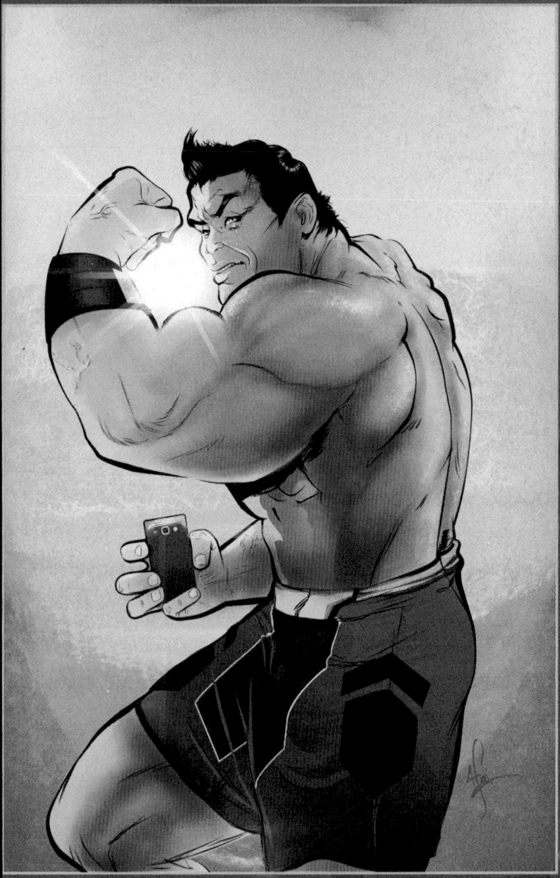

2 VARIANT BY AFUA RICHARDSON

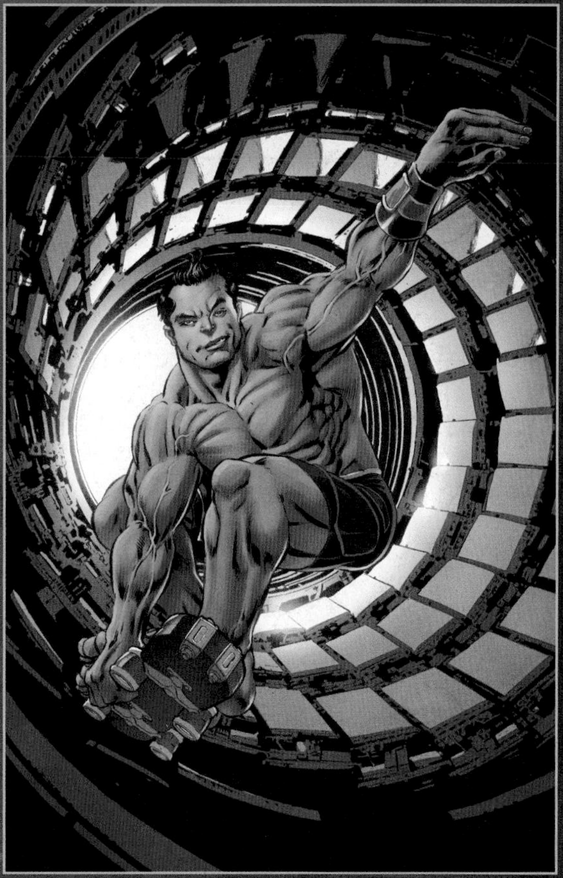

3 VARIANT BY MIKE PERKINS & ANDY TROY

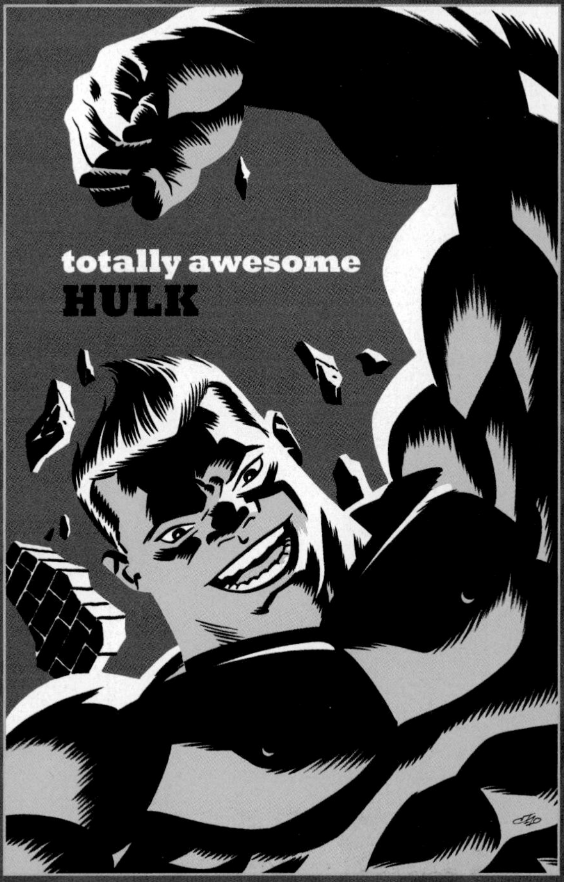
totally awesome
HULK

3 VARIANT BY MICHAEL CHO

4 WOMEN OF POWER VARIANT BY
MEGHAN HETRICK

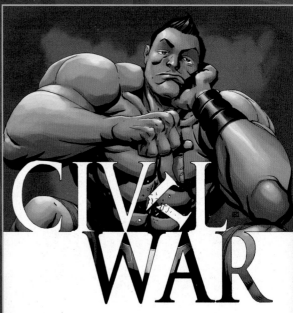

5 CIVIL WAR VARIANT BY
KHOI PHAM & CHRIS SOTOMAYOR

3 1901 05845 5892